SECOND CHAMBERS

THE LIBRARY OF LEGISLATIVE STUDIES

General Editor
Philip Norton

ISSN 1460-9649

A series of new and recent books exploring the role of legislature in contemporary political systems. The volumes typically draw together a team of country specialist to provide in-depth analysis.

Parliaments in Contemporary Western Europe
edited by Philip Norton

Volume 1: *Parliaments and Governments in Western Europe*
Volume 2: *Parliaments and Pressure Groups in Western Europe*
Volume 3: *Parliaments and Citizens in Western Europe*

Delegation and Accountability in European Integration
The Nordic Parliamentary Democracies and the European Union
edited by Torbjörn Bergman and Erik Damgaard

The Uneasy Relationships between Parliamentary Members and Leaders
edited by Lawrence D. Longley and Reuven Y. Hazan

Parliaments in Asia
edited by Philip Norton and Nizam Ahmed

Conscience and Parliament
edited by Philip Cowley

The New Roles of Parliamentary Committees
edited by Lawrence D. Longley and Roger H. Davidson

Members of Parliament in Western Europe
Roles and Behaviour
edited by Wolfgang C. Müller and Thomas Saalfeld

Parliaments in Western Europe
edited by Philip Norton

The New Parliaments of Central and Eastern Europe
edited by David M. Olson and Philip Norton

National Parliaments and the European Union
edited by Philip Norton

Second Chambers

editors

NICHOLAS D.J. BALDWIN
DONALD SHELL

LONDON AND NEW YORK

First published in 2001 by
FRANK CASS AND COMPANY LIMITED

Published 2006 by Routledge
2 Park Square, Milton Park, Abingdon, Oxfordshire OX14 4RN
711 Third Avenue, New York, NY 10017

First issued in paperback 2016

Routledge is an imprint of the Taylor and Francis Group, an informa business

British Library Cataloguing in Publication Data

Second chambers
1. Legislative bodies – Upper chambers
I. Baldwin, Nicholas II. Shell, Donald III. Journal of
Legislative Studies
328.3'1

ISBN 0 7146 5144 3

Library of Congress Cataloging-in-Publication Data

Second chambers / editors, Nicholas D.J. Baldwin, Donald Shell.
p.cm.
Includes bibliographical references and index.
ISBN 0-7146-5144-3 (cloth)
1. Legislative bodies–Upper chambers. I. Baldwin, Nicholas. II. Shell, Donald. III. Title.
JF541.S39 2001
328.3'1–dc21 2001003645

This group of studies first appeared in a Special Issue of *The Journal of Legislative Studies*, Vol.7, No.1 (Spring 2001), [Second Chambers].

Publisher's Note

The publisher has gone to great lengths to ensure the quality of this reprint but points out that some imperfections in the original may be apparent

ISBN 13: 978-1-138-98152-2 (pbk)
ISBN 13: 978-0-7146-5144-6 (hbk)

Contents

Introduction

DONALD SHELL

Previous volumes of 'Legislative Studies' have been devoted to legislatures in particular parts of the world, for example Asia or the Nordic countries. In such cases little attention has been given to second chambers. This is unsurprising. Second chambers generally command much less attention than first chambers. They invariably have less power and their significance within the political system of which they are a part is often very marginal. Furthermore, many legislatures, indeed a substantial majority in the world as a whole, have no second chamber at all. Much of the scholarly writing on legislatures over the last century has assumed that second chambers will gradually disappear. Such bodies have been viewed as hangovers from a pre-democratic past, tolerated because of tradition, nostalgia or for reasons of patronage. Eventually they would surely vanish altogether.

But that has not been the case. Arguably second chambers are becoming more rather than less significant in the contemporary world. As Louis Massicotte shows in his contribution to this volume, the trend that was evident earlier this century towards the elimination of second chambers appears to have been arrested. Within the last decade the number of second chambers has actually grown. In particular, newly democratising countries have been as likely to opt for a bicameral as for a unicameral legislature and in so far as a unicameralist trend did exist it was only evident in small countries or in countries where the second chamber that had existed was associated with an undemocratic regime swept away in revolution.

Second chambers may still generally be very much the junior partner to their respective first chambers but at least in some cases their significance has been increasing. Perhaps this is because they are being more closely examined. Sometimes it is necessary to look hard and probe with determination before the influence of a second chamber can be discerned. Their work is often done in a more obscure and hidden way than that of first chambers. They rarely make the headlines in newspapers, and the fate of governments does not generally hang on the outcome of second chamber votes. But a number of recent studies have drawn attention to the role they play, and in doing so illustrated that this is not without significance.

The relative significance of second chambers may be enhanced by the apparently diminished significance of first chambers. Ever since Viscount

Bryce famously wrote of the 'decline of legislatures' in 1921 this has been a recurrent theme of scholarly debate. Most would now agree that the picture is too problematic to permit so simple and pithy a summary verdict as Bryce implied. But as the work of governments has become more complex, so the tasks faced by legislatures in keeping pace has been more difficult, and despite their efforts their capacity to do so has probably diminished. Second chambers may therefore play a supplementary role in helping to fulfil the broad and varied responsibilities of parliamentary bodies.

Furthermore, there is a growing awareness of the complexity of the notion of representation. What is the relationship between representing territory and representing people? If elections produce chambers that appear 'unrepresentative' in terms of gender or ethnicity or other variables, such as age and education, can and should second chambers be looked to as a means of enriching the representative quality of a parliament? Meg Russell explores the issue of territory in relation to second chambers and Bob Borthwick examines the various ways in which second chambers are composed. Michael Rush produces some evidence about the relative composition of second chambers in terms of socio-economic composition, but, as he points out, this is an area where the basic information for comparative studies is at present still very limited. Michael Rush also provides some comparisons between the resources and facilities available to members of second chambers. Again, attention given to these matters in the past has tended to focus very much on first chambers.

But where second chambers do have significance attached to their role, or to their membership, then the question of their relationship to their partner first chamber is likely to assume a greater importance. Roger Scully argues that intercameral relations have a more far-reaching impact on the political system than is generally realised takes up this issue. Compared to first chambers, second chambers are much more diverse in their structure. Almost all first chambers are directly elected, but second chambers may be composed through indirect as well as direct election, and they may also of course be appointed or at least contain an appointed element. Indeed, having different categories of membership is much more common for second chambers than it is for first chambers. These are issues explored by Samuel Patterson and Anthony Mughan, who also examine the way chambers relate in bicameral systems. Their conclusion emphasises the role of second chambers in sustaining legitimate constitutional order.

The focus of this volume is on second chambers in the contemporary world. But second chambers do have a long history, and arguably the ideas on which they are based have an even longer history. This is explored briefly in the first contribution, on the history of bicameralism. Some might argue that bicameral structures have only come into existence where some group has been powerful enough to insist on this, and that they have survived in the main because there has been insufficient determination to remove them. But varied rationales have also been advanced in support of bicameralism and among these there has been continuity as well as discontinuity. Where a revolution of some kind sweeps away a whole constitutional order, then a clear preference for unicameralism in the new order may well result. But there have also been a few cases where after sustained public debate, and outside the context of a general constitutional upheaval, a shift from bicameralism to unicameralism has taken place. Louis Massicotte examines some of these.

Second chambers have a long history. They are extremely varied in the structure they take, and their role is often disputed. They are frequently institutions under threat. Their reform is widely advocated, yet on the whole little is done to bring about such reform. The reform or removal of such bodies tends to receive more public attention, and probably more scholarly attention, than the actual work they do. This volume is an attempt to shed a little more light on this neglected area.

University of Bristol

The History of Bicameralism

DONALD SHELL

Any examination of the history of bicameralism must look at the ideas upon which the concept is based, not simply its varied institutional forms. The ideas that underlie the concept of bicameralism, or which have been used to provide justifications for second chambers, are much older than the institutions that may be classified as bicameral. The latter, the institutional arrangements, first arose in the medieval period in various European countries. They arose out of a particular conception of society and out of a need for kings to consult with the 'great and the good' of their day. Parliaments came into existence to serve this practical purpose, and they took a bicameral structure because different forms of consultation were deemed appropriate with different sections or orders of society. The earliest recognisable legislature is the English parliament. This emerged first in a unicameral or single chamber form but then became bicameral in the early fourteenth century. Separate representation for nobility and the church from that of the remainder of society was the *raison d'être* for the two chambers becoming distinct. But once parliament had taken this form various arguments were put forward as justifications for the structure that had come into existence. Thus the intellectual roots of bicameralism do not lie simply in the need for the different classes of society, or different estates of the realm, to be separately represented in different parliamentary chambers.

Instead they lie in much more ancient notions going back to the dawn of government as a rational endeavour of the human mind and spirit. What are these? Two ideas in particular stand out. First that the power of government should not be concentrated in a single individual or a single institution, or even a single class of people. Rather there should be a blend or a mixture of sources which contribute to the authority exercised by government. This is, of course, a very general idea which can be given more precise expression in a variety of ways. In more modern parlance we think in terms of 'checks and balances', and the theories which underlie bicameralism have frequently drawn on such language for their justification. The second powerful idea concerns the need for wisdom in government, and hence the

Donald Shell is Senior Lecturer in Politics at the University of Bristol desirability of hearing counsel from various sources, but with special attention being given to the wise, the experienced, the distinguished, the elderly and the meretricious. Government is not simply about the exercise of power; it is also about sound judgement and persuasion based on reasoned argument.

GREECE AND ROME

Both these fundamental ideas were first espoused in ancient Greece. Quite why in the fifth century BC men first conceived of government in terms of man-made republics rather than the rule of gods or kings will not detain us here. But what has been described as the 'originality of this astounding people' suddenly gave birth to new concepts as humans began self-consciously to think about the basis and the purpose of government.[1] Aristotle's analysis, which was both descriptive and normative, identified three major forms of government, monarchy, aristocracy and democracy, the rule of the one, the few and the many. Any of these practised exclusively would be likely to degenerate into a pathological or deviant form. Hence, good government required that all three be blended together in a mixed or balanced form. Precisely how the blend was given effect in ancient Greece is not relevant to our purpose here. It would be misleading to try to draw any direct parallel between the Assemblies and the Councils of Athens and other city-states, and governments that existed centuries later. But henceforth wherever men reflected on the structure and form of government, wherever they sought to put forward justifications for the institutional arrangements they wished to defend or to advocate, the ideas first formulated in ancient Greece have reverberated in their considerations.[2]

This was true for the Roman Republic. The name of its most famous institution, the Senate, has been bequeathed to most of the second chambers that exist in the contemporary world. Here we see the accretion of authority based on a reputation for wisdom and sagacity born out of experience and intelligence, qualities linked with either high birth or high achievement. For this reason the Senate, though not initially or in a formal constitutional sense intended as a significant source of legal authority, gradually assumed a dominant role as the central steering authority within the Republic. At first it was there to give advice to the Magistrates or Consuls. But it became the body that directed rather than advised.[3] Its members served for life and as an institution it was closely linked with the patrician families. It was not a 'second chamber' in a bicameralist sense. But the reputation it gained for bringing wisdom and experience to bear on the business of government has evoked the interest and admiration of apologists for second chambers ever since.

ENGLAND, EUROPE AND THE MIDDLE AGES

Hence scholarly writing about fifth century Greece and second century Rome has provided a potent source of guidance to subsequent political thinkers who wrestled with the question: what constituted a good form of government? In Britain from the time of Magna Carta to the franchise reforms of the nineteenth and twentieth centuries, the single most dominant model for interpreting the constitutional arrangements was the so-called classical theory of mixed government. The king represented monarchy, the House of Lords the aristocratic element, and the House of Commons the democratic element within society. The health of this constitutional trinity required that each of these three co-ordinate powers remained in balance with the other. If any were to be eclipsed then the danger of tyranny, oligarchy or excessive influence from the unruly masses would arise.

It would, however, be a mistake to think that this theory was in some way responsible for the creation of the institutions which it sought to explain and justify. Rather, parliament simply crept into existence, an institution that arose to meet the very practical necessity for some means to exist by which the monarch could consult with those whose relative status or power within the community made such consultation prudent.[4] From the Anglo Saxon Witans, meetings of the wise, to the Great Council of the Nation, to the modern-day House of Commons and House of Lords, there is a continuous line of development. But these arrangements have been born out of circumstance, practice and necessity rather than deliberate design. The division of parliament into two Houses arose gradually in the thirteenth and fourteenth centuries. First it became necessary for the Great Council to include not just mighty magnates and august prelates, but also those who in some sense represented the shires and cities of the land. From time to time those who brought pleas on behalf of the Commons would withdraw, perhaps meeting separately from the Lords. In 1377 the Commons for the first time elected its own Speaker. A two-chamber parliament had emerged. The mixed theory of the constitution drawn from classical times offered a supportive interpretation of these arrangements.

In the thirteenth and fourteenth centuries similar bodies arose all over Europe. As rulers found that in practice they needed to obtain the consent of such bodies, so in turn these bodies began to exercise some control over rulers. The way was open for them to become deliberative bodies with regular meetings, and for the notion of representation to arise. In most of medieval Europe society was seen as composed of distinctive estates, most commonly three in number, clergy, nobility and others. In some cases the three estates met together, in others they met separately. In Sweden four estates were recognised, nobles, clergy, burgesses and peasants, and each met in its own chamber.

England was unusual in two major ways. First, because parliament gradually grew in strength without eliminating the power of the crown. And, second, because two distinctive chambers emerged, both of which developed a recognised legitimacy. In France, by contrast, the Estates-General were sidelined by the monarch, meeting only twice between 1307 and 1789. The monarchy tended towards absolutism until it disappeared in the political earthquake of the French revolution. In Poland, on the other hand, the Sejm 'gobbled up the monarchy', first obtaining the right to appoint the monarch and then declining to allow the crown the degree of autonomy necessary for the business of government to be effectively executed.[5] The monarchy simply faded away. In England, by contrast, a tension between parliament and the crown continued. This erupted in the seventeenth century in civil war, and then abated with the powers of the crown gradually coming to be exercised by ministers whose primary responsibility was to parliament (and thence to the people) rather than to the person of the monarch.

If this was one way in which English experience was unusual, another was the development of two chambers, both of which exercised definite power. From the fourteenth century the Lords of Parliament received individual summonses to attend because of their personal status while the members of the lower House attended because they were representatives of communities, called to give assent to taxes on behalf of those from whom the crown derived its revenues. English bicameralism was never deliberately designed, but once it had emerged its continued existence was underpinned by the understanding based on the classical theory of the constitution.

In this the House of Lords was frequently viewed as an intermediary between the Commons and the monarch, a 'screen and a bank between the Prince and the People'.[6] Such thinking ran on through the seventeenth-century upheavals. Though during the puritan revolution the House of Lords was abolished (in 1649), schemes were soon being advanced for its return, albeit perhaps in a very different form. Even Cromwell argued the need for a body to interpose between the House of Commons and the executive. Among the ideas debated in this most fertile period of constitutional argument were life peers, peers nominated by the Commons, the removal of all bishops, and the advent of a suspensory rather than absolute veto for the upper House. The poet John Milton thought there should be two perpetual aristocracies, one military and one civil.[7] But such excitements receded as the Restoration was consolidated. The old House of Lords was brought back, but as a decidedly junior partner in a firmly established two-chamber parliament.

This did not, however, prevent the continued dominance of the classical theory of the English constitution. Indeed, in order to sustain and strengthen the acceptance of that theory, many proposals were put forward for reform of the House of Lords between the seventeenth-century restoration and the

Great Reform Act of 1832. These were not aimed at making the House less aristocratic and more democratic. That would have been to violate the balance so vital to the mixed theory of the constitution. Rather, they were designed to enhance the capacity of the second chamber to continue to play its traditional role within a balanced constitution, maintaining it as an institution independent of the crown, one representing property over and against the community as a whole. Indeed, of greater concern than any desire to democratise the system was the perceived need to prevent the House of Lords from losing the independence essential for it to fulfil the balancing role demanded of it by the classical theory of the constitution. Through the appointment of bishops and the creation of new peerages, the crown was seen as having too great an influence over the House. Until the nineteenth century there were never enough peers by succession to give the House any real independence from the crown.[8] But by the nineteenth century, when its hereditary composition was sufficient to give it such independence, it lacked the authority to assert such independence. Burke initially feared the power of the crown and wished to strengthen the Lords to counter this, not because he had any respect for the idea of hereditary legislators, but because realistically he recognised the chamber as a source of countervailing power. But later in his career his fear was more of the people and the power wielded in their name by the Commons.

The passage of the Great Reform Act of 1832 aggravated such fears but also made clear the supremacy of the democratic element in the constitution and catalysed agitation against the House of Lords for its undemocratic nature. The classical theory of the constitution was at an end. From the time of the Cromwellian revolution until 1832 it had 'effectually precluded the growth of democratic criticism of the House of Lords'.[9] Before examining the subsequent development of such criticism, and indeed why it took another 170 years before the predominantly hereditary nature of the House was finally removed, we ought first to consider how a wholly new rationale for bicameralism consistent with democratic principles was developed in the New World.

AMERICAN CONSTITUTION-MAKING

From the early seventeenth century onwards the colonists in North America had begun to establish their own governments. From then until the American revolution these were modelled on the English pattern, and as in England the classical or mixed theory of the constitution was viewed as normative. Bicameral legislatures were established, but with no aristocracy and every desire to avoid the creation of an aristocracy, what basis could there be for the membership of second chambers? Upper Houses were 'supposed to embody something other than the people', but it was not always clear what this something other could be.[10] Most states looked to substantial property qualifications for the members of, or for the electors to, second chambers. If first chambers represented people, second chambers represented property, almost as a substitute for wisdom and experience, for whereas 'wisdom and integrity were difficult to measure, property was not'.[11] What the colonists wanted was an independent senatorial class in small upper Houses where members would serve lengthy terms. The notion that a second chamber was a necessary bridge between the power of the people and the power of the executive was widespread. This required that the second chamber retain its independence. The failure of the House of Lords to remain adequately independent of the British crown opened up the British constitution to substantial criticism; it no longer properly embodied the values of the classical mixed constitution.

In the American states the theory of mixed government was coming under challenge by the 1770s. The values on which the colonies system of government had been based for over a century were at variance with those of England. 'With a more democratic franchise, more upward mobility, less polarised income distribution, and no established Church or aristocracy of blood'[12] it was not surprising that, at least in some quarters, advocates of unicameralism emerged. However, prevailing opinion still accepted the predisposition towards bicameralism at the time of the Philadelphia Convention – where the need for a second chamber was virtually unquestioned – and in the course of debate there the Founding Fathers in effect formulated a whole new justification for a second chamber. The arguments were spelt out in the Federalist Papers,[13] and these still provide a very clear, vigorously expressed cogent defence of the principle of bicameralism.

The need for checks and balances was spelt out in Paper 51, where the argument used embraced the idea that the two branches of the legislature should be composed in fundamentally different ways. Paper 62 then built on this and outlined the purposes of a second chamber. First, a second chamber was necessary as a constitutional safeguard because those who administer government may 'forget their obligations to their constituents, and prove unfaithful to their important trust'. Hence, a second branch of the legislative assembly would 'double the security of the people by requiring the concurrence of two distinct bodies'. This danger of concentrating power in the hands of a single group has frequently been emphasised. John Stuart Mill spoke of the 'evil effect produced upon the mind of any holder of power, whether an individual or an assembly, by the consciousness of having only themselves to consult'.[14]

Second was the need to afford a breathing space in the legislative process to allow for second thoughts. This derived from the fact that there was a 'propensity of all single and numerous assemblies to yield to the impulses of sudden and violent passions, and to be seduced by factious leaders into intemperate and pernicious resolutions'. Examples of such behaviour (it was said) could be cited without number. A body which is to correct this infirmity ought to be smaller and more stable than the lower chamber; hence the need for longer terms and partial renewal of the membership of the second chamber. Again this argument has been widely articulated (though one might say usually made with less passion or intemperate language!). And the next two arguments deployed in support of the principle of a second chamber also concerned the ability of its members to bring a different perspective to bear on the role of a legislature from that provided by a first chamber. 'Another defect to be supplied by a Senate lies in a want of due acquaintance with the objects and principles of legislation', the purpose of which was not only to serve the happiness of the people, but also to be based on knowledge of how such could be attained. And, fourth, a second chamber was necessary to provide for greater constancy because 'a continual change even of good measures is inconsistent with every rule of prudence'. The danger of 'mutable government' was: 'Laws so voluminous that they cannot be read, or so incoherent that they cannot be understood'. Another 'effect of public instability is the unreasonable advantage it gives to the sagacious, the enterprising and the moneyed few over the industrious and uninformed mass of the people'. This concern for the quality and consistency of legislation has recurred in much discussion about the role of second chambers, as has concern that second chambers should be so composed that people with special experience and maybe particular virtue should be there. John Stuart Mill spoke of one House representing popular feeling, the other personal merit; the upper House should have members with special training or knowledge, a chamber of statesmen in contrast to a people's chamber.

Paper 63 added two further reasons which have found a less general applicability. First was the desirability of the Senate having special responsibility in regard to foreign affairs, where its small size would imbue members with a greater sense of personal responsibility for its decisions, and where the need for sagacity and experience was greater. Such qualities were more likely to be found in a Senate than in a popularly elected chamber. Finally, a Senate, because of the longer term its members would serve, should have a greater sense of responsibility, and thus be less likely to give way to irregular passions or be misled by 'the artful misrepresentations of interested men'. It was assumed that the Senate would be a 'temperate and respectable body of citizens' who would encourage the triumph of reason, justice and truth in the public mind.

These arguments were all consistent with the idea that a second chamber should be a small and stable body, heavily endowed with wisdom and experience, and intent on providing disinterested service to the community. But as debate developed at the Philadelphia Convention so a whole new rationale for a second chamber emerged, one based on the concept of federalism to which the Convention gave birth. This was of course the famous 'great compromise' whereby the interests of the large and the small states could be reconciled. An instrument for helping to effect such reconciliation was the proposed Senate. The essence of the compromise was that while the lower House would be elected on a popular basis proportionate to the electorate as a whole, the Senate would provide an equal representation for the states irrespective of their size. And with the Senate's membership fixed at two per state it would remain a relatively small body. Furthermore, the members would be chosen not directly by the people, but by the state legislatures. Thus the Senate became not only small, but also more select and more insulated from the raw views of the populace than the House. Its members would be 'refined through a filtration process of election to ensure that the wisest and most experienced in society were selected'.[15] It was clearly envisaged that the Senate would be a powerful body, though there remained a good deal of confusion and uncertainty over the exact nature of the institution that was to be established. However, it was clear that a whole new justification for a bicameral legislature had been invented. The Senate with the states equally represented in it had a crucial part to play in this new formulation of federalism. The states had direct representation as states in the Senate, which in turn had a direct input to legislation, senior appointments and international treaty making.[16] The prestige of the Senate was to grow. Riker has argued that initially it was intended to be a 'peripheralising influence' on American federalism, an intention reinforced by the fact that senators could be instructed by their states and could be recalled if necessary. But these practices lapsed. As the prestige of the Senate grew its members were soon able to resist pressures to oust them. Very few forced resignations occurred, while primary elections and public canvasses grew in popularity, and though state legislatures could in theory ignore or override the results of these, in practice this became more and more difficult to do. Eventually the 17th Amendment was ratified in 1913, universalising a situation already widespread by providing for the direct popular election of senators in all states.[17]

EUROPE AGAIN – INTO THE MODERN PERIOD

The American revolution thus gave rise to debates about constitution making that in effect provided a double justification for second chambers, one based on traditional arguments for checks and balances and senatorial wisdom, and the other based on the newly invented concept of federalism. At the same time the French revolution swept away the old order and elevated the 'sovereignty of the people' into the over-riding principle of government. Sovereignty was indivisible and hence the representative body of the nation could not possibly be other than unicameral. The indefatigable constitution maker, the Abbé de Sieyes, made his oft-quoted remark: 'If a second chamber dissents from the first, it is mischievous; if it agrees it is superfluous.' This phrase, according to Herman Finer, stopped thought by stunning the mind, and he suggested an appropriate answer would be: 'If the two assemblies agree so much the better for our belief in the wisdom and justice of the law; if they disagree, it is time for the people to reconsider their attitude'.[18] France's own searing experience in the aftermath of the revolution inclined the country quite quickly to introduce a second chamber, and, though this was later swept away, from 1875 the country has had a bicameral system. The French Senate has generally been composed by indirect election, representing the land and territory of the country, while the first chamber has represented the people.

Elsewhere in Europe the aristocratic character of second chambers diminished. One hundred years ago the hereditary principle still played a part in the membership of second chambers in Austria, Germany, Hungary, Russia and Spain (as well of course as Britain), though only in Hungary were hereditary peers still in a majority. In Portugal hereditary peers who had already taken their seats were allowed to remain under constitutional reforms of 1885, but as they died their heirs were excluded. Bishops still sat in the second chambers of all these countries. But the trend was clear. Hereditary and episcopal members were removed as constitutional change took place. Already at the turn of the century some countries had second chambers largely composed of members appointed for life; the Italian Senate, for example, consisted of distinguished persons nominated for life by the king, with the only hereditary members being princes of the royal family. Scandinavian countries had moved furthest towards democratising their second chambers, with varied forms of election having become the norm. Norway was unusual; its 1814 Constitution provided that the elected first chamber should appoint a quarter of their own number to serve as a second chamber – if indeed this could properly be classified as a second chamber. In Holland the aristocratic part of the 'second' chamber was removed in 1848, and a part-appointed and part-elected chamber constituted. Confusingly, however, this chamber though weak in terms of power, was designated the 'First' chamber because it was heir to the pre-1848 aristocratic chamber, which had of course been regarded as the pre-eminent chamber. How very Dutch!

Constitution making in nineteenth-century Europe also reflected the influence of America. In Switzerland a second chamber with a membership based on the cantons was established in 1848, while in 1871 Germany adopted a federally constituted Bundesrath, to which the Bundesrat is the direct heir. Elsewhere the establishment of a second chamber invariably accompanied the creation of new federal systems. These were constituted either with equal representation of the federal units (as in America) or unequally (as in Switzerland and Germany). As the age of empire ended, many newly independent countries opted for bicameral legislatures. Frequently this was integral to the creation of federal systems, but in the absence of federalism, second chambers were still widespread. Imitation and tradition have no doubt had their part to play in this process. Inertia too can contribute to the continuation of a second chamber even when its role has become extremely marginal. Britain illustrates this well, while also being a special case, the House of Lords retaining a substantial hereditary membership (well over half the nominal membership) until 1999.[19]

BICAMERAL OR UNICAMERAL?

The frequent association of second chambers with pre-democratic institutions of an aristocratic kind, or with appointment rather than election, has resulted in many becoming weak bodies, lacking any clear sense of legitimacy. Where this is the case the question naturally arises: should bicameralism be abandoned in favour of unicameralism? A number of countries have abolished their second chambers – New Zealand did in 1950, Denmark in 1956 and Sweden in 1971 – but these have without exception been small unitary states, having populations of no more than five million.[20] When Portugal adopted a new Constitution in 1976, the second chamber was removed, leaving that country with a population of some ten million – the largest Western democracy currently without a second chamber. Many former communist countries have opted for bicameral legislatures. Some countries having abolished their second chambers now face some pressure for the return of such bodies. There is certainly no clear trend towards single chamber legislatures in the contemporary world. The whole process of democratisation has not been accompanied by any repudiation of second chambers.

This may seem surprising. It is after all not difficult to recognise the strength of arguments against bicameralism. If in a parliamentary system both chambers have real power and divergent memberships, then the principle of a cabinet being sustained in office through retaining the support of a majority, and carrying through the policies that the majority are prepared to support, may be jeopardised. Even where the responsibility of prime minister and cabinet is recognised as being exclusively to the first chamber, the principle of democratic accountability may appear weakened by the interference of a second chamber. If, to prevent this, second chambers have their powers removed and become rather weak bodies, then their continued existence may well be questioned on the grounds that they have become marginal to the political system. Arguments of this kind can easily be reinforced by drawing attention to the confusion, inefficiency and delay which can arise as draft legislation is shuffled back and forth between two chambers. Why cannot one chamber be organised in such a way as to provide adequate scrutiny of legislation and public accountability of the government?

Such arguments may remind us of the comment made by Walter Bagehot writing of the nineteenth-century House of Lords when he suggested: 'With a perfect lower House it is certain that an upper House would be scarcely of any value'.[21] The fact is that now, as then, and throughout history, no first chamber can be considered so virtuous. Checks and balances are needed, and so is wisdom. These qualities were emphasised in ancient Greece and Rome, and have never lost their relevance. They may of course be infused into politics and government by means other than second chambers. In modern democracies the judiciary may provide more effective 'checks' than any parliamentary chamber is able to give. But it may be more difficult to ensure 'balance' is also available, and here the role of a second chamber may remain significant. Certainly in modern society government activity has become more complex. Balancing diverse views and interests in the complex web of policy-making, especially, for example, where difficult ethical issues are also involved, may be best served in a legislative chamber where the mighty force of party is a little muted. Given too that good 'governance' demands more of policy-makers in terms of mobilising support and winning co-operation from private interests, a second chamber composed differently from the first may have a worthwhile role to play. Democratic governments cannot achieve their aims through the use of public power alone. Winning support through persuasion is vital. A chamber that represents varied interests, either explicitly and formally, or implicitly and informally, may have a vital role in mobilising support.

The history of bicameralism is not simply the history of those parts of legislatures or parliaments that have been designated second chambers. Too frequently second chambers are spoken of as if they were mere appendages to first chambers, to be treated as isolated institutions, often as historical hangovers. In fact it is important to see them in relation to the first chambers that are part of the same bicameral structure. The history of bicameralism must therefore take some account of the changes that first chambers have been undergoing. Several points are worth making in this context.

First we note the rise not only of the professional politician, but also of the career politician. There are much greater pressures on elected members of first chambers, more of whom either believe their work as members should be full time, or find it necessary in practice to make it full time. But not only are those who have become members of first houses more likely to be full-time politicians; they are also more likely to have been virtually full-time politicians long before they arrive in a parliamentary chamber. A higher proportion than in the past have made their living in politics. They have been political researchers, or they have worked for a political party, or perhaps they have followed what Anthony King has described as a 'politics-facilitating occupation'.[22] Their goal has been to enter politics, and life has been organised very deliberately with that end in view. This narrows the range of experience represented by members of first chambers.

Another change lies in the nature of political campaigning. Not only has this become overtly continuous between elections, but it is also conducted in a very much more sophisticated manner, with party leaders ever more dominant in the control they exercise over their party candidates. The technicians of modern democracy orchestrate the party faithful in strictest possible unison. This stifles debate within parties, and often – if more indirectly – between parties too. Intense party competition imposes a style of debate which focuses at least as much on isolating and undermining the opponent's case as on establishing one's own. Adversarial politics often makes genuinely open debate difficult to achieve. A second chamber, precisely because it is insulated somewhat from the focal point of politics, may allow for such debate.

Finally there is an increasing tension between the varied roles a first chamber must fulfil. These always have been varied, but in the past it has not been so difficult to hold them in a sort of creative tension with each other. Thus in parliamentary systems the directly elected House must maintain a government, but must also hold that government to account. The latter task may too readily be subordinated to the former. The pressure placed on majority party members to close ranks and to refrain from criticism of government has increased. The patronage powers available to party leaders can be deployed to reinforce top-down party cohesion.

In his book *Modern Democracies*, published in 1921, Lord Bryce devoted part of chapter 64 (which deals with second chambers) to a section entitled 'Reasons which in our time increase the need for a second chamber'.[23] In this he reminds readers of the previous and oft-quoted chapter, 'the Decline of Legislatures', which had described the dissatisfaction he claims was felt by 'nearly every free people' with representative legislatures of his day. In dealing with second chambers he develops this argument, and in so doing seeks to strengthen his case for second chambers. Thus, 'Legislatures contain too little of the stores of knowledge, wisdom and experience which each country possesses'.

The reasons he offers for this resonate with much contemporary discussion of legislatures, even if the language in which they are expressed is different. The demands placed on members have become so 'toilsome and exacting ... the fatigue of elections ... is far greater ... the pressure from constituents is so heavy ... many men exceptionally qualified for public service ... who are deficient in fluency of speech or other popular arts [hopeless on television?] do not offer themselves as candidates'. Furthermore, 'the defects aforesaid tend to grow more dangerous because the functions thrust upon governments are becoming more numerous and complex', which increasingly demand 'the power of steady and penetrating thinking'. All this of course was taken as signifying the need for a second chamber that could compensate for some of these defects, a chamber that would be 'a kind of reservoir of special knowledge and ripened wisdom'.

Now it would be easy to dismiss this as simply showing what an elitist approach to politics prevailed in the good Viscount's mind. After all, his chapter on the decline of legislatures has frequently been the butt of criticism for its sweeping relegation of institutions much of whose history since has been marked by rather robust good health. And yet his criticisms may alert us to some of the benefits that perhaps almost unnoticed have been made available through second chambers. In principle a second chamber ought to provide for the mobilisation into a legislature of people whose experience is different, decidedly different, from that which is normal for the first chamber. The argument here would be that if a second chamber is going to exist at all it ought to be so composed that its membership is dissimilar in important respects from that of the first chamber. If bicameralism entails mere lookalike chambers then the argument for unicameralism is strengthened. There is no point in mere duplication. A second chamber should be complementary to its first chamber. But given that that is so, the argument in modern sizeable democracies for the existence of two chambers is convincing.

CONCLUSION

This brief history of bicameralism has sought to indicate the major ideas which have been used to support two chamber legislatures, and to illustrate a little how these have been worked out in different ways. Second chambers arose in pre-democratic times to represent the aristocratic and other high orders of society. For centuries the task of representing aristocracy was deemed sufficient justification for second chambers. As democratic ideas began to spread so second chambers came under strain. Some were removed, while the membership of others underwent adjustment, though usually retaining an elitist character. However, a wholly new justification for second chambers as institutions intrinsic to the success of federal states emerged from the American revolution. Today the most powerful second chambers are found in federal states, though the extent to which they safeguard in practice the interests of the states may be slight. Perhaps it is surprising that second chambers remain so widespread. Many have little clear legitimacy and must be considered as weak or insignificant, mere adjuncts to first chambers. But it would be easy to underestimate their influence, as well as the difficulties involved in their removal. Furthermore, there are reasons for arguing that modern democracies have greater need than ever for both political 'checks and balances' and for wisdom in policy-making, qualities the value of which were first recognised in ancient Greece and Rome. Second chambers may be viewed as entirely concerned with the self-interested defence of particular groups, usually elite groups of some kind. But it ought nevertheless to be recognised that arguments of many kinds have been deployed in support of the bicameral principle. Some at least of those arguments have real strength.

NOTES

1. S. Finer, *The History of Government*, vols.1–3 (Oxford: Oxford University Press, 1997), p.316.
2. See especially Kurt Von Fritz, *The Theory of the Mixed Constitution in Antiquity* (Columbia, OH: Columbia University Press, 1954)
3. Von Fritz, *The Theory of the Mixed Constitution in Antiquity*, ch.7.
4. See R. Butt, *History of Parliament: The Middle Ages* (London: Constable, 1989).
5. See Finer, *The History of Government*, vol.2, esp. ch.8.
6. Quoted in C.C. Weston, *English Constitutional Theory and the House of Lords 1556–1832* (London: Routledge & Kegan Paul, 1965), p.25.
7. Weston, *English Constitutional Theory and the House of Lords 1556–1832*, p.79.
8. 'For the first time in its history it contained in the nineteenth century, an overwhelming majority of members who had been born, and not created peers'. A. Pollard, *Evolution of Parliament* (London: Longman, 1920), p.304.
9. Weston, *English Constitutional Theory and the House of Lords 1556–1832*, p.1.
10. G.S. Wood, *The Creation of the American Republic* (Charlotte: University of North Carolina Press, 1969), p.163.
11. Wood, *The Creation of the American Republic*, p.217.
12. Finer, *The History of Government*, p.1489.
13. J. Jay and J. Madison, *The Federalist or the New Constitution* (Everyman edition, London: J.M.Dent).
14. J.S. Mill, *Considerations on Representative Government* (London: Everyman, 1861), p.325.
15. Wood, *The Creation of the American Republic*, p.553.
16. Finer, *The History of Government*, pp.1514–16.
17. W.H. Riker, 'The Senate and American Federalism', *American Political Science Review*, 49 (1955), pp.452–69.
18. H. Finer, *The Practice of Modern Government*, vol.1 (London: Methuen and Co, 1946), p.684.
19. See D.R. Shell, 'The Second Chamber Question', *Journal of Legislative Studies*, 4 (1998), pp.17–32.
20. On these see L.D. Longley and D. Olson, *Two into One: The Politics and Processes of National Legislative Cameral Change* (Boulder, CO: Westview Press, 1991).
21. W. Bagehot, *The English Constitution* (London: Fontana/Collins, 1963 (1867)), ch.3, pp.133–4.
22. A. King, 'The Rise of the Career Politician in Britain and its Consequences', *British Journal of Political Science*, 11 (1981), pp.249–85.
23. Lord Bryce, *Modern Democracies,* vol.2 (London: Macmillan, 1921).

Methods of Composition of Second Chambers

R.L. BORTHWICK

Interest in the question of the appropriate composition of second chambers has been highlighted in the United Kingdom in recent years as the issue of the reform of the country's House of Lords has returned to a high place on the political agenda. Towards the end of 1999, the composition of the Lords was strikingly altered by the removal from its membership of the overwhelming majority of hereditary members. This action, undertaken in the House of Lords Act, constituted a remarkably decisive step on an issue that had defeated all attempts to deal with it for most of the preceding 90 years. When, in 1911, the powers of the Lords were reduced, the issue of composition had been tantalisingly left for the future.[1] Aside from the introduction of life peers and the admission of women in 1958 and of a procedure for hereditary peers to renounce their peerages in 1963, the composition of the House had shown itself remarkably resistant to reform.

Thus in 1999 one of the most eccentric arrangements for composing a second chamber was substantially altered. Even then, however, hereditary peers did not disappear from the Lords completely. Pending a decision on the long-term future composition of the house, it was agreed that ten per cent of the number of hereditary peers would be retained. This rather untidy arrangement was agreed to as part of the bargaining process through which the House agreed in effect to dispense with the remaining nine-tenths of its hereditary membership without provoking any last-ditch resistance.[2] Meanwhile, a Royal Commission had been set up to look at the future of the House. High on its agenda was the issue of composition. When the Commission reported in January 2000,[3] much of the interest centred on its recommendations in this area. In its deliberations it evidently paid some regard to ways in which other second chambers were composed, though in the end such comparative study does not appear to have produced much desire to draw directly on overseas experience. As Shell points out, given the time scale within which the Commission was required to operate, it is not entirely surprising that its horizons were relatively limited.[4]

R.L. Borthwick is Senior Lecturer in the Department of Politics, University of Leicester

In a sense, the Report of the Royal Commission on the Reform of the House of Lords provides part of the background to a consideration of the ways second chambers are composed elsewhere in the world. What follows draws heavily on the excellent sources provided by the work of Meg Russell. In a series of publications she has provided a mine of information on second chambers, and all who trawl in these waters owe her a debt of gratitude.[5] In looking at how second chambers across the world are composed, it is convenient to treat the subject under a number of headings. Perhaps the most basic issues are the size of such bodies and the length of terms of office of their members. Discussion of these is followed by a survey of the basis of the composition of second chambers and then an examination of how members are selected.

SIZE

The House of Lords in its pre-1999 reform state was unusual in a number of ways, one of which was its size. At the time of the 1999 changes its membership, at least on paper, was in excess of 1,200. Not only was it the largest second chamber in the world but it was also one of the very few that was larger than its partner first chamber. Even if one disregards those who did not attend for one reason or another, its membership was still in excess of 800. As Russell points out, the norm is very much for first chambers to be larger, and often substantially larger than second chambers.[6] Even after the removal of the bulk of the hereditary peers, the House remains large by international standards with a membership at the time of writing of almost 700 when the additional working peers announced in April 2001 are included. Thus it remains very large (and is likely to increase) and bigger than the House of Commons.

By comparison, other second chambers tend to be much smaller: the largest is the French Senat with a membership of 321. Of the others in Russell's selection of 20 major systems, only the Italian Senato exceeds 300 and 11 of her sample have a membership of 100 or less. Included in this last group are some of the best known of second chambers, including the US Senate with its 100 members, the German Bundesrat which, even after unification and the incorporation of the eastern Lander, has only 69 members, and the Australian Senate with its 76 members.

In their survey of second chambers, Patterson and Mughan calculate that, excluding the House of Lords, the average size of second chambers is 83. They provide details of 61 countries with second chambers and of these nine have a membership between 100 and 200 and only six, apart from the House of Lords, have a membership in excess of 200.[7] It is true that many of those countries with smaller second chambers have much smaller populations than the UK, for example, Austria, Belgium and Switzerland. But India, with its much larger population, has only 245 members in its Council of States.[8]

In most cases the membership of second chambers is fixed, at least in the absence of some change in the constitutional landscape. Thus the US Senate had 96 members for almost half a century after the addition of Arizona to the Union in 1912 and then moved quickly to 100 with the addition of Alaska and Hawaii in 1959. Pending the admission of another state or the granting of full representation to the District of Columbia, the Senate will remain at 100. In many other systems too there is a clear fixed size to the second chamber, particularly, as we shall see later, where this is related to the basis of composition, for example, 76 in Australia, 69 in Germany or 178 in the Council of the Federation in Russia. In a minority of cases there is no fixed size to the second chamber. This is usually as a result of the possibility of a variable number of appointed or *ex-officio* members (as in Italy, or of course in the most extreme example, the UK). In the 20 countries listed in detail by Russell, the size of the second chamber was fixed in 15 of them.

LENGTH OF TERMS

The British House of Lords has been unusual in that the great bulk of its members were there for life (the only exception being the bishops of the Church of England). One of the few other second chambers which had a similar system was the Canadian Senate whose members, once appointed, used to be there for life, but since 1965 they have had a mandatory retirement age of 75.

In most systems, however, the norm is a fixed period of office. Often these terms will be longer than for the country's first chamber. Thus United States Senators serve six years compared to the two years of Representatives. Six years can be regarded as a fairly common length of term: it applies in places such as Australia, India, Mexico and the Netherlands. But, as Patterson and Mughan point out, 'two-thirds of all members of upper houses serve terms of five years or less'.[9] In France Senators serve nine-year terms, longer than most other countries with fixed terms. It is worth noting, however, that if the proposals of the Wakeham Commission for the British House of Lords are eventually accepted, then the members of the reformed house will serve 15-year terms, much longer than is to be found elsewhere.

In some systems, however, there is no fixed term of office. This may be because the second chamber can be dissolved at the same time as the lower house. Thus in Belgium and Italy elections for the second chamber take place on the same day as those for the lower house, and so the term of office of members of the second chamber is up to a maximum of five years. In Austria and Germany members of the second chamber have no fixed term of office because the membership of those bodies will change when there is a change in the composition of the legislature (in the case of Austria) or government (in the case of Germany) of any of the constituent units.

In France, as in a number of other countries, one finds staggered terms so that one-third of French Senators are chosen every three years. This is paralleled in countries such as the United States, where one-third of the Senate is elected every two years, and Australia, where half the Senators in each state are elected every three years. It follows that second chambers composed in this way are never dissolved. The same is true of systems like Germany where the second chamber is composed of representatives from the constituent units.

BASIS OF COMPOSITION

In systems that are bicameral it is normal to compose the second chamber in some way that is different from the way in which the first chamber is chosen. One of the few exceptions to this rule is Italy, where both houses of parliament are chosen in essentially the same way.[10] Since the norm for first chambers is to be based on representation of individuals and population, it is perhaps not surprising that many second chambers have, as their basis of composition, territory in some form or other. This is especially likely to be the case where a country has a federal constitution, since the representation of the constituent units is likely to be important.

The United States Senate, for example, has always been composed on the basis of equal representation for the constituent states. This was an important part of securing agreement to the constitution when it was drafted in 1787; the way in which the Senate was to be composed was seen as a protection for the smaller states who feared that their voice would not be heard sufficiently in a lower house chosen on the basis of population. Similarly, the Australian Senate has equal representation for each of its constituent states (with lesser representation for territories), as does the Council of the Federation in Russia. In other cases, however, there may be variation in the representation for the constituent units. In the case of Austria each province has between three and 12 seats in the country's Bundesrat. Similarly in Germany, each Land has from the three to six seats in the second chamber depending on its size.

In some cases the connection between territory and second chamber representation is less clear-cut. Thus in Canada members of the Senate have a notional connection with provinces even though they are appointed to their positions and thus the concept of representation is not a strong one. In other cases, the link with territory may take the form of providing a link with local government. Thus in France the Senate is chosen in a series of electoral colleges composed of local councillors and members of the country's lower house, the National Assembly. This system is based on population but with representation biased in favour of rural areas. The Senado of Spain is composed of a mixture of directly and indirectly elected members: 208 of its members are directly elected on the basis of four (or in some cases three) members from each province; the remaining members are elected indirectly by regional assemblies.

Territory may be the most common basis for composing second chambers but it is by no means the only one. In its pre-1999 form the British House of Lords reflected, however dimly, the idea, once much more common, that parliamentary chambers represented estates of the realm. Thus the upper chamber was composed of Lords temporal and spiritual and balanced, in some way, the representatives of the Commons. Such notions sit uncomfortably with modern ideas of equality. Even in a fully reformed House of Lords, however, it seems likely that the Anglican Church will continue to have a special place.[11] There may be other groups whom it is useful to have represented in the second chamber. Thus in Belgium the Senat represents the linguistic communities that make up that country with the bulk of the membership either directly or indirectly elected to represent the Flemish and French populations.

One of the most ambitious attempts to find a different basis for composing a second chamber is to be found in Ireland where the Seanad is composed predominantly, at least in theory, of representatives of five 'vocational' panels. However, although groups within these vocational areas may nominate candidates for election, nominations may also be made by members of the two Houses of Parliament. More crucially, as Russell points out, members of the vocational groups have no vote in the elections, the electorate 'comprises members of the incoming Dail, outgoing Seanad and local councillors'.[12] In practice this part of the membership of the Seanad is totally dominated by the political parties, 'the chances of being elected on purely vocational grounds are virtually nil'.[13]

The Irish second chamber also contains members elected by graduates of the country's two main universities and a number of members appointed by the Prime Minister. The latter reflects a feature that is to be found in a number of countries. In India the President has power to appoint up to 12 members of the upper house, while in Italy a President of the Republic may appoint up to five life members during his period of office. *Ex-officio* members can also be found in some second chambers. For example, former presidents may have membership of the upper house as in Italy, or, most famously, Chile. The archbishops and senior bishops of the Anglican Church fall into this category in the UK, as do the children of the monarch in Belgium.

HOW CHOSEN

Passing reference has already been made to the different ways in which second chambers can be chosen. Leaving aside those who are *ex-officio* members of a second chamber, the basic choice is between appointment and election. Apart from a number of former British colonies in the Caribbean, second chambers composed exclusively or predominantly of appointed members are quite rare. The British House of Lords and the Canadian Senate are the major examples. The latter is composed of members chosen formally by the Governor General but in reality by the Prime Minister. As we have seen there is a connection between those appointed and the provinces to which they are attached. However, as Russell points out, the most important feature of the appointments is less the provincial connection than the party label:

> There is no tradition in Canada of Prime Ministers making appointments to the Senate from outside their own party ... seats in the Senate are almost invariably given as a prize for long party service, rather than to individuals who necessarily have a record in, or commitment to, the region they are appointed to represent.[14]

The interim House of Lords that emerged from the first stage of reform in 1999 is also essentially a nominated house. Its membership now consists overwhelmingly of members who have been appointed to membership. It could be argued that the house now has an element of election in that 75 of the 92 hereditary peers who have survived for the moment were chosen by their colleagues in the various party groupings. This, however, is election only in the most formal sense.

Some form of election is now the normal way of filling second chambers. Elections may be direct or indirect. Examples of direct election are to be found in the United States, where the electoral system is the same as that used for the lower house,[15] and Australia, where the electoral system used for the Senate is more proportional than that used for the lower house. According to Patterson and Mughan, in only 19 countries are all members of the second chamber directly elected.[16] Among these are Switzerland, Japan, Mexico and some of the newer democracies of eastern Europe, such as Poland. Elsewhere selection may be a mixture of direct and indirect election or by the latter method alone.

Indirect election normally involves some combination of local councillors, state legislatures or governments and/or members of the lower house of the national legislature. In India the bulk of the members of the second chamber are chosen by state legislatures. In Austria, they are chosen by the provincial assemblies. In the Netherlands, the provincial councils choose the members of the second chamber (confusingly called the first chamber) from among their own members. Germany provides a slightly different version whereby the members of the Bundesrat are members of the Länder governments. In this last case the actual individuals who attend meetings of the Bundesrat vary depending on the subject matter: 'in practice all members of the Land cabinet will be either members or deputy members of the Bundesrat'.[17]

In light of the fact that election, either direct or indirect, is overwhelmingly the most common method of choosing the great majority of members of second chambers, the hesitation shown by the Wakeham Commission on this topic is rather surprising. In their report the Commission spoke of a second chamber of some 550 members with the possibility of a minority of members elected in some way to reflect the nations and regions of the UK. Three schemes were offered with varying numbers to be elected (65, 87 or 195) and no agreement on the method to be used.

CONCLUSION

This brief survey has attempted to show something of the considerable variety to be found in the way that second chambers are composed. In so far as one can speak of what is typical in this area, it would be that second chambers are almost always smaller than their equivalent first chamber, and in many cases very small indeed. The terms of office of their members, where these are prescribed, tend to be longer than in the lower house.

The most commonly found basis for composition is probably territory in some form, this being especially the case in federal systems. As we have seen, second chambers are composed in a variety of ways with election, direct or indirect, playing a part in a majority of cases,[21] but with appointment also being a prominent feature.

In the light of this evidence, it is perhaps surprising that the UK appears to be destined to continue with a second chamber whose composition is likely to be overwhelmingly on the basis of appointment. Even if some way is indeed found of taking this power of patronage – in full or in part – out of the hands of the prime minister of the day and giving it to an 'independent' appointments commission, the UK will still be out of step with most of those countries with which it would normally be compared. Moreover, there seems to be a reluctance to prescribe a maximum membership for the British House of Lords. Although the Wakeham

Commission spoke of a reformed house of around 550 members, the evidence so far from the interim arrangements is of a house growing in size with each batch of new appointments. Other countries are clearly able to arrange these matters very differently.

NOTES

1. The preamble to the 1911 Parliament Act spoke of the act being merely a temporary measure pending a full scale reform of composition.
2. For a discussion of this see D. Shell, 'Labour and the House of Lords: A Case Study in Constitutional Reform', *Parliamentary Affairs,* 53/2 (2000), pp.290–310.
3. *Report of the Royal Commission on the Reform of the House of Lords: A House for the Future*, Cm 4534, London, 2000.
4. Shell, 'Labour and the House of Lords', p.302.
5. These were first in a series of publications by The Constitution Unit during 1998 and 1999, for example, M. Russell, *Second Chambers Overseas: A Summary.* The fruits of her labours were brought together in M. Russell, *Reforming the House of Lords: Lessons from Overseas* (Oxford: Oxford University Press, 2000).
6. Russell, *Second Chambers Overseas,* p.3. According to the same source the only other examples of countries with second chambers larger than the first are Kazakstan and Burkina Faso.
7. S.C. Patterson and A. Mughan, 'Senates and the Theory of Bicameralism', in S.C. Patterson and A. Mughan (eds.), *Senates: Bicameralism in the Contemporary World* (Columbus, OH: State University Press, 1999), pp.4–5.
8. See Table 1 in Russell, *Second Chambers Overseas*, pp.13–21.
9. Patterson and Mughan, 'Senates and the Theory of Bicameralism', p.5.
10. Russell, *Reforming the House of Lords, Lessons from Overseas*, p.29.
11. *Report of the Royal Commission on Reform of the House of Lords,* para. 15.9. It should be added that the Commission recommended that other faiths should also be represented in the reformed House.
12. M. Russell, *A Vocational Upper House? Lessons from Ireland* (London: The Constitution Unit, 1999), p.3.
13. J. Casey, *Constitutional Law in Ireland* (London: Sweet & Maxwell, 1992), p.100, quoted in Russell, *A Vocational Upper House? Lessons from Ireland,* p.6.
14. M. Russell, *An Appointed Upper House: Lessons from Canada* (London: The Constitution Unit, 1998), p.5.
15. Of course, prior to the passage of the 17th Amendment in 1913, Senators were chosen by state legislatures, though that system had begun to break down prior to 1913. See B. Sinclair, 'The Coequal Partner: The U.S. Senate', in Patterson and Mughan (eds.), *Senates*, pp.36–7.
16. Patterson and Mughan, 'Senates and the Theory of Bicameralism', p.5.
17. Russell, *Reforming the House of Lords: Lesson from Overseas*, p.61.
18. In 34 out of 61 cases according to Patterson and Mughan, see 'Senates and the Theory of Bicameralism', p.5.

Socio-Economic Composition and Pay and Resources in Second Chambers

MICHAEL RUSH

Who the members of second chambers are and what resources they have to fulfil their role or roles as members of a legislature are relatively neglected topics. The least neglected aspect of composition is, of course, party affiliation, but that apart, little attention has been paid to socio-economic composition, with one or two notable exceptions, such as the United States Senate and the UK House of Lords. In the latter case, however, far more attention has been focused on its hereditary membership than on more conventional socio-economic criteria. As for resources, here the focus has been largely on first rather than second chambers and, where the latter have been examined, principally on elected rather than non-elected chambers.[1] Yet both are important – socio-economic composition has important implications for theories of representation and the concept of representative government and may influence attitudes and legislative behaviour; the level of resources has more mundane but equally important implications for the effectiveness of legislators and legislatures.

The information available on the socio-economic composition of second chambers and the resources available to their members is limited, but sufficient can be gleaned from various sources to enable a useful picture to emerge, a clear sense of how much second chamber members and resources match those of first chambers. Data on various aspects of composition and resources were therefore gathered on 14 countries – Australia, Austria, Belgium, Canada, France, Germany, the Republic of Ireland, Italy, Japan, the Netherlands, Spain, Switzerland, the United Kingdom, and the United States – but systematic data was not available on every country in respect of the aspects of composition and resources covered, as the subsequent tables demonstrate.

Michael Rush is Professor of Politics at the University of Exeter. He gratefully acknowledges the assistance of Meg Russell of the Constitution Unit, University College, London, Sue Blunden and Wayne Hooper of the Australian Senate, Senate Administration of the Canadian Senate, Verona NiBhroinn of the Irish Senate, and Rosa Ripollés Serrano of the Spanish Senate.

THE SOCIO-ECONOMIC COMPOSITION OF SECOND CHAMBERS

There is a long-standing and widespread literature on elites and elite theory that has invariably included members of legislatures.[2] However, where it deals with legislatures, much of this literature centres on first chambers and elected chambers. Furthermore, the amount of systematic and directly comparable information that is available is limited in range and scope. For example, virtually no such information is available on the educational backgrounds of members of second chambers. On the other hand, enough information can be found on age, gender and occupation to facilitate meaningful comparison.

Age

One of the crucial factors that affects the age profiles of members of second chambers is that a number of countries have a higher minimum age qualification for the second chamber than for the first. This is the case in Canada, India, Mexico and the United States – all of which impose a minimum age of 30; France, Liberia, Malaysia, the Philippines and Romania – minimum age 35; and Italy and the Czech Republic – minimum age 40.[3] In addition, in Switzerland's qualifications for members of the Council of State, including a minimum age qualification, are fixed by each canton and therefore vary. These age qualifications are clearly reflected in Table 1, with more than half (53 per cent) of the French Senate aged 61 or more, compared with less than a fifth (19.4 per cent) of the members of the National Assembly; in Italy, where two-thirds (66 per cent) of Senators are aged 51 or more, compared with less than two-fifths (37.3 per cent) of Deputies; and in Switzerland, where 71.7 per cent of the members of the Council of State are aged 51 or more, but only 54 per cent of members of the Nationalrat. This contrasts with Australia and Belgium, where the minimum age qualification is the same for both

TABLE 1
AGE PROFILES OF MEMBERS OF SECOND CHAMBERS IN FIVE COUNTRIES

	Australia		Belgium		France		Italy		Switzerland	
Age gp.	Upper cham.	Lower cham.	Upper cham.	Lower cham.	Upper cham.	Lower cham.	Upper cham	Lower cham.	Upper cham	Lower cham.
21-30	1.3	2.0	2.8	3.3	0.0	0.0	0.0	1.4	0.0	1.0
31-40	14.5	17.7	18.3	22.0	0.0	8.7	0.0	20.5	0.0	6.0
41-50	28.9	40.8	36.6	35.3	13.1	27.0	34.0	40.8	28.3	39.0
51-60	39.5	33.3	32.4	32.7	33.9	44.9	44.1	26.7	63.0	47.0
61-70	15.8	6.1	9.9	6.7	34.3	16.5	15.2	10.6	8.7	7.0
70+	0.0	0.0	0.0	0.0	18.1	2.9	6.7	0.0	0.0	0.0
Total	100.0	99.9	100.0	100.0	100.0	100.0	100.0	100.0	100.0	100.0

Source: Inter-Parliamentary Union website – http://www.ipu.org/parline-e/reports/htm.

houses. Even in Australia, however, Senators are clearly older on average: more than half (55.3 per cent) are aged 51 or more, compared with two-fifths (39.4 per cent) of Australian MPs. In Belgium there is virtually no difference – 42.3 per cent of Senators and 39.4 per cent of Deputies are aged 51 or more. The Australian–Belgian difference may well be a function of terms of office – only three years for MPs but six years for Senators in Australia, compared with five years for both Senators and Deputies in Belgium. Russell points out that the average age of members of second chambers is also higher in countries where membership of the second chamber normally comes towards the end of an individual's career, political or otherwise, as is the case in Canada and the UK, or where membership is dependent on holding some other office, as is the case in France (mostly local office) or Germany (membership of a Land government).[4] Noting that members of second chambers are generally elected or appointed for longer terms of office than their first chamber counterparts, Russell comments: 'Once the higher average age of Senators is taken into account a picture already begins to emerge of more mature and deliberative parliamentary chambers with a less adversarial atmosphere'.[5] This comment is no less applicable to other aspects of socio-economic composition.

TABLE 2
PROPORTION OF WOMEN MEMBERS IN FIRST AND SECOND CHAMBERS

Country	First chamber	Second chamber	Mode of elect. etc. of second chamber
Australia	22.3	32.1	Direct election – PR (STV)
Austria	26.8	20.3	Indirect election by prov. Ass. – PR
Belgium	23.3	28.2	Mixed – most directly elected – PR
Canada	19.9	30.5	Appointed
France	10.9	6.3	Indirect election: electoral colleges in depts. – maj.(2 ballot)
Germany	30.9	18.8	Appointed
Ireland	12.1	22.4	Mixed – most indirectly elected – PR
Italy	11.1	8.0	Most elected – FPTP + PR (75/25%)
Japan	7.3	17.1	Direct election – FPTP + PR (40/60%)
Netherlands	36.0	26.7	Indirect election – PR (party list)
Spain	28.3	22.8	Mixed – most directly elected – maj/pref. vote
Switzerland	23.0	19.6	Direct election – mostly maj.
UK	18.4	15.6	Mostly appointed, some hereditary
US	12.9	9.0	Direct election – FPTP

Source: IPU website.

Notes: The Netherlands is the only country to reverse the usual terminology of first or lower chamber and second or upper chamber, so the Eerste Kamer (First Chamber) is the upper house and the Tweede Kamer (Second Chamber) is the lower house.

Gender

It is a well-established fact that women are under-represented, usually significantly so, in legislatures and this is true of the 14 countries included in Table 2 in respect of both first and second chambers. However, as the table also shows, although five clearly have a lower proportion of women in the second chamber, five have a higher proportion and the remaining four are close to parity, with a less than four per cent difference.[6] It is therefore not surprising that there is no difference on average in the proportion of women in first and second chambers: the mean for first chambers is 20.4 per cent and for second chambers 19.9 per cent.

It has been clearly shown that proportional representation (PR), especially when combined with a party list system, results in the selection and election of more women legislators, whereas first-past-the-post or simple plurality electoral systems militate against the selection and election of women.[7] This is very clearly supported by the data in the table in the case of first chambers: seven of the eight countries with an above-average proportion of women use PR and party list systems, except for Germany, which uses this system to elect half the members of the Bundestag, and Australia, which uses the alternative vote, a majoritarian system, for elections to the House of Representatives. Although both Italy and Japan use a German-style added-member system, only a quarter and a third of the members respectively are elected by this method and this probably accounts for the lower proportion of women members. The only other country to use PR is Ireland, but it uses the single transferable vote, which is less helpful to women candidates. The situation with second chambers is similar, but less clear cut, since it is complicated by the use of indirect elections and systems of appointment. However, no second chamber with a below average proportion of women members uses a pure form of PR. More interesting are the five cases where the second chamber has a higher proportion of women than the first chamber in that, with the exception of Canada, all use some form of PR, either alone in direct elections (Australia and Belgium) or indirectly (Ireland), or in combination with the simple plurality (Japan). In fact, Japan is a particularly interesting case: whereas a majority (two-thirds) of the members of the House of Representatives are elected by simple plurality, a majority (three-fifths) of the House of Councillors are elected by PR using a preferential system, which may enhance the chances of women being elected. In contrast, Spain, with a lower proportion of women in the second chamber, uses PR for the Chamber of Deputies and a majoritarian system for the Senate. Canada, where the proportion of women is more than ten per cent higher in the Senate than the House of Commons, is an example of the power of appointment being deliberately used to shift the balance. A similar, though less marked, effort has been made in the UK since the election of the Labour government in 1997. Russell points out that, of the 477 life peers in the House of Lords in the summer of 1999, 87 or 18.2 per cent were women and that, of the 181 life peers created between May 1997 and November 1999, 19.9 per cent were women.[8] The removal of most of the hereditary peers, as a result of the passing of the House of Lords Reform Act in November 1999, therefore inevitably involved an increased proportion of women in the upper house.

Occupation

Two features stand out in the occupational data in Table 3: first, there is a basic similarity in the occupational profiles of the two senates; and, second, both senates are very similar to their respective lower chambers. In the Belgian and French Senates teachers constitute the largest single occupational group and the next four groups are the same, though not in the same order. What marks off the French Senate is the much higher proportion of farmers, a consequence almost certainly of the over-representation of rural areas in the constitution of the French upper house. The similarities between the upper and lower houses in both countries is also apparent, with the same four occupations heading the list in Belgium and three of the four in France. There are, however, differences, notably the much higher proportion of the 'liberal professions', mostly lawyers, in both lower houses.

The Italian Senate displays some of the same characteristics as its Belgian and French counterparts, with an occupational similarity between the first and second chambers, but differing in detail with, for example, more journalists/writers/publishers in the Italian Parliament. However,

TABLE 3
OCCUPATIONS OF MEMBERS OF THE BELGIAN AND FRENCH PARLIAMENTS

	Belgium		**France**	
Occupation	**Senate**	**Ch. of Deps.**	**Senate**	**Nat. Ass.**
Teachers	23.9	27.3	21.8	25.6
Private sector employees	21.1	19.3	12.8	16.6
Civil servants	18.3	14.7	13.4	16.8
Liberal professions	12.7	24.7	12.1	31.2
Medical professions	9.9	0.0	13.7	}
Business/trade/industry	5.6	0.0	10.0	}
Self-employed	4.2	10.0	0.0	}
Farmers	1.4	0.0	10.9	} Others 9.7
Others	1.4	0.0	0.0	}
Retired	1.4	1.3	0.0	}
Journ./writers/publishers	0.0	1.3	0.0	}
Unemployed	0.0	1.3	5.3	}
Total	99.9	99.9	100.0	99.9

Source: IPU website.

teachers (if that category and 'academics/researchers' are combined) and the legal profession again figure prominently. The Swiss Parliament offers more of a contrast, with lawyers heading the list in the Council of State or upper house, but with twice the proportion found in the Nationalrat and farmers are also more common in the latter. However, there are fewer teachers in the Swiss Parliament than in the other three legislatures.

TABLE 4
OCCUPATIONS OF MEMBERS OF THE ITALIAN AND SWISS PARLIAMENTS

A. ITALY

Occupation	**Senate**	**Ch. of Deps.**
Academics/researchers	15.6	9.2
Legal professions	15.6	17.4
Others	13.6	15.5
Civil servants	6.7	6.3
Managers	6.7	10.0
Journs./writers/publishers	6.3	6.8
Medical professions	6.3	6.5
Teachers	6.3	6.3
Retired	5.4	2.2
Politicians	5.1	0.0
Private sector employees	5.1	5.9
Farmers	4.4	8.5
Trade unionists	2.9	1.7
Engineers	0.0	1.9
Business/trade/industry	0.0	1.7
Total	100.0	99.9

B. SWITZERLAND

Occupation	**Council of State**	**National Council**
Legal professions	41.3	20.0
Others	15.2	13.5
Business/trade/industry	8.7	9.0
Politicians	6.5	1.5
Teachers	6.5	10.0
Association staff	4.3	3.5
Economists	4.3	4.0
Self-employed	4.3	11.0
Housewives	2.2	1.0
Journs./writers/publishers	2.2	2.5
Medical professions	2.2	5.5
Private sector employees	2.2	0.0
Farmers	0.0	11.5
Civil servants	0.0	3.5
Engineers	0.0	3.5
Total	99.9	100.0

Source: IPU website.

TABLE 5
THE PROVISION OF SALARIES, PENSIONS, REVIEW MACHINERY FOR AND THE FULL-TIME/PART-TIME STATUS OF MEMBERS OF SECOND CHAMBERS

Country	Salaried	Higher or lower than 1st chamber	Pension scheme	Regular review or indexed	Full-time or part time
Australia	Yes	Equal	Yes	Yes	Full-time
Austria	Yes	Equal	No	Yes	Full-time
Belgium	Yes	Equal	Yes	Yes	Full-time
Canada	Yes	Equal	Yes	Yes	Full-time
France	Yes	Equal	Yes	Yes	Full-time
Germany	No	Not applic.	No	No	Part-time
Ireland	Yes	Less	Yes	Yes	Mostly part-time
Italy	Yes	Equal	Yes	Yes	Full-time
Japan	Yes	Equal	Yes	Yes	Full-time
Spain	Yes	Equal	Yes	Yes	Full-time
Switzerland	Yes	Equal	Yes	Yes	Full-time
UK	No	Not applic.	No	Not applic.	Mostly part-time
US	Yes	Equal	Yes	Yes	Full-time

Sources: Australia, Canada, Ireland and Spain – staff of the legislature concerned; remainder IPU website; additional information from Meg Russell.
Note: No information was available on the Dutch Eerste Kamer.

Of course, differences between countries are to be expected and, no doubt, were systematic data on more countries available, other contrasts would emerge. Yet the data that are available suggest two conclusions: first, that there are more similarities than differences, both between chambers in a particular country and between second chambers in different countries; and, second, that second chambers, probably more so than first chambers, fulfil the cliché that members of legislatures in liberal democracies are mostly male, middle-aged and middle class.

PAY AND PENSIONS

The contrast between the UK and other countries, with the partial exception of Ireland and special exception of Germany, could not be more marked in the data shown in Table 5. The German Bundesrat is an exception because its members are members of, nominated by and represent the Land governments and, as such, are paid salaries and provided with pension schemes by those governments. Eleven of the 12 remaining countries pay members of their second chambers a salary; ten of the 12 pay the same salary to members of the upper and lower houses; ten provide a pension scheme; and ten regard being a member of the second chamber as a full-time position. Only Senators in Ireland are paid less than members of the lower house and most Irish Senators are part-time rather than full-time. Nonetheless, the contrast with the House of Lords could not be starker.

There is no difficulty in explaining this contrast, however. Historically, the House of Lords originated as a body representing the landed aristocracy, whose wealth obviated the need for payment. In contrast, some members of the House of Commons were originally paid wages or expenses by their constituents, but the practice had largely died out by the end of the fifteenth century and MPs remained unremunerated until 1912.[9] The payment of MPs, when it came, stemmed not from principle, but from expedience, from the particular needs of Labour and Liberal-Labour MPs, most of whom had little or no personal income, unlike the great majority of MPs.[10] All that had changed as far as members of the House of Lords were concerned was that many more now drew their wealth from manufacturing, commerce and finance, rather than the land; there was neither need nor pressure to pay them. But linked to this was a widespread view that full-time politicians were and are an undesirable phenomenon, a view strongly echoed in the report of the Royal Commission on the Reform of the House of Lords (the Wakeham Commission) in January 2000. The Commission took the view that a reformed second chamber 'should contain a substantial proportion of people who were not professional politicians … [and that] part-time membership … should continue to be facilitated'.[11] It therefore recommended not a salary but payment based on attendance. However, the total payment possible should not exceed the basic salary of a backbench member of the House of Commons,[12] although it did recommend that members who chaired 'significant committees' should be paid a salary,[13] a practice widespread in other legislatures in both first and second chambers.

RESOURCES

In 1967, in reference to British MPs, Bernard Crick wrote: 'Clearly a Member should be able to draw on public funds, or be reimbursed from them, for those essentials he needs to do his job properly: secretary, office, postage, telephone and travel'.[14] At that time British MPs could claim free travel for journeys between London, their constituencies and their homes (introduced to cover only journeys between London and their constituencies in 1924), limited postage (only to government departments, local authorities and health authorities in their constituencies), and telephone calls in the London area (an historical anomaly). There was no provision for secretarial or other staff, and office accommodation, much of it shared, was available to fewer than half the members, including ministers, although such cost of staff and other expenses could be claimed against tax.[15] The major omission

TABLE 6
THE RESOURCES AVAILABLE TO MEMBERS OF SECOND CHAMBERS

Country	Office	Staff	Travel	Subsist.	Tel.	Internet	Postage	Station	Elect. all
Australia	Suite	3	Yes	Yes	Yes	Yes	Yes	Yes	Yes
Austria	Yes	Allow	Yes	Yes	Yes	Yes	Yes	Yes	No
Belgium	Yes	1–2	Yes	Yes	Yes	Yes	Yes	Yes	Gen. all
Canada	Suite	4–5	Yes	Yes	Yes	Yes	Yes	Yes	n.a.
France	Yes	3	Yes	Yes	Yes	Yes	Yes	Yes	Gen. all
Germany	No	No	Yes	Yes	Limit.	Limit.	No	No	No
Ireland	No	Limit/ shared	Yes	Yes	Limit.	Limit.	Yes	Yes	n.a.
Italy	Yes	2	Yes	Yes	Yes	Yes	Yes	Yes	No
Japan	Yes	Yes	Yes	Yes	Yes	Yes	Yes	Yes	Gen. all
Spain	No	Party groups	Yes	Yes	Yes	Yes	Yes	Yes	No
Switzerland	Yes	Yes	Yes	Yes	Yes	Yes	Yes	Yes	No
UK	Limit.	All.	Yes	Yes	Yes	Yes	Yes	Yes	n.a.
US	Suite	15–40	Yes	Yes	Yes	Yes	Yes	Yes	Gen. all

Sources: Australia, Canada, Ireland and Spain – staff of the legislature concerned; remainder IPU website; additional information from Meg Russell.
Note: No information was available on the Dutch Eerste Kamer.

from Crick's 'shopping list' was subsistence to enable MPs to meet the expenses, other than travel, of attending parliament, especially those with constituencies more than commuting distance from London. Developments and improvements in all these areas came soon after Crick wrote, or rather republished, these words, since the first edition of *The Reform of Parliament* was published in 1964. And, not surprisingly, there have continued to be improvements since, especially after a proper distinction between salary and expenses was drawn in 1972.[16] Crick's list, plus the provision of subsistence, provides an appropriate basis for comparing the resources available to members of second chambers.

No attempt has been made in Table 6 to provide detailed information for all the countries covered, since it was not available in each case, but in some cases more detail is provided to give some indication that the provision of resources varies significantly. There is no doubt, for instance, that the resources available to Australian, Canadian, French and American Senators are extensive, especially to the latter in terms of staff. Comparison, however, is complicated by the fact that resources are provided by different means in different countries. For example, the provision of staff, subsistence, travel, postal and telephone services may be provided directly, or covered by a general expenses allowance, or by specific allowances, or by reimbursement. Where resources are provided by allowances, general or specific, they may be subject to varying degrees of checking and auditing and may or may not be taxable. In some cases, a proportion of the salary is tax-free as a contribution towards expenses, and so on. Nonetheless, it is possible, as the data in Table 6 indicate, to produce a reasonably clear picture of the range and extent of the resources available to members of second chambers

Members of the German Bundesrat are again a special case, since they are provided with resources in their capacity as members of a Land government, so that, travel and subsistence apart, there is either no or only limited provision for separate resources in their role as members of the second chamber. There are also differences between those second chambers whose members are elected and therefore have constituents to represent or, at least in the case of France, indirectly elected, but nonetheless regarded as representing identifiable territories and interests. However, this does not apply to Irish Senators, even though they represent functional groups in society, nor does it apply to Italian Senators, even though they are directly elected (but it does not apply to Italian MPs either). In some cases separate provision is made for maintaining an office and staff in the constituency and meeting other constituency expenses, in others resources are provided through an adjustment to the general allowance based on the number of electors. It is also a common practice for additional resources to be provided for party groups in many legislatures (or for parties other than the governing party or parties) and second chambers are no exception.[17]

Irish Senators and members of the House of Lords fare least well compared with members of second chambers in other countries. Both are mostly part-time and neither has constituents. Yet the Irish Senate has become busier in recent years and the House of Lords meets more often than any other of the legislative chambers in the countries covered, other than the UK House of Commons. The general trend is for legislatures to become busier and for their members to be full-time, either in the sense that they have no other occupation or that being a member of the legislature is very much their principal occupation. This trend can be seen not only at national level, but in sub-national legislatures as well.[18] An inevitable concomitant of this is for better and more extensive resources to be introduced. This was recognised by the Wakeham Commission in that it recommended that additional office accommodation and secretarial resources should be provided for members of a reformed House of Lords[19] and that the existing travel and subsistence allowances should be reviewed 'with a view to ensuring that regular attendance is economically viable to [members] who live outside London'.[20] Such improvements, however, would hardly bring the UK into line with second chambers elsewhere; the House of Lords would remain an exception.

CONCLUSION

Second chambers have much in common with first chambers in terms of composition and the provision of the pay and resources available to their members. However, their members tend to be older, particularly where a higher minimum age qualification applies than for membership of the first chamber. Some second chambers actually have a higher proportion of women members, but women remain significantly under-represented. In other aspects of socio-economic composition the available evidence suggests that second chambers do not, on the whole, differ markedly from first chambers.

The norm as far as pay and resources are concerned is for members of second chambers to be full-time, salaried legislators, with a high level of resources in a number of cases and adequate resources in most others. However, the German Bundesrat apart, the UK House of Lords stands out as a major exception and every indication is that it will remain so for the foreseeable future.

NOTES

1. See, for example, M. Rush, 'The Pay, Allowances, Services and Facilities of Legislators in Eighteen Countries and the European Parliament: A Comparative Survey', Review Body on Senior Salaries, *Report No. 38: Review of Parliamentary Pay and Allowances*, Cm. 3330-II, July 1996, Vol.2: Surveys and Studies, pp.38–59 and T. Stark, 'International Comparisons on the Remuneration of Members of Parliament, Review Body on Senior Salaries, *Report No. 38*, pp.60–68.
2. See G. Mosca, *The Ruling Class*, trans. H.D. Kahn, ed. A. Livingston (New York: McGraw-Hill, 1939; originally published 1896); V. Pareto, *The Mind and Society*, trans. A. Bengiorno and A. Livingston, ed. A. Livingston (New York: Harcourt-Brace, 1925; originally published 1916); R. Michels, *Political Parties: A Sociological Study of the Oligarchical State of Modern Democracy*, trans. E. and C. Paul (New York: Dover, 1962; originally published 1911); C. Wright Mills, *The Power Elite* (Oxford: Oxford University Press, 1956); T.B. Bottomore, *Elites and Society* (London: Watts, 1964); G. Parry, *Political Elites* (London: Allen and Unwin, 1969); D.R. Matthews, *The Social Background of Political Decision-Makers* (New York: Random House, 1965); D.R. Matthews, *US Senators and their World* (New York: Vintage, 1960); J.D. Barber, *The Lawmakers: Recruitment and Adaptation to Legislative Life* (New Haven, CT: Yale University Press, 1965); W.L. Guttsman, *The British Political Elite* (London: McGibbon and Kee, 1963); and H. Best and M. Cotta (eds.), *Parliamentary Representatives in Europe 1848–2000: Legislative Recruitment and Careers in Eleven European Countries* (Oxford: Oxford University Press, 2000).
3. M. Russell, *Reforming the House of Lords: Lessons from Overseas*, (Oxford: Oxford University Press, 2000), p.33, and Inter-Parliamentary Union website – www.ipu.org. All Latin American states with bicameral legislatures modelled on the US Constitution have a higher age qualification for senators: Argentina, Colombia and Uruguay – 30; Bolivia and Brazil 35; and Chile and Paraguay – 40.
4. Russell, *Reforming the House of Lords*, p.4. In August 2000 the average age of members of the House of Lords was 68. House of Lords website – www.parliament.uk/ld.
5. Russell, *Reforming the House of Lords*, p.103.
6. It is likely that for electoral and legislative recruitment reasons the proportion of women MPs

in the British House of Commons will fall at the 2001 election, possibly to the extent of leaving the House of Lords with a higher proportion of women than the Commons.

7. See M. Gallagher and M. Marsh (eds.), *Candidate Selection in Comparative Perspective: The Secret Garden of Politics* (London: Sage, 1988); P. Norris and J. Lovenduski, *Political Recruitment: Gender, Race and Class in the British Parliament* (Cambridge: Cambridge University Press, 1995); and P. Norris, 'Legislative Recruitment', in L. LeDuc, R.G. Niemi and P. Norris (eds.), *Comparing Democracies: Elections and Voting in Global Perspective* (London: Sage, 1996).
8. Russell, *Reforming the House of Lords*, p.326.
9. See C. Townsend, *History of the House of Commons: From the Convention Parliament of 1688–89 to the Passage of the Reform Bill in 1832* (London: Henry Colburn, 1843), Vol.II, pp.362–72; and E. Porritt, *The Unreformed House of Commons* (Cambridge: Cambridge University Press, 1909), vol.I, ch.XII.
10. The catalyst in this process was a court judgment in 1909 (the Osborne Judgment) that declared payments by trade unions to MPs illegal.
11. The Royal Commission on the Reform of the House of Lords (the Wakeham Commission), *A House for the Future*, Cm. 4534, Jan. 2000, para. 10.18.
12. *A House for the Future*, paras. 17.9–11.
13. *A House for the Future*, para. 17.12.
14. B. Crick, *The Reform of Parliament* (London: Weidenfeld and Nicolson, 2nd rev. edn. 1968; first edn. published 1964), pp.66–7.
15. For an account of the development of pay and resources at Westminster see M. Rush and M. Shaw (eds.), *The House of Commons: Services and Facilities* (London: Allen and Unwin, 1974) and M. Rush (ed.), *The House of Commons: Services and Facilities, 1972–1982* (London: Policy Studies Institute, 1983); and M. Rush and D. Jones, 'Services and Facilities' in D. Shell and D. Beamish (eds.), *The House of Lords at Work: A Study of the 1988–89 Session* (Oxford: Clarendon Press, 1993), pp.308–24.
16. See Review Body on Top Salaries, *Ministers of the Crown and Members of Parliament*, Cmnd. 4836, Dec. 1971, para. 33.
17. This is the case in most continental European legislatures. The opposition parties in the House of Lords (currently the Conservatives and Liberal Democrats) and the crossbench group of peers receive grants to support them in carrying out their parliamentary duties.
18. See M. Rush, 'The pay, allowances, services and facilities of legislators in sub-national legislatures: a comparative survey', Review Body on Senior Salaries, *Report No. 47: Initial Pay, Allowances, Pensions and Severance Arrangements for Members of the Scottish Parliament, National Assembly of Wales and Northern Ireland Assembly*, Cm. 4188, March 1999, pp.87–105.
19. Review Body on Senior Salaries, *Report No. 47*, para. 17.15.
20. Review Body on Senior Salaries, *Report No. 47*, para. 17.17.

Fundamentals of Institutional Design: The Functions and Powers of Parliamentary Second Chambers

SAMUEL C. PATTERSON and ANTHONY MUGHAN

There is a powerful sense in which, if you have seen one parliamentary body, you have seen them all. Of course, there are many differences in detail – of constitutional form, organisation, rules, influence, habits, standards of appropriate conduct. Nevertheless, on a wide canvas representative assemblies around the world have much in common. They are collective decision-making bodies that follow long-standing, widely shared practices and procedures epitomised in the British Parliament and the United States Congress and replicated, with variations, in many countries. These two famous, even maternal, parliaments have metamorphosed in many ways over the centuries.

Still, it seems likely that if Edmund Burke or William Pitt could be resurrected to visit today's British House of Commons, or if Henry Clay could sit in today's US House of Representatives, they would be at home. In 1999, parliaments remained in 178 countries, according to the tally kept by the International Parliamentary Union headquartered in Geneva; today (2000) the figure is 177. The family resemblance among these parliamentary entities is very marked. But, of course, there are differences in the institutional design and performance of parliaments, and these lie at the heart of parliamentary analysis.

The upper houses of the world's parliaments, most commonly called senates, have not been given much attention by scholars or commentators.[1] Accordingly, the relevant legislative literature is not generally very informative as to the powers and functions of these institutions. Of course, the most venerable of upper houses, the US Senate and the British House of Lords, have been studied by scholars and receive considerable public notoriety.[2] More recently, greater attention has been focused on bicameralism and senate institutions.[3] Despite the notable inattention to

Samuel C. Patterson is Professor Emeritus, Political Science, Ohio State University and Anthony Mughan is Professor of Political Science and Director of the Undergraduate International Studies Program at Ohio State University upper houses, these institutions have persisted, and in many ways they are thriving today.

Of course, most of the world's parliaments are unicameral – they have only one house.[4] When the Inter-Parliamentary Union took its regular inventory of national parliaments in 1999, it found 67 bicameral institutions, almost 38 per cent of parliaments. Since 1997, upper houses have been established in Algeria, Liberia, Morocco, Nigeria, Senegal and Slovenia; the Congo Sénat did not come into existence as expected; and in late 1999 the Pakistani Senate was dissolved, along with the National Assembly, in a military coup. In short, the number of senates is growing.

DEMOCRATIC FERTILITY FOR UPPER HOUSES

Upper houses are to be found in all parts of the world. Most of the national legislatures in the western hemisphere are bicameral, so there are senates not only in the United States, Canada and Mexico, but also in the South American countries of Argentina, Bolivia, Brazil, Chile, Colombia, Paraguay, Uruguay and Venezuela (as well as in several Central American and West Indian republics). Upper houses exist in the parliamentary assemblies of the major western European countries, including Austria, Belgium, France, Germany, Ireland, Italy, the Netherlands, Switzerland and the United Kingdom. In the 1990s, as the countries of the old Soviet bloc established democratic parliaments, many, including the Czech Republic, Croatia, Poland, Romania, Russia and Yugoslavia, created upper houses.

Senates are more widely scattered elsewhere in the world, but they are significant parliamentary institutions in Western Pacific countries such as Australia, Japan, Malaysia and the Philippines, and in the Asian countries of India, Pakistan and Thailand. Again, a number of small countries in the Middle East (such as Jordan) and Africa (such as Ethiopia, Namibia or South Africa) have parliaments with upper houses. It is very likely that the geopolitical location of upper houses has some bearing on their power and influence, in as much as the potential for senate power is doubtless greater in large, major countries where areal representation is important and where democratic policy-making is on a firm footing.

Upper houses vary strikingly in size. The senates of small countries and island republics are the smallest – Belize has a Senate of only eight members. The US Senate, with 100 senators, is somewhat larger than the average upper house, but a number of other senates are also quite large; the upper houses in France, India, Italy, Japan, Spain, Thailand and the UK have more than 200 members. The size of the British House of Lords was pruned by about half (from 1,325 to 671) through the enactment of a House of Lords bill in November 1999 that denied hereditary peers automatic membership in the House (although the number had risen to 693 by May 2001). In so far as size reflects effective political representation, it may have some bearing on the power and influence of upper houses.

More important than size itself to the power of senates is likely to be the ways in which the members are chosen. The more democratic senates, where all or most members are elected by the people, directly or indirectly, are likely to carry greater weight in the parliamentary arena than those senates whose members are appointed. Today, senators are directly or indirectly elected in 38 senates (57 per cent); in 21 senates (31 per cent), all members are directly elected by the citizens. In 19 senates (28 per cent), the membership is entirely appointed, where senators are named by the monarch, the head of state or the chief executive. In some of these, like the Canadian Senate, the powers of the upper house, while perhaps weak, are not trivial, but many appointed senates appear to be puppet bodies, with membership largely perfunctory or honorary and lacking a constituency base.

The democratic fertility of the milieu in which senates reside doubtless impinges on the scope of their functions and their relative power. The large and diverse republics enjoying a fecund tradition of constitutionalism and grassroots democracy tend to be those in which a vibrant parliamentarism flourishes, and with it a relatively active and influential upper house. But a democratic environment does not necessarily lead to senate power; other structural and organisational properties need to be taken into account. These properties include the constitutional structure, the design of the parliamentary institution, the nature of government and opposition in parliament, the policy space in which lawmakers operate, and the internal organisational contours of the legislative houses.

'SYMMETRIC' AND 'ASYMMETRIC' BICAMERALISM

Because only a few bicameral parliaments have been studied with any care, it is not easy to distinguish strong and weak upper houses across the board. Nevertheless, it is possible to characterise broadly the relative power dispersion between the two houses of parliament, at least in the light of the constitutional assignment of powers and functions to the lower and upper houses. We have determined to array upper houses on a continuum from 'symmetric' (where the two houses are coequal, exercising the same powers and functions), on one end of the continuum, to 'asymmetric'

FIGURE 1
SYMMETRY OF CONSTITUTIONAL POWERS OF UPPER HOUSES

Co-equal with Lower House	Co-equal with Restrictions	Limited Exclusive Powers, Veto	Delay and Advisory	Subordinate to Lower House
Italian Senato Liberian Senate Mexican Cámara de Senadores Nigerian Senate Romanian Senatul Swiss Ständerat United States Senate	Argentine Senado Australian Senate Belgian Sénat Haitian Sénat Indian Rajya Sabha Malaysian Dewan Negara Nepalese Rastriya Sabha Pakistani Senate Philippine Senado South African National Council	Brazilian Senado Chilean Senado Colombian Senado German Bundesrat Venezuelan Senado	Austrian Bundesrat Canadian Senate Czech Senat Jordanian Majlis al-Aayan Netherlands Eerste Kamer Thai Wuthisapha	British House of Lords French Sénat Irish Seanad Eireann Japanese Sangiin Polish Senat Russian Soviet Federatsii Spanish Senado

(where one house is subordinate to the other), on the other end.[5] We collected information about the powers and functions of 36 national upper houses as a basis for comparison and analysis (see the Appendix for details).

Figure 1 shows the distribution of senates according to the relative dispersion of power between the lower and upper houses of bicameral parliaments. At one end of this continuum are senates that are constitutionally coequal with the lower houses (sometimes called 'egalitarian bicameralism'), followed by senates that are 'coequal with restrictions'; the most common restriction gives priority to the lower house in considering financial legislation. On the one hand, some of these senates, such as those in Liberia, Nigeria, Haiti or Pakistan are not robust institutions (in fact, the Haitian and Pakistani senates have recently been suspended, the Haitian pending national elections and the Pakistani pending reorganisation following the military coup). But theoretically they were established as coequal bicameral bodies. In short, these senates perform the same functions and have the same powers as the lower houses, although the parliaments as a whole are weak.

On the other hand, the coequal condition embraces a number of very powerful upper houses – in polities such as Italy, Switzerland, the United States of America or Australia. The Italian Senato della Repubblica is on a par with the lower house in legislative powers, and it uniquely plays the same role as the lower house in the confirmation of the prime minister and cabinet ministers, and in consideration and approval of financial legislation. Accordingly, the Italian parliament is described as a case of 'perfect bicameralism'.[6] The legislative powers of the Swiss Ständerat are exactly the same as those of the lower house, and both houses play the same role in the selection of the federal council, whose chairman serves as president of the confederation (a post that circulates annually among the seven federal council members).

The United States Senate is frequently characterised as the most powerful upper house in the world. Although the US Constitution requires that tax legislation be initiated in the House of Representatives, this has proved a fairly nominal provision and the Senate has as much financial power as the House, if not more. And, despite the fact that the US Senate was founded as a federal house, composed of two senators from each state and originally chosen by the state legislatures, that body soon evolved into a national legislative institution on an equal footing with the lower house. Indeed, the contemporary US Senate is 'the more visible and more prestigious chamber'.[7] By the same token, the Australian Senate is overwhelmingly on a par with the House of Representatives save for formal constitutional provisions prohibiting the Senate from amending tax or budget bills. But the Senate has unlimited power to return bills to the House unapproved, and in this event the House's only recourse is to invoke the deadlock procedures.[8] Like the US Senate, the Australian Senate came to be a national institution rather than a states' house, but unlike the individualistic US Senate the Australian Senate has evolved as a highly partisan body.[9]

Some senates have law-making powers like those of their lower houses, but these senates may both be constrained with respect to financial legislation and have the constitutional authority to exercise some powers exclusively. The South American countries of Brazil, Chile, Colombia and Venezuela epitomise this institutional situation. For example, the senates in these four polities are accorded certain judicial powers, such as impeachment and trial of the president or other government officials. In the instance of the German Bundesrat, the exclusive power concerns the states, or Länder. Composed of state officials numbered in proportion to the state populations who vote *en bloc*, the Bundesrat may veto legislation adopted by the lower house if state interests are paramount. Its absolute veto power applies to about half of all bills the Bundestag may pass, and other legislation may be delayed by the upper house.[10] Thus, the Bundesrat is, especially within the realm of state-related legislation, a powerful house, and uniquely 'a very federal house'.

As Figure 1 indicates, some upper houses are largely advisory, or may only delay the passage of laws. Such is the nature of the so-called 'persisting vote' in the Austrian lower house, whereby majorities may override Bundesrat rejection of bills. Although the appointed Canadian

Senate flexed its muscles between 1984 and 1993, demonstrating its potential legislative power, normally it has played the role of revising and delaying legislation adopted by the House of Commons.[11] The senates in the Czech Republic, Jordan, the Netherlands and Thailand have some legislative role, but in the end only a suspensive veto of actions by the lower houses. In the Netherlands' Eerste Kamer, government bills may not be amended.

Finally, there are upper houses that are fully subordinate to the lower houses – in the UK, France, Ireland, Japan, Poland, Russia and Spain. The British House of Lords, despite the drastic reduction of its hereditary membership in 1999, remains an anachronism. In recent years, it has made various constructive contributions to legislation through deliberation, delay, amendment and compromise, but it is the popular lower house that generally prevails.[12] The French Sénat truly has been a 'chamber of reflection', enjoying only limited legislative power. It 'exercises influence by engaging in dialogue with the lower house and suggesting amendments ... but deputies in the National Assembly have the last word'. Still, despite this limited formal power, the upper house, 'combining persuasion and amendment, negotiation and accommodation, pressure and retreat, reflection and imagination ... has managed to carve out a place for itself'.[13]

The Polish and Spanish senates are subordinate to the lower houses, where the final legislative decisions are rendered. The Polish Senat reviews legislation adopted by the lower house, the Sejm, but that body may, in turn, override or reject the senate's actions. Thus, the Polish upper house has been something of a puzzle to observers, 'an institution in search of a mission'.[14] The Spanish Senado 'falls among the weakest of democratic upper houses'. It can perform an advisory function, engage in inquiries and oversight of the executive, and play some role in the selection of governmental personnel. But its legislative role is minimal; its legislative actions can be overridden by a majority vote in the lower house, and it can, in any event, only delay legislation.[15]

The condition of symmetrical vs. asymmetrical bicameralism provides a basis for assaying the power of upper houses in relation to their counterpart lower houses. But the more global influence of upper houses may be assessed in light of other significant conditions. Among these is the constitutional structure in which parliament operates, and its institutional design.

STRUCTURAL ENVELOPE AND INSTITUTIONAL DESIGN

Are upper houses more likely to be influential in federal or in unitary systems of government? And are upper houses prone to greater power

TABLE 1
CONSTITUTIONAL STRUCTURE AND PARLIAMENTARY DESIGN

Parliamentary institution is:	**Constitutional system is:**	
	Unitary	**Federal**
Unicameral	111 (70.3%)	0 (0%)
Bicameral	47 (29.7%)	20 (100%)
Total number	158	20

Note: In the 1990s, constitutions were adopted in Cameroon (1996), Chad (1996), Madagascar (1992), and Malawi (1994) providing for the establishment of senates, but these provisions have not been implemented; these parliaments are counted as unicameral. The Norwegian Stortinget is counted here as unicameral, though in passing legislation it divides into two chambers, the 124-member Odelsting and the 41-member Lagting. Upper houses were abolished in New Zealand (1950), Denmark (1953), and Sweden (1971). The Slovenian parliament is counted here as bicameral, but in fact its upper house, the National Council, has only an advisory and not a law-making function.
Sources: See Appendix.

because bicameral parliaments are simply designed to be more powerful than unicameral parliaments? Again, are upper houses likely to be stronger in presidential systems where there exists a separation of powers between the executive and legislative branches of government, or in parliamentary systems where the executive and legislative entities are closely tied together? These questions are not easy to answer with certainty.

All the parliaments in the federal systems of this world are bicameral. According to the most recent inventory of the Inter-Parliamentary Union, the existing 20 federal systems unanimously deploy two house legislatures. But bicameralism is not limited to federal systems; very nearly a third (29.7 per cent) of the unitary countries also practise bicameral parliamentarism (see Table 1). Moreover, as Table 1 shows, of the 67 two-house parliaments, 47 (70.1 per cent) are located in unitary countries. Still, the upper houses that are widely acknowledged to be the strongest function in federal environments – in Switzerland, the United States, Australia, perhaps Belgium, and Germany – among unitary systems, only the Italian senate is accorded comparable legislative power. Of the upper houses considered in this analysis that are nominally subordinate to the lower houses – in Britain, France, Ireland, Japan, Poland, Russia and Spain – all are unitary except Russia.

There does seem to be a relationship between the intercameral dispersion of legislative power and executive structure. In Table 2, we compare presidential and parliamentary systems in the light of the symmetry or asymmetry of power between houses of parliament. The senates that are coequal with the lower house function mainly in presidential systems, while the subordinate senates are located in parliamentary regimes. Presidential systems that accord separate constitutional powers to executive and legislative institutions appear, *ceteris paribus*, to foster autonomous senates on a par with lower houses; when government and parliament are intermingled, as in parliamentary systems, the government's connection to the lower, popularly elected lower house is likely to pre-empt a strong upper house.

TABLE 2
EXECUTIVE STRUCTURE AND UPPER HOUSE POWER

Upper House Power is:	Executive Structure is: Presidential	Parliamentary with a President	Parliamentary
Co-equal with Lower House (N = 7)	United States Senate Liberian Senate Mexican Cámara de Senadores Nigerian Senate Swiss Ständerat	Italian Senato Romanian Senatul	
Co-equal with Restrictions (N = 10)	Argentine Senado Philippine Senado South African National Council	Haitian Senát Indian Rajya Sabha	Australian Senate Belgian Sénat Pakistani Senate Malaysian Dewan Negra Nepalese Rastriya Sabha
Limited Exclusive Powers, Veto (N = 5)	Brazilian Senado Chilean Senado Colombian Senado Venezuelan Senado	German Bundesrat	
Delay & Advisory (N = 6)		Austrian Bundesrat Czech Senat	Canadian Senate Jordanian Majlis al-Aayan Netherlands Tweede Kamer Thai Wuthisapha
Subordinate to Lower House (N = 7)		French Sénat Irish Seanad Eireann Polish Senat Russian Soviet Federatsii	British House of Commons Japanese Sangiin Spanish Senado
Total number	12	11	12

Sources: See Figure 1 and Appendix.

GOVERNMENT AND OPPOSITION

Senates in which the executive power enjoys a firm parliamentary majority are less likely to carry influence over public policy. When a government has unqualified support from its fellow partisans in the parliamentary houses, the structure of political conflict tends to be that of government vs. opposition, rather than that of an independent parliament exercising influence on the policies and programmes of the government of the day. The American Senate is a powerful legislative body partly because presidents, even if they belong to the majority Senate party, cannot be certain of majority support for their policy initiatives. But the textbook case here involves the Australian Senate, where minority party representation deflects control by the major party caucuses and accords the Senate considerable leverage over the legislative agenda, budget bills and public policy generally. The adoption of proportional representation for Senate elections has meant that only rarely have governments won clear Senate majorities, producing a kind of 'divided government' in which a government with an unmistakable governing majority in the House of Representatives must satisfy dissenting parties and interests in the Senate.[16]

More fundamentally, the government, or the head of state, may utterly dominate the parliamentary institution. At the extreme, the members of the upper house may be appointed by the executive. In 1999, 40 per cent of the world's upper houses (27 of 67) contained appointed members; in 24 per cent (16 of 67) a majority of the members were appointed (all the members of 14 upper houses were appointed). Naturally, there is a correlation between the mode of selecting senators and the legislative equality of the upper house with the lower. In short, the popularly elected senates are much more likely to enjoy powers coequal with those of the lower house, and, conversely, appointed senates are likely to be subordinate to the lower house, or merely advisory. Many of these appointed senates are located in small countries such as Barbados, Jamaica, Jordan, Malaysia or Thailand. The Canadian Senate is an anomaly – an appointed body operating in a fairly large parliamentary democracy. Canadian senators are formally appointed by the governor-general, that peculiar figure standing in for the British monarch who is the powerless official Canadian head of state. In reality, senators are hand-picked by the prime minister, who may adjust the Senate's membership in harmony with the government party majority in the House of Commons.

If governments ease the influence of upper houses by virtue of appointing their membership, a variety of conditions may prevail in which the upper houses can constrain the executive. In Italy, prime ministers and cabinets must receive a vote of confidence in both parliamentary chambers – the Camera dei deputati and the Senato della repubblica. In principle, the upper house could declare 'no confidence' in the prime minister and cabinet, which would precipitate the resignation of the government; in practice, this kind of drama is largely played out in the lower house. No other upper house is accorded the confirmatory power enjoyed by the Italian Senato. It is true that the upper house of the Japanese Diet – the Sangiin, or House of Councillors – may play a role in the designation of the prime minister and cabinet, but if the upper house majority disagrees with the lower, or if the upper house fails to make a decision, 'the decision of the House of Representatives shall be the decision of the Diet' (Constitution of Japan, Art. 67). But, of course, in other parliamentary systems it is the lower house, not the upper, that provides the setting for the confirmation or dismissal of governments. And, it probably goes without saying that, in presidential regimes, the formal role of the legislative institution lies in the limited case of impeachment and removal of a sitting chief executive from office. Latin American senates (in Brazil, or Colombia, or Venezuela) may be empowered to conduct trials of government officials, or impeach the president.

POLICY SPACE

If the policy space of a legislative house is wide – if it can roam across the spectrum of public policy issues, broadly enmeshed in policy-making – then that house is powerful. If the house's policy space is narrow or cramped, or diminishing, then the house is weak. In parliamentary systems, the role of the upper house is generally constrained because most bills introduced are government bills, and legislation (especially financial bills) tends to originate in the lower house. Some senates – in Argentina, Belgium, Britain, the Czech Republic, Ireland, Malaysia, the Netherlands, South Africa or Thailand, may not amend or reject tax or budget bills passed by the lower house.

A *leitmotif* of a senate's legislative power is its law-making activity. Influential senates have high levels of legislative activity; weak senates are relatively inactive. Accordingly, influential upper houses like the US and Italian senates exhibit activity levels about the same as their lower houses. Weak upper houses are less active – for instance, the Polish senate meets only about half as many days as the lower house. The German Bundesrat is very active within the scope of its law-making powers, which concern the affairs and government of the Länder. The house meets only 12–15 times a year, but when it is in session it has a very full agenda. Few bills are actually initiated by the Bundesrat, but the lion's share of government bills must be scrutinised by the upper house. Today, about half of all bills require Bundesrat consent.[17] The stronger upper houses are persistently active legislatively, and many are becoming more so. But legislative activity can wax and wane; for instance, the Canadian Senate underwent a remarkable period of legislative activism from the mid-1980s until the mid-1990s. By 1997 the period of Senate activism had clearly diminished, and the Senate for the most part has reverted to its traditional less visible and less overtly partisan form of behaviour.[18]

Amending activity can be particularly crucial for upper houses. The US Senate is a hotbed of amending activity – 'senators are free to offer as many amendments as they wish, and amending marathons are frequent'.[19] In Germany, the upper house scrutinises government bills before they are introduced in the Bundestag, and upper house amendments may be incorporated into these bills prior to their consideration by the lower house.[20] The Australian Senate has made liberal use of its amending power; during a session of the mid-1990s, '157 bills attracted 1,812 successful Senate amendments at an average of 11 amendments per bill'.[21] Similarly, the French Sénat is heavily involved in amending activity, and 'the National Assembly accepts 50 to 85 percent of the amendments adopted by the Senate'.[22] In contrast to these senates with considerable amending power are those senates whose competence to amend bills is limited. For example, the Irish upper house cannot amend financial legislation passed by the lower house. Although both houses of the Dutch parliament must approve legislation, the upper house cannot amend government bills passed by the lower house. Again, the South African National Council of the Provinces, the nation's upper house, has no authority to amend tax or appropriations bills passed by the lower house.[23]

INTERNAL STRUCTURE

Other things being equal, the complexity of the internal structure of legislative bodies is likely to be correlated with institutional strength. Complex internal structure primarily embraces the organisation of parties and leaders, and the committee system. The two central features of internal structure – party and committee – both overlap and interact. In many senates, party and committee structures are mutually reinforcing, with committee memberships finely tuned to replicate the party group composition of the parent body. In parliamentary systems where this is the case, committees may exert considerable influence over legislation because the partisan structure of the house is built into them. Indeed, in Italy, majority party coalition confidence in committee decision-making is so great that committees may enact legislation on their own, *in sede deliberante*. In contrast, where the legislative parties are weak, committees may constitute the prevailing power centres. In the US Senate, with its relatively weak parties poorly linked to the extra-parliamentary party leadership, committees chaired by individualistic senators exert enormous influence in the house's legislative process.

Committee power depends upon a division of legislative labour in which senators can acquire expertise and authority with respect to a finite realm of legislation. Most senates have fewer than 20 permanent, or standing, committees. Here are some examples of the sizes of senate committee systems:

Australian Senate	16 committees
Czech Senat	9 committees
French Sénat	6 committees
German Bundesrat	17 committees
Italian Senato	13 committees
Japanese Sangiin	17 committees
Polish Senat	14 committees
US Senate	18 committees

Committee organisational practices vary in some interesting ways. The Australian Senate standing committees are organised in pairs; eight subject areas are divided into a pair of committees, one a reference committee to conduct inquiries and the other a legislation committee to consider government expenditure, legislation, and administration. Commonly, standing committee organisation conforms to the contours of the departmental structure of the executive branch, so that there is a committee on agriculture, on the interior, on defence, on education and so forth. But the six standing committees of the French Sénat have very broad jurisdictions, particularly the committees on social affairs and cultural affairs.

The formal rules governing parliamentary structure and action may derive from the constitution, extraordinary laws or the standing orders or rules of procedure adopted by the parliamentary houses. Crucially important is the reconciliation of legislative differences between the senate and its counterpart, the lower house. Two basic processes address what happens when the houses of a bicameral legislature adopt different versions of legislation or disagree on amendments: (1) a joint committee, usually called a conference committee, is appointed consisting of members of each house, who hammer out a compromise bill for each house to adopt; and (2) a shuttle system, referred to in France as the *navette*, in which a disputed bill is considered alternately by the two houses until agreement is reached. These intercameral proceedings provide a venue for the senates and lower houses to flex their legislative muscle.

In the case of the US Congress, most disputed bills shuttle between the Senate and the House of Representatives until each house has adopted them in the same form, or the bills fail. But intercameral disagreements over major bills tend to be resolved by conference committees – joint House–Senate committees composed of members of the substantive committees who first considered the legislation, appointed for the particular bill. In the conference committee environment, the Senate version of bills tends to be favoured.[24] In France, where the lower house, the Assemblée Nationale, makes the ultimate legislative decision when there is disagreement between the two houses, bills may shuttle between the houses until agreement is reached, and the two versions are identical. If agreement cannot be reached after two attempts by each house, the government may intervene, invoking the involvement of a joint conference committee composed of seven deputies and seven senators. For various reasons, in this environment the upper house is favoured.[25]

In Germany, a permanent joint conference committee called the Mediation Committee, composed of 16 members chosen by each house, may resolve intercameral differences. In this reconciliation process, the Bundesrat tends to have 'a weightier bargaining position than the Bundestag', but in practice the Mediation Committee procedure has not been invoked frequently.[26] In Australia, intercameral disagreement can yield drastic results if members persist; if there is deadlock, if the Senate fails twice to pass a House bill, a 'double dissolution' may be precipitated and national elections called for members of both houses. In summary, the parliamentary procedures for resolving differences between a senate and its lower house provide one instance in which the formal rules may impinge on senate power.

CONCLUDING REMARKS

In this chapter we have spelled out the more important constitutional and political factors enhancing, moderating or sometimes negating upper houses' performance of their policy-making, or influencing, function. It is an exercise in boundary drawing, not in detailed mapping of the role played in government by individual senates, or types of senate. Filling in the detail, searching for regularities and integrating into the study of government this hitherto largely ignored institution are the tasks that remain to be undertaken.

At the same time, we must not lose sight of the fact that influencing policy is not the only or, some would say, most important function of senates. At least two others can be identified and both relate to upper houses' ability to influence policy as well as to achieve other desired goals, like creating and sustaining a legitimate constitutional order. The first is their role as guarantor of institutional stability and the second their representational function. As a start, both these functions can profitably be subjected to the same boundary-drawing exercise in which we have engaged in this discussion. By way of example, let us first briefly examine the stability function. Above all, senates can act as guarantors of institutional continuity and constitutional integrity. They often play a key role in constitutional revisions, for instance. Senate approval, usually by a qualified majority, is commonly a prerequisite for amendments to be accepted, as well as for the appointment of constitutional judges, witness the two-thirds endorsement needed in the US Senate for the appointment of Supreme Court justices. In European countries like France and Germany, senates not only appoint a number of the justices to the constitutional court themselves, but also submit cases to it directly. Similarly, they often appoint top state officials directly, or at least have to agree to their appointment.

The same complexity can be seen in the representational function of senates. Beyond issues of direct election, indirect election or appointment, there is the problem of the constituencies which senators represent and their role in legitimising the constitutional order in the eyes of these constituencies. In this regard, perhaps the most important characteristic of senates on a global scale is their structural flexibility. In practice they represent a diversity of types of constituency and thereby guarantee parliamentary representation for collective entities that institutions resting on individually based 'one person, one vote' formulae cannot. This is important to the goal of achieving a balanced, responsive and stable democratic government in a wide variety of societal contexts. Most commonly, it is regional, territorially defined interests that are accommodated and protected in upper houses, but these institutions can also be structured around the representation of professions and social groups. The Irish Senate, for instance, has members elected by the universities. In Africa, traditional elites have reserved seats in a number of upper houses. In Burkina Faso, there are 22 representatives from the different religious communities as well as from the 'traditional community'.

In sum, senates are complex entities, and indeed are becoming more complex as their number in the world increases. The unprecedented attention now being given to them, typified by this special issue of this journal, is to be welcomed despite it highlighting how much needs to be done to integrate this institution into the systematic study of political outcomes.

NOTES

1. A number of studies of upper houses, or 'second chambers', came into existence in the first two decades of the twentieth century. See H.B. Lees-Smith, *Second Chambers in Theory and Practice* (London: Allen & Unwin, 1923); J.A.R. Marriott, *Second Chambers: An Inductive Study in Political Science* (Oxford: Clarendon Press, 1910); and H.W.V. Temperley, *Senates and Upper Chambers: Their Use and Function in the Modern State* (London: Chapman and Hall, 1910). Contemporary work tends to be restricted to a single national institution, but see J. Mastias and J. Grangé, *Les secondes chambres du Parlement en Europe occidentale* (Paris: Economica, 1987).
2. As, for example, in D. Shell, *The House of Lords* (New York: Harvester Wheatsheaf, 2nd edn. 1992), or B. Sinclair, *The Transformation of the U.S. Senate* (Baltimore, MD: Johns Hopkins University Press, 1989).
3. See S.C. Patterson and A. Mughan (eds.), *Senates: Bicameralism in the Contemporary World* (Columbus, OH: Ohio State University Press, 1999), which considers upper houses in nine national parliaments – in Australia, Britain, Canada, France, Germany, Italy, Poland, Spain and the United States; and G. Tsebelis and J. Money, *Bicameralism* (New York: Cambridge University Press, 1997), which mainly considers intercameral negotiations in selected parliaments.
4. L. Massicotte's chapter on 'Unicameralism: A Global Survey and a Few Case Studies', in this volume provides a valuable overview.
5. The most sophisticated effort to identify 'strong' and 'weak' bicameralism is A. Lijphart, *Democracies: Patterns of Majoritarian and Consensus Government in Twenty-one Democracies* (New Haven, CT: Yale University Press, 1984). Also, see M. Cotta, 'A Structural-Functional Framework for the Analysis of Unicameral and Bicameral Parliaments', *European Journal of Political Research*, 2 (1974), pp.201–24.
6. C. Lodici, 'Parliamentary Autonomy: The Italian Senato', in Patterson and Mughan (eds.), *Senates*, pp.225–59.
7. For a succinct summary of the US Senate's role, see B. Sinclair, 'Coequal Partner: The U.S. Senate', in Patterson and Mughan (eds.), *Senates*, pp.32–58, quote at p.38.
8. J. Uhr, 'Generating Divided Government: The Australian Senate', in Patterson and Mughan (eds.), *Senates*, pp.93–119. Also see J. Uhr, *Deliberative Democracy in Australia: The Changing Place of Parliament* (New York: Cambridge University Press, 1998).
9. For instance, see D.M. Farrell and I. McAllister, 'Legislative Recruitment to Upper Houses: The Australian Senate and House of Representatives Compared', *Journal of Legislative Studies*, 1 (1995), pp.243–63.
10. See W.J. Patzelt, 'The Very Federal House: The German Bundesrat', in Patterson and Mughan (eds.), *Senates*, pp.59–92; and U. Thaysen, *The Bundesrat, the Länder and German Federalism* (Washington, DC: American Institute for Contemporary German Studies, 1994).
11. C.E.S. Franks, 'Not Dead Yet, But Should It Be Resurrected? The Canadian Senate', in Patterson and Mughan (eds.), *Senates*, pp.120–61.
12. See D. Shell, 'To Revise and Deliberate: The British House of Lords', in Patterson and Mughan (eds.), *Senates*, pp.199–224.
13. J. Mastias, 'A Problem of Identity: The French Sénat', in Patterson and Mughan (eds.), *Senates*, pp.162–98; quotes at pp.162–3 and 195. See also J. Mastias, *Le Sénat de la Ve République* (Paris: Economica, 1980).
14. D.M. Olson, 'From Electoral Symbol to Legislative Puzzle: The Polish Senat', in Patterson and Mughan (eds.), *Senates*, pp.301–32; quote at p.327.
15. C. Flores Juberías, 'A House in Search of a Role: The Senado of Spain', in Patterson and Mughan (eds.), *Senates*, pp.260–300; quote at p.284.
16. See Uhr, 'Generating Divided Government: The Australian Senate', esp. pp.98–103.
17. See Patzelt, 'The Very Federal House: The German Bundesrat', pp.76–7; Thaysen, *The Bundesrat*, pp.21–2.
18. See Franks, 'Not Dead Yet, But Should It Be Resurrected? The Canadian Senate', p.145.
19. Sinclair, 'Coequal Partner: The U.S. Senate', p.47.
20. Patzelt, 'The Very Federal House: The German Bundesrat', p.76.

21. Uhr, 'Generating Divided Government: The Australian Senate', p.111.
22. Mastias, 'A Problem of Identity: The French Sénat', p.177.
23. See G. O'Brien, 'South Africa's New Upper Chamber', *Canadian Parliamentary Review*, 20 (1997), pp.16–18.
24. See L.D. Longley and W.J. Oleszek, *Bicameral Politics* (New Haven, CT: Yale University Press, 1989).
25. J. Money and G. Tsebelis, 'The Political Power of the French Senate: Micromechanisms of Bicameral Negotiations', *Journal of Legislative Studies*, 1 (1995), pp.192–217. Also, see Tsebelis and Money, *Bicameralism*; and J. Money and G. Tsebelis, 'Cicero's Puzzle: Upper House Power in Comparative Perspective', *International Political Science Review*, 13 (1992), pp.25–43.
26. Patzelt, 'The Very Federal House: The German Bundesrat', p.78.

APPENDIX

FUNCTIONS AND POWERS OF SELECTED PARLIAMENTARY UPPER HOUSES

Country & House	Constitutional System	Size	Term (Years)	Selection	Functions & Powers
Argentine Senado	Federal	72	6	Three senators are directly elected in each province; half the membership is chosen every 3 years.	Law-making power co-equal to that of the lower house, except that the Chamber of Deputies has exclusive purview regarding tax legislation and bills concerning military recruitment.
Australian Senate	Federal	76	6	Half of the members are elected every 3 years; except for 4 senators representing the federal territories who serve only 3-year terms; each of the 6 states elects 12 senators by proportional representation.	Role in law-making co-equal with that of the House of Representatives; may not initiate or amend financial bills, but may return any legislation to the lower house requesting amendments; bicameral deadlock precipitates delay, elections, and joint sessions of the two houses.
Austrian Bundesrat	Federal	64	5-6	The state parliaments send a number of delegates to the upper house based on the state's population; federal councillors serve terms corresponding to the term of the state legislature.	Handles legislation in the same manner as the lower house, but the lower house may override *Bundesrat* rejection of bills by a majority vote, referred to as a'persisting vote'. If the upper house takes no action on bills passed by the lower house, after 8 weeks they may become law with upper house approval.
Belgian Sénat	Federal	71	4	40 members are popularly elected; 31 members are indirectly chosen within the Dutch and French-speaking communities or are co-opted from the royal family.	Bills issuing from the monarch or the government are introduced in the lower house, and on ordinary legislation the lower house has the final word. The upper house is excluded from consideration of bills concerning naturalisation, ministerial liability, budgeting, and determining the size of the army. But the senate and lower house are on an equal footing regarding basic federal and constitutional legislation
Brazilian Senado	Federal	81	8	One-third and two-thirds directly elected every 4th year, alternately, from the states and the federal district.	Co-equal with the Chamber of Deputies regarding ordinary legislation; but the upper house has exclusive power concerning trials of government officials, appointment of specified government and diplomatic officials, and establishing the debt limits for governmental units.

Country & House	Constitutional System	Size	Term (Years)	Selection	Functions & Powers
British House of Lords**	Unitary	697	Life	92 hereditary peers; 579 life peers; 26 clergy.	Financial bills must originate in the House of Commons; the Lords cannot alter financial bills once they are approved by the lower house; Lords amendments to other bills may be rejected by the House of Commons, and final approval of bills may only be delayed by the House of Lords.
Canadian Senate	Federal	104	Life	Appointed by the governor-general on the recommendation of the prime minister; senators are expected to retire at 75; equal representation is accorded each of the country's main regions.	Primarily revises the details of bills, and delays final passage, but has the constitutional power to reject bills passed by the House of Commons; may not initiate money bills; committees may conduct influential investigations.
Chilean Senado	Unitary	48	8	38 are elected, half every 4 years, two from each region or district; 9 are appointed; former presidents are life senators.	Co-equal legislative powers, but bills of pardon or amnesty must originate in the senate, and that body may not originate bills concerning taxes, spending, or recruitment; prohibited from engaging in oversight of government acts; has some exclusive judicial powers.
Colombian Senado	Unitary	102	4	100 directly elected in the country at large; 2 elected from Indian communities.	Co-equal law-making powers, except that revenue bills cannot, and bills involving international relations must be initiated in the senate; the upper house has various exclusive powers including declaration of war, selection of judicial officers, and matters concerning the president's office-holding (including impeachment trials).
Czech Senat	Unitary	81	6	One-third directly elected every 3 years from single-member districts.	Bills may originate in either the senate or the Chamber of Deputies, but budget bills are considered only by the lower house; the senate must act on a bill within 30 days or it is presumed enacted.
French Sénat	Unitary	321	9	One-third indirectly elected every 3 years; senators chosen by popularly elected electoral colleges in each department, the number of seats based on department population; election by majority in departments with 4 senators or less, by proportional representation in departments with 5 or more senators.	Generally subordinate to the National Assembly, but with somewhat greater influence regarding 'organic laws' and financial bills. The senate may initiate bills or propose amendments, but the final decision rests with the lower house. The senate conducts investigations and engages in oversight, but cannot dismiss the government.

Country & House	Constitutional System	Size	Term (Years)	Selection	Functions & Powers
German Bundesrat	Federal	69	Varies	Appointed by the 16 Länder (state) governments; terms are not fixed, but depend on the office-holding of the state governments.	Veto over legislation affecting state powers; if a bill fails by a two-thirds vote in the Bundesrat, only a two-thirds vote in the lower house can override the defeat; exercises a voice in the position taken by German ministers in the Council of Ministers of the European Union.
Haitian Sénat	Unitary	27	6	One-third directly elected every 2 years, 3 senators elected from each of nine departments.	Co-equal with lower house, except that budget or tax bills must be introduced in the lower house; the senate has exclusive powers regarding judicial selection, and serves as a court for impeachment charges.
Indian Rajya Sabha	Federal	245	6	233 elected by state legislatures, one-third every 2 years; 12 distinguished citizens appointed by the president.	Bills may originate in either house, except that money bills must be first introduced in the lower house; both houses convene together to resolve differences.
Irish Seanad Eireann	Unitary	60	5	49 elected indirectly by functional or occupational groups, 11 appointed by the prime minister.	Subordinate to lower house, the senate's role is limited to delay and amendments of lower house actions. Constitutional amendments and financial legislation must be initiated in the lower house, and the latter cannot be amended by the upper house.
Italian Senato	Unitary	326	5	315 directly elected; 9 appointed by the President of the Republic, 2 ex-*officio* members (former Presidents); majority vote for 75% of the seats, proportional representation for 25%.	The Chamber of Deputies and the Senate are co-equal law-making bodies; committees may enact legislation (in *sede deliberante*); the prime minister and cabinet must be confirmed by both houses of parliament.
Japanese Sangiin	Unitary	252	6	Half directly elected every 3 years, 152 from the prefectures and 200 from the country at large.	Role greatly overshadowed by the lower house; the budget must be introduced and passed by the lower house. If the upper house fails to approve a budget or treaty within 30 days, it becomes law without upper house action.
Jordanese Majlis al-Aayan	Unitary	40	4	Appointed by the king.	Government bills are initiated in the Chamber of Deputies, but to become law bills must be passed by both houses. If the upper house rejects a bill twice, it may be enacted by a two-thirds vote of both houses meeting jointly.

Country & House	Constitutional System	Size	Term (Years)	Selection	Functions & Powers
Liberian Senate	Unitary	26	9	Directly elected by counties.	Co-equal law-making powers.
Malaysian Dewan Negara	Federal	69	3	26 elected by state legislators, two from each state or territory; 43 appointed by the monarch.	Bills may originate in either house, except that money bills must originate in the lower house; money bills may be enacted without the approval of the upper house.
Mexican Cámara de Senadores	Federal	128	6	Half directly elected every 3 years; an alternate is elected for each senator; may not be re-elected.	Bills may originate in, and must be passed by both houses, and a two-thirds vote of each house is required to override a presidential veto.
Nepalese Rastriya Sabha	Unitary	60	6	35 elected by the lower house, 15 chosen by local electoral colleges, a third every 2 years; 10 named by the king.	Financial bills must originate in, and be passed by, the lower house, but otherwise all laws must be adopted by both houses.
Netherlands Eerste Kamer	Unitary	75	4	Chosen by members of provincial councils.	Government bills are introduced in the lower house. Although both houses must approve measures, the upper house may not amend bills adopted by the lower house; the right of interpellation is accorded members of both houses.
Nigerian Senate	Federal	109	4	Directly elected from each state and the capital territory.	Bills must be passed by both houses to become law, and presidential vetoes can only be over-ridden by two-thirds votes in both houses; confirms presidential appointments.
Pakistani Senate***	Federal	87	6	14 elected by provincial assemblies, 8 by members of the lower house from the tribal areas, 3 from the federal capital, and 5 by provincial assemblies from religious scholars and professionals; half are elected every 3 years.	Bills may originate in either house, but money bills must originate in the lower house; senate-amended bills may be enacted by a majority vote in a joint session of the two houses.
Philippine Senado	Unitary	24	6	Half directly elected at large every 3 years.	Money bills must originate in the lower house, but the senate may adopt amendments; presidential vetoes can be overridden by a two-thirds vote of members of both houses.

Country & House	Constitutional System	Size	Term (Years)	Selection	Functions & Powers
Polish Senat	Unitary	100	4	Two senators directly elected from 47 of the 49 provinces; 3 senators are elected for Warsaw and Krakow.	Subordinate to the Sejm; may initiate legislation, propose amendments, or veto bills, but the lower house makes final legislative decisions; the senate must act on ordinary bills within 30 days, and consider budget amendments within 20 election is by majority vote days; only the Sejm may vote to override a presidential veto, but only the senate may approve or block a national referendum.
Romanian Senatul	Unitary	143	4	Directly elected from 42 multi-member constituencies.	The senate has the same constitutional powers as the lower house; in conferring powers and functions, the Constitution addresses both houses of parliament simultaneously.
Russian Soviet Federatsii	Federal	178	Varies	Members are representatives from the executive and legislative branches of federation members, two from each of 89 federal territorial units; terms vary by republic or region.	Powers limited to approving border changes, martial law, external deployment of the military, calling presidential elections, removing an impeached president, and appoint high court judges; bills must be introduced in the lower house, and are considered enacted if the upper house does not act within 14 days.
Slovenian Drzavnisvet	Unitary	40	5	Indirectly elected.	The upper house is accorded only an advisory role in the Constitution, and does not have full law-making powers.
South African National Council	Federal	90	5	Ten members from each province elected by provincial legislators.	Exercises general legislative power, but appropriations and tax bills must originate in the lower house, and may not be amended by the upper house. National councillors participate in choosing the President of the Republic, who is elected by a joint sitting of the two houses of parliament.
Spanish Senado	Unitary	257	4	208 elected directly from 52 multi-member constituencies in the provinces, Ceuta, and Melilla; 49 indirectly elected by the legislative assembly of the 7 autonomous communities.	May propose constitutional reforms; may amend or veto bills adopted by the Congress of Deputies (with in 2 months for ordinary bills and 20 days for urgent bills), but the final decision is made by the lower house; may engage in oversight of the executive, but the government is responsible only to the lower house.
Swiss Ständerat	Federal	46	4	Two members directly elected from each of 20 cantons; 1 member elected from each of 6 half cantons.	Has the same functions and powers as the lower house; both houses meet jointly for various purposes, including choosing the chancellor and considering laws on federal elections.

Country & House	Constitutional System	Size	Term (Years)	Selection	Functions & Powers
Thai Wuthisapha	Unitary	262	4	Appointed by the king.	All bills must first be introduced in the lower house. House-passed bills may be considered by the upper house for no more than 60 days (30 days for money bills) but the senate must approve the annual appropriation bill within 15 days, or the bill is adopted without senate approval.
United States Senate	Federal	100	6	Two senators elected in each of the 50 states, by direct popular vote since 1913; before 1913, senators were chosen by state legislatures; one-third are elected every two years.	Law-making power, including initiating legislation, co-equal with the lower house; confirms presidential appointees; must ratify treaties; may impeach the president for 'high crimes and misdemeanors'.
Venezuelan Senado	Federal	57	5	54 directly elected, 2 from each state and the federal district; 3 former Presidents of the Republic appointed for life.	Both houses exercise general lawmaking powers, but the senate has particular powers to initiate bills related to treaties, to authorise government property transactions, military missions, and absenting the president from the country, and bring the president to trial.

Notes:

* Thirty-one upper houses – those in Algeria, Antigua & Barbuda, Bahamas, Barbados, Belarus, Belize, Bolivia, Bosnia-Herzegovina, Burkina Faso, Cambodia, Croatia, Dominican Republic, Ethiopia, Fiji Islands, Gabon, Grenada, Jamaica, Kazakstan, Kyrgyzstan, Lesotho, Mauritania, Morocco, Namibia, Palau, Paraguay, Saint Lucia, Senegal, Swaziland, Trinidad & Tobago, Uruguay, and Yugoslavia – are not included in this compilation because of insufficient information.

** On 11 November 1999 the British parliament enacted the House of Lords Bill, which excludes hereditary peers from automatic membership in the House. The new legislation provides that the hereditary peers elect 90 of their number – in addition to the two office holders – who will continue as members of the House until a new method for selecting members is determined.

*** Pakistan's parliament was dissolved by a military coup in October 1999.

Sources: Inter-Parliamentary Union, *World Directory of Parliaments* (Geneva: Inter-Parliamentary Union, 1999), *and Chronicle of Parliamentary Elections* (Geneva: Inter-Parliamentary Union, Vols. 26-30); S.C. Patterson and A. Mughan (eds.), *Senates: Bicameralism in the Contemporary World* (Columbus: Ohio State University Press, 1999); R.L. Maddex, *Constitutions of the World* (Washington, DC: Congressional Quarterly, Inc., 1995); and various country parliamentary web sites as listed in the web pages of the Inter-Parliamentary Union, at http://www.ipu.org. As of 1999, 178 national parliaments were counted by the Inter-Parliamentary Union; 67 (38%) were bicameral. In 2001 these figures were 177 and 66 (37%) respectively.

Responsibilities of Second Chambers: Constitutional and Human Rights Safeguards

MEG RUSSELL

Second chambers – even those which are otherwise weak – are often given particular responsibility for protecting the constitution. This responsibility flows naturally from both of the original models of second chambers – as either conservative or federal houses.[1] This contribution discusses the constitutional and human rights roles of second chambers in seven Western democracies. The chambers selected are intended to represent a spectrum of different models, and a range from effective to ineffective upper houses. The countries considered are Australia, Canada, France, Germany, Ireland, Italy and Spain.

The original purpose of this comparative piece was to inform the debate on House of Lords reform in the United Kingdom. The constitutional role of the House of Lords is limited, although the Lords does have the power to veto a bill which attempts to extend the life of a parliament. However, the chamber does see one of its roles as constitutional protection, and at times has taken a particular interest in constitutional matters.[2] The house is also closely linked to the judiciary, acting – through the Law Lords – as the UK's highest court of appeal. The House of Lords, and members appointed from it to the Judicial Committee of the Privy Council, perform many of the functions which in other countries are assigned to supreme courts.

The proposed reform of the House of Lords, coming alongside other major constitutional reforms in the UK – including devolution and the coming into force of the Human Rights Act – offers a major opportunity to re-evaluate the constitutional role of the upper house. This opportunity was to a large extent missed by the Royal Commission on the Reform of the House of Lords, which reported in January 2000.[3] As this study shows, the UK's arrangements are highly unusual, with many upper chambers playing a stronger role in constitutional protection. Connections between the judiciary and the upper house are also relatively common in parliaments overseas, though in quite a different form to that in the UK.

Meg Russell is a Senior Research Fellow at the Constitution Unit, University College, London

The role played by second chambers when changes to the constitution are made is considered first. Then the links between the upper chamber and the judiciary – which generally comprise involvement in senior judicial appointments – and the role which second chambers occasionally play in other public appointments are looked at briefly, followed by another constitutional protection role – the right enjoyed by members of many second chambers to seek review of potentially unconstitutional bills. First, a short summary is included of the composition and powers of the seven second chambers under consideration.

THE SEVEN SECOND CHAMBERS

Some summary details of the seven second chambers which form the focus of this article are given in Table 1.[4] The chambers represent a range from very powerful to relatively powerless where ordinary legislation is

TABLE 1
SEVEN SECOND CHAMBERS

	Composition method	**Members represent**	**Power over ordinary Bills**
Australia: Senate	Directly elected by single transferable vote.	States	Total veto.
Canada: Senate	Appointed by Governor General on advice of PM.	Provinces	Total veto.
France: Sénat	Indirectly elected, by electoral college dominated by local councillors.	Départements	System of shuttle and mediation may delay bills, but lower house has last word.
Germany: Bundesrat	Appointed by state governments from amongst their members.	Länder (states)	Total veto over bills affecting states (around 60 per cent of bills), otherwise delay only.
Ireland: Seanad	Most elected by councillors and MPs in five 'vocational' categories, plus six elected by university graduates and 11 appointed by the Taoiseach (Prime Minister).	Majority represent vocational groups	Three months' delay.
Italy: Senato	Majority directly elected by similar system to lower house, on same day. Small number of appointed and *ex officio* members.	Regions	Total veto.
Spain: Senado	Around four-fifths directly elected - by semi majoritarian system, remainder elected by members of regional assemblies.	Provinces and regions	Two months' delay (20 days for urgent bills).

concerned. Whilst the chambers in Australia, Canada and Italy have the power to veto bills, and in Germany this applies to over half of bills, in Spain the upper house may delay legislation for as little as 20 days. In Ireland and France, and in Germany for non-state-related bills, the upper house also enjoys only the power of a relatively short delay. The chambers considered are composed in a variety of ways. The Canadian Senate is appointed, whilst the Australian and Italian upper houses, and a majority of members in the Spanish Senado, are directly elected. Some form of indirect election is employed in four cases, with links between local government and the upper house in both France and Ireland, with state governments in Germany and with regional assemblies in Spain. In most cases the upper house is expected to perform some kind of territorial function, which is demonstrated by the representation of regions, provinces or states.[5]

One of the critical aspects of composition is the impact which the election or appointment system has on the political balance of the upper house. In Italy and Spain, for example, the majority of upper house members are elected on the same day as the lower house, using a system which tends to advantage the parties that go on to form the government. Similarly in Ireland the Taoiseach's nominees are used to guarantee the government a majority in the Seanad. This creates a very different political dynamic to that in Australia, for example, where the proportional system in the upper house tends to give no party overall control. In France the complex design of the electoral college and voting system for the Sénat gives a permanent advantage to parties of the centre-right. The Socialists have never had a majority in the upper house, and the parties supporting the 1997 government in the lower house held only 29 per cent of seats in the Sénat in 1999.

These features of the powers of the upper house, its composition, territorial role and political balance, set the scene for consideration of the chamber's role in constitutional matters. This is the focus of the remainder of the article.

AMENDING THE CONSTITUTION

The United Kingdom is one of only three Western democracies without a written constitution.[6] Constitutional change therefore has a less well defined meaning in the UK than in most other countries. The recent changes in the UK, such as the establishment of the Scottish Parliament and National Assembly for Wales, the passing of the Human Rights Act, or the reform of the House of Lords itself, would in most countries have required amendments to the written constitution. Such changes would have had to go through a more rigorous approval process than ordinary legislation.

In the UK some limited acknowledgement is given to the importance of constitutional bills. By convention bills considered to be 'first-class constitutional measures' take their committee stage on the floor of the House of Commons.[7] However, no special conditions – such as a qualified majority, for example – need be met for such bills to pass. With the exception of a bill to extend the life of a parliament, the House of Lords has no more power over constitutional bills than any other. The limited powers of parliament over these bills are a result of the ill-defined nature of the constitution and of constitutional amendment in the British system.

In all the countries considered here, bills to amend the constitution are subject to a tougher approval process than ordinary legislation, which often includes particular powers for the upper house. In all cases the upper house either has a veto over constitutional bills, or these are subject to other safeguards such as automatic referendums. The arrangements for the seven countries, and for the UK, are summarised in Table 2.[8]

In many cases constitutional amendments must pass in both houses, not only by the simple majority that applies to ordinary legislation, but by a tougher 'qualified' majority. In Italy an absolute majority (that is, a majority of all members of the house, not just those voting) is required, and in Germany a majority comprising two-thirds of members of each house is necessary. In Spain ordinary constitutional bills should pass by a three-fifths majority in each chamber, and if this is not achieved the bill is sent to a joint mediation committee. This is in stark contrast to the chamber's relatively weak powers over ordinary bills. If, following mediation, a constitutional bill is supported by a two-thirds majority in the lower house, it may pass with only an absolute majority in the Senado. This still gives the upper house the opportunity to block the bill, but allows strong support in the lower house to outweigh weaker support in the upper house. In any case, a referendum may be called on a constitutional bill in Spain if one-tenth of members of either house request it within 15 days of the bill passing. A similar arrangement exists in Italy, where a referendum may be called by one-fifth of members of either house, by a petition of 500,000 electors or by five regional assemblies, unless a two-thirds majority passed the bill in both chambers.

In France, no qualified majority is required for constitutional amendments. However, the Sénat has far more power in this area than over ordinary bills. Whilst the lower house may have the last word, after mediation, on ordinary bills, the Sénat has an absolute veto over constitutional bills. These are also subject to either a referendum, or a joint sitting of parliament which must pass them by a three-fifths majority. This

TABLE 2
THE ROLE OF THE UPPER HOUSE IN PASSING CONSTITUTIONAL AMENDMENTS

	Legislative process in upper house	**Chamber's power to call referendum**	**Other safeguards**
Australia	Must pass by absolute majority,[1] but Senate may may be overruled after a delay.	None	All constitutional changes are subject to referendum.
Canada	Senate can delay for only six months.	None	All constitutional changes are subject to agreement by provincial legislatures.
France	Pass by simple majority only, but Sénat has absolute veto.[1]	None	All constitutional changes subject to referendum or approval by joint parliamentary sitting.
Germany	Must pass by a two-thirds majority.[1]	None	None
Ireland	Same as ordinary legislation.	None[2]	All constitutional changes are subject to referendum.
Italy	Must pass twice, second time by an absolute majority.[1]	If not passed by two-thirds majority in both houses, one-fifth of Senators may request referendum.[1]	In some circumstances, referendum may also be called by 500,000 electors or five regional assemblies[3]
Spain	Must pass by a three-fifths majority[1] – or else by two-thirds majority in lower house and absolute majority in Senado.[4]	One-tenth of Senators may request referendum within 15 days.[1]	None
UK	Same as ordinary legislation, except House of Lords has veto of bill to extend life of a parliament.	None	None

Notes: 1. Same applies in lower house.

2. Seanad has power to petition for a referendum on any bill of 'national importance', but a referendum is automatic on constitutional change.
3. A similar provision also allows for referendums to propose the repeal of any existing law.
4. Major constitutional changes, including changes to the status of the monarchy, or citizens' rights, this process must be followed by dissolution of both houses of parliament, and repeated after fresh elections. They are then also subject to a referendum.

not only applies to bills amending the constitution, but also to 'organic' bills. These are bills of a constitutional nature, which do not require an actual amendment to the constitution – a bill to change the electoral system would be an example. Similar categories of 'organic' bills exist in several other countries but are not necessarily subject to such stringent restrictions as constitutional change. In Spain the Senado actually has less power over organic bills than over ordinary legislation.

Thus in Germany, France, Italy and Spain the upper chamber can act as a real block to constitutional change. The implications of this will be discussed shortly. However, it is also worth considering briefly the systems where the second chamber does not hold such a threat. In Canada the Senate can veto all ordinary legislation, but not constitutional bills. This arrangement was put in place in 1982, as part of the Canada Act (which provided a modernisation of the Canadian constitution), and limited the delaying power of the upper house over constitutional bills to six months. This was in fact an admission of the failure of the Senate to act as an effective territorial chamber.[9] Instead of seeking the provinces' approval through the Senate, this approval is now required directly through provincial assemblies. The new arrangements have created a situation where the constitution is very 'rigid' and difficult to change. Ironically, attempts to reform the Senate itself are now frustrated by this rigidity.[10]

The system to change the Australian constitution is quite similar to that in Canada. Unlike all other legislation, the Senate does not have a veto over constitutional change. However, this is compensated by the requirement to seek approval by the states. In Australia this is done through a referendum, which must be supported by at least half of those voting in at least four of the six states. It must also be supported by a majority of voters overall. This also creates a rigid system; of the 42 questions put to such referendums, only eight have been agreed.[11] Similarly in Ireland a referendum is required to change the constitution. This provides a safeguard against parliament, which has no more power over constitutional changes than over other bills, taking rash or politically motivated action in this area.

Returning to the countries where the second chamber can have an impact, this has often created a real obstacle to reform. As with blocking of ordinary legislation, the chamber's behaviour over constitutional amendments will be highly dependent on its political balance. In countries such as Spain and Italy, where the political balance in the second chamber tends to mirror that in the first, a change which has been agreed by the lower house will not generally hit problems in the upper house. However, in others, such as Germany and France, political tensions between the chambers can require careful negotiation of constitutional changes, and even result in total blockage of government proposals.

The requirement in Germany to obtain a two-thirds majority in each chamber for constitutional change is designed to ensure that such proposals have cross-party support. Except in the case of a 'grand coalition' of left and right (such as that of 1966–69), no government would hold such a large majority of seats.

Despite this stringent condition, there have been more than 40 constitutional changes agreed since 1949.[12] A large proportion of these have changed the relationship and relative powers of the federal and state levels. These have generally resulted in an increase of powers to the centre.[13] All these changes have had to be negotiated with state governments through the Bundesrat. Although states – and in particular their parliaments – have forfeited some powers in this process, state governments have conceded the changes, since their position in the upper house means they retain a veto on federal legislation. However, there have been clashes between the state and federal levels over constitutional change. An example was the threat from the Länder to use the Bundesrat to block constitutional changes resulting from the Maastricht Treaty. A coalition of Länder from across the political spectrum joined together to claim rights for the states in European decision-making. The result was the inclusion in 1992 of a new Article 23 of the Basic Law, giving the Bundesrat additional powers over EU matters. This was extracted from the federal government as a condition for agreeing the changes they required.[14]

In France the resolution of differences between the chambers over constitutional matters has been less harmonious. The Sénat has at times used its veto to block government proposals completely. Such problems have recently troubled Lionel Jospin's Socialist government over several key proposals. One example was the government's *Parité* legislation, which sought to amend the Constitution to guarantee equal rights for men and women to elected office. This was given unanimous support in the lower house and received personal endorsement from the Gaullist President Chirac. The government planned to hold a joint session of parliament at Versailles on International Women's Day in March 1999 to endorse the change. However, these plans were thwarted when the Sénat heavily amended the proposals in January. A weakened version of the reform was eventually agreed in late June. This prompted a furious response from the press over the Sénat's conservative attitude.

Another recent battle between the government and the Sénat was over proposals to limit the number of elected offices which the Constitution allows citizens to hold. This is an issue which cuts to the heart of French political culture, and particularly to parliament, where many members hold multiple mandates.[15] The first constitutional amendment on the *cumul des mandats* was successfully passed in 1985. This introduced a limit of two senior political positions (member of parliament, MEP, regional council member, mayor of a major municipal council, and so on) which an individual could hold at any one time. The proposal of the Jospin government was to limit this further to preclude members of parliament from holding an executive office such as mayor. This would have an impact on a large number of sitting members in both houses. This required an 'organic' bill and although it passed the lower house with the support of the Socialist majority, it was vigorously opposed by the Sénat in its notional role as the local government house. Senators conceded only that a limit of three elected offices could be held, such that one of these was with a municipal authority covering less than 3,500 inhabitants (there are 22,000 such authorities in France). Government was forced to accept this position, which represented little change from the current law. The Sénat also opposed proposals to limit to two the number of mandates which could be held by local representatives. However, since this could be dealt with through ordinary legislation it was passed without the consent of the chamber in April 2000.

The Sénat's opposition to such proposals illustrates the difficulty which the government could face in implementing major constitutional change. Members of the Sénat have opposed, for example, greater devolution of powers to regional government, or rationalisation of the local government system. Crucially they are also opposed to their own reform, and have an absolute power to block it. For example, in 1991 the Socialist government proposed some relatively minor amendments to the composition of the Sénat, which would have more closely related geographical representation in the chamber to population. These changes, which would have reduced the stranglehold of conservative rural areas over the house, were rejected by the Sénat without debate.[16] Similar proposals put by the Jospin government were also rejected by the upper house and subsequently abandoned.

JUDICIAL AND OTHER APPOINTMENTS

The House of Lords, as well as acting as a parliamentary chamber, forms the UK's highest court of appeal. The members of the chamber include up to 12 serving 'Lords of Appeal in Ordinary', commonly known as 'law lords'. As well as sitting in the House of Lords, the law lords also sit as members of the Judicial Committee of the Privy Council. These two bodies between them fulfil the roles that Constitutional and Supreme Courts serve in other countries. An additional link between the chamber and the judiciary is created by the role of the Lord Chancellor, who is not only the head of the judiciary, and a serving cabinet minister, but also acts as the presiding officer of the upper house.

It is relatively common overseas for the parliamentary upper house to have a role in overseeing the judiciary. However, other countries observe more strictly the doctrine of 'separation of powers', and do not allow dual membership of the judiciary and legislature. Instead the relationship between the parliamentary and judicial branches of government operates at arms length.

The commonest link between these branches is for upper house members to have responsibility for approving senior judicial appointments. This applies in particular to the appointment of members of Constitutional and Supreme Courts, who are the ultimate arbiters in constitutional disputes. In some countries – such as the Russian Federation and the US – this duty is borne by the upper house alone. In others it is shared equally with the lower house. Four examples of countries where the upper house shares this responsibility are Germany, France, Italy and Spain.

In each of these countries a Constitutional Court is responsible for overseeing the protection of the constitution, and resolving constitutional disputes between different branches or levels of government.[17] The role of these bodies is further discussed in the next section. In each case the upper house plays a major part in the appointment of members of the court. Thus in Germany the two chambers each elect half the members of the court, on a two-thirds majority. This ensures that the successful candidates have broad political support. The Bundestag and Bundesrat alternate in electing the president of the court. In Spain a similar system applies, with one-third of the court elected by each chamber on a three-fifths majority. In France each chamber is responsible for one-third of appointments, but these are made by the president of the chamber. The presidents of the chambers – particularly of the Sénat – are powerful figures in French politics, as this role indicates.[18] In Italy the two chambers meet in a joint session to elect one-third of members of the Constitutional Court.[19]

Thus, in each of these cases the upper house – and lower house – are tied into the appointment of the highest court which will at times adjudicate constitutional matters. In addition, second chambers may have other responsibilities for the judiciary. In Italy and Spain the two houses of parliament share responsibility for appointing part of the body which is responsible for day-to-day judicial oversight and appointments. In Italy a joint session of the two chambers is responsible for appointing one-third of this body, whilst in Spain the two chambers appoint one-fifth of members each. This creates an indirect line of accountability between the entire judicial system and parliament.

The upper house may also share responsibility for other public appointments and government positions. In Italy the Senato is involved in the election of the head of state – the President of the Republic is elected by a special session including members of both houses of parliament, alongside regional representatives. In Spain both houses must approve the candidate for Ombudsman (*Defensor del Pueblo*) – candidates are proposed by a joint committee, and must be approved by both houses on a three-fifths majority.[20] In Canada this responsibility extends to other public appointments, including the Official Languages Commissioner, Information Commissioner, and Privacy Commissioner, whose appointments must be approved by both houses of parliament.

PROTECTING RIGHTS AND THE CONSTITUTION

As well as blocking bills which seek to amend the constitution, some second chambers have powers to challenge the constitutionality of other bills. This operates through members of the chamber referring bills to the Constitutional Court, on the basis that they breach some provision of the constitution. In some cases this power is used frequently.

In Spain, for example, there are six routes by which a bill may be referred to the Constitutional Court. These are referral by: the Prime Minister, the Ombudsman, a judge, a regional government or parliament, a group of 50 lower house members, or a group of 50 Senators. The opportunity for groups of parliamentarians to make such appeals means an opposition party may use this right if it can find a constitutional provision which may be used to object to the bill. This can be an effective weapon against the government, and create a strong incentive for government to act within the constitution. Given the weak powers of the Senado, and its permanent government majority, it has been suggested that 'in practice [the Constitutional Court] has often become an alternative and, in some ways, more effective Second Chamber'.[21]

Likewise, the Constitutional Court in Germany can 'almost be described as a third legislative body'.[22] It has a *de facto* power of amending legislation and can nullify acts which do not comply with the Basic Law. Various laws have been referred to the court by opposition parties, and struck down as a result.[23] The Bundesrat has the power to make referrals to the court, as do individual Länder. However, the stronger position of the upper house in the German legislative system means that it has recourse to the court on matters of substance less frequently than its Spanish counterpart. Because the Bundesrat has the power to veto all legislation covering matters under the control of the Länder, or affecting their finances, many of its referrals to the court relate simply to whether a bill is one which falls into this category. There have been several supportive decisions in the Constitutional Court on which forms of legislation the Bundesrat can veto. This has helped increase over time the proportion of bills which require upper house consent.[24]

In France bills may be referred to the Constitutional Council by a group of 60 lower house members or 60 Senators, or the president of either house. As in Spain and Germany this may be used as a weapon by the opposition. For example, during the 1980s 'recourse to the Constitutional Council became automatic when legislation was adopted against the advice of the Senate'.[25] However, where objections to a bill can be justified on constitutional grounds this can also act as an important safeguard.

Until 1974 in France the right to refer a bill to the Constitutional Council lay only with the presidents of the two houses, rather than the members. In 1971, in a landmark case, the president of the Sénat used his power for the first time to refer a bill on the issue of freedom of association. This required an interpretation of the preamble of the constitution, which referred to the 1789 Declaration of the Rights of Man and the Citizen. The ruling, against the bill, was seen as equivalent to the establishment of a French Bill of Rights.[26]

Ever since this time the Sénat has seen itself as a protector of individual rights and freedoms, and has frequently referred bills to the Constitutional Council on these grounds.[27] Although it has won several victories it is questionable to what extent these referrals were motivated by human rights, rather than political, objections. Whilst the Sénat has frequently sought to protect individual freedoms, it has been notably less proactive in the protection of collective rights. Referrals invariably come from the political groups, in both chambers. The Sénat's reputation as a protector of civil liberties has therefore been described as 'an exaggeration if we look closely'.[28]

The same cannot be said of the Australian Senate, which has a long record of legislative scrutiny on human rights grounds, unparalleled in the lower house. Despite the absence of an Australian Bill of Rights, two committees in the Senate scrutinise all legislation against a set of human rights criteria. Both committees operate in a scrupulously bipartisan way, and have won many victories to protect the rights of Australians.

The Australian Senate Standing Committee on Regulations and Ordinances has operated since 1932, and for 50 years it was the main legislative scrutiny committee in parliament. It has been suggested 'that the Senate's pioneering role in the scrutiny of delegated legislation is ... a rare and early example of an Australian parliamentary institution leading the world'.[29] The committee scrutinises all forms of delegated legislation against a strict set of criteria, including human rights requirements. The Scrutiny of Bills Committee was established in the Senate in 1981, as a result of Senators' concerns that delegated legislation was receiving closer scrutiny than other bills. The criteria against which this committee scrutinises bills are an extension of those used by the older committee. The committee's role, set down in Senate standing orders, is to ensure that bills do not:

- trespass unduly on personal rights and liberties;
- make rights, liberties or obligations unduly dependent upon insufficiently defined administrative powers;
- make rights, liberties or obligations unduly dependent upon non-reviewable decisions;
- inappropriately delegate legislative powers;
- insufficiently subject the exercise of legislative power to parliamentary scrutiny.

Both committees meet weekly and scrutinise all legislation as soon as it is introduced to parliament (often resulting in bills being considered whilst still passing through the lower house). They are both supported by legal advisers, and publish weekly reports for Senators. Where issues of concern are contained within a bill or instrument the committee will write to the relevant minister asking for a response, which will also be reported to the Senate. This often results in the government making amendments. Alternatively, members of the Senate may use the committees' reports to propose amendments to ordinary legislation, or to propose annulment of problematic delegated legislation.

The committees are well respected, and play an important role in protecting personal liberties and civil rights. They retain the support of Senators by sticking rigidly to their terms of reference and not getting embroiled in primarily political disputes (although the publication of their reports may equip others to do so). The Scrutiny of Bills Committee identifies potential problems in around 40 per cent of bills.[30] The Regulations and Ordinances Committee proposes rejection of several instruments per year, and during the almost 70 years of its existence the Senate has always accepted its view. Over time the committee has achieved changes to rules which would have reduced a person's right to trial by jury, allowed officials other than judicial officials to issue search warrants, and enabled officials to enter premises without identification.[31] In contrast, there is no parallel mechanism in the lower house for considering the human rights implications of legislation, or for detailed scrutiny of secondary legislation.

CONCLUSIONS

Second chambers often have a powerful constitutional role. While they may be no more powerful than first chambers in this respect, they may have powers over constitutional matters which exceed their powers over ordinary bills. This is an acknowledgement of the seriousness of constitutional change, and the need to gain a broad consensus when this is planned. The veto power of the upper house – whether as a conservative house or a house representing the provinces, regions or states – is appropriate in these circumstances.

The only truly effective territorial chamber amongst those discussed is the German Bundesrat.[32] The Bundesrat's approval is required for all constitutional amendments, and this is used as a mechanism for gaining the support of the German states. This arrangement makes constitutional amendments achievable relatively quickly, whilst ensuring broad support. Other federal states such as Canada and Australia also require support from their constituent territories for all constitutional change. The fact that the upper house is not an effective territorial chamber means that they require extra-parliamentary approval mechanisms. These are cumbersome and have resulted in rigidity in these countries' constitutions. Genuinely territorial chambers might have eased this situation.

The attitude of a second chamber to constitutional amendments is liable to be shaped by its general attitude to the government. This is largely a matter of party politics. Thus a second chamber which can block constitutional change, but which is rarely controlled by government, can also introduce rigidity. This is the case in France, where the Sénat has a total veto on constitutional change. The Sénat's in-built conservative bias creates a particular problem for Socialist governments, but also results in a general inability to move beyond the old political order. Devolution to France's regions, and upper house reform, are impossible to achieve without the Sénat's consent.

The systems in Italy and Spain combine parliamentary approval of constitutional amendments with the recourse to a referendum if a significant minority of parliamentarians is opposed. However, the requirement to seek approval by the upper house is less likely to be an obstacle, as government tends to have a majority there, as well as in the lower house. In the French system the recourse to a referendum could offer a more genuinely consensual procedure than blockage by the Sénat. However, in France a referendum on constitutional change cannot be called until after both chambers have reached agreement.

Second chambers – or at least their members – may also have other methods of protecting the constitution. Frequently they are involved in the appointment of members of Constitutional Courts, which act as final arbiters in constitutional disputes. In the UK it is members of the House of Lords themselves who will be responsible for such arbitration, in the shape of the law lords. In other countries such an arrangement would not be contemplated as it would be seen as a breach of the separation of powers between parliament and the courts.

As well as being involved in the appointment of Constitutional Courts, members of upper houses may also refer matters to the courts for their consideration. In Germany, France and Spain groups of parliamentarians from either chamber may refer legislation which they suspect breaches the constitution. Although this mechanism may be used by opposition parties to try and undermine government policy, it may also offer a real constitutional protection where the upper house cannot veto ordinary bills. It is therefore used frequently in France and Spain by members of both houses. Where a party can find genuinely constitutional – rather than purely political – grounds to oppose a law, they can be successful. In Australia, where this parliamentary appeal route is not available, members of the upper house nonetheless play an important role in guarding individual liberties, through the operation of two Senate committees with a human rights focus.

All of the examples given illustrate the anomalous position of the UK's House of Lords. The chamber has no particular powers of constitutional protection, whilst the presence of the law lords in the chamber may become more problematic as they are drawn into resolution of human rights and devolution disputes.[33] The reform of the chamber offers an opportunity to re-evaluate its role in the UK constitution, with potential lessons to be learnt from the operation of parliaments overseas.

NOTES

This contribution is an adaptation of a chapter in the author's book *Reforming the House of Lords: Lessons from Overseas* (Oxford: Oxford University Press, 2000). Permission to adapt it and reproduce it here has kindly been given by Oxford University Press.

1. For discussion of these two models see G. Tsebelis and J. Money, *Bicameralism* (Cambridge: Cambridge University Press, 1997).
2. See D. Shell, *The House of Lords* (London: Harvester Wheatsheaf, 1992), pp.168–70, for a discussion of the role of the House of Lords during the abolition of the Greater London Council in 1984–85, for example. For a discussion of the House of Lords' role in human rights see A. Reidy, *The House of Lords: In Defence of Human Rights* (London: Constitution Unit, 1999).
3. *A House for the Future, Royal Commission on the Reform of the House of Lords*, Cm 4534 (2000). For a critique of the Royal Commission's proposals see M. Russell and R. Cornes, 'The Royal Commission on Reform of the House of Lords: A House for the Future?', *Modern Law Review* 64/1 (2001), pp.82–99.
4. For a full description of the composition, role and functions of these chambers see Russell, *Reforming the House of Lords.*
5. For a fuller discussion of territorial representation and functions in upper houses, see M. Russell, 'The Territorial Role of the Upper House', this volume.
6. The other two are Israel and New Zealand, both of which have single chamber parliaments.
7. This does not necessarily imply a better quality of scrutiny for such bills. For example, in

1997 the Labour government tried to break with convention and send the Scotland Bill and Government of Wales Bill to standing committee. This did not happen, following opposition from the Conservatives. Ironically, however, there were times during the consideration of these bills when there were fewer members in the chamber for a committee of the whole house than there would have been in a standing committee.

8. For information about the constitutional role of upper chambers in 20 Western democracies, see Russell, *Reforming the House of Lords*, ch.2.
9. The role of the Canadian Senate as a territorial chamber is discussed in Russell, 'The Territorial Role of the Upper House'.
10. For a discussion of Senate reform attempts in Canada see Russell, *Reforming the House of Lords*, ch.11.
11. See *Constitutional Change: Report of the House of Representatives Standing Committee on Legal and Constitutional Affairs* (Canberra: Parliament of the Commonwealth of Australia, 1997).
12. See P. James, 'The Federal Framework', in P. James (ed.), *Modern Germany* (London: Routledge, 1998).
13. See K. Sontheimer, 'The Federal Republic of Germany (1949): Restoring the Rechtsstaat', in V. Bogdanor (ed.), *Constitutions in Democratic Politics* (Aldershot: Gower, 1988).
14. See C. Jeffery, 'German Federalism in the 1990s: On the Road to a "Divided Polity"?', in K. Larres (ed.), *Germany Since Unification* (Basingstoke: Macmillan, 1998).
15. In January 1999, 163 of the 321 members of the Sénat held positions as local mayors. In addition 20 senators were regional councillors and 140 were departmental councillors, including 45 regional and departmental presidents.
16. See D. Maus, 'Libres Propos sur le Sénat', *Pouvoirs*, 64 (1993), pp.89–97, or Russell, *Reforming the House of Lords*, ch.11.
17. In France this body is known as the 'Constitutional Council'. In other countries it is known as the 'Constitutional Court'.
18. The Sénat President is formally the second most powerful figure in the French Republic, with responsibility for deputising for the President. The Sénat President acted as temporary President of the Republic in 1969, following the resignation of General de Gaulle, and in 1974, following the death of Georges Pompidou. The power of the Sénat President is discussed in Russell, *Reforming the House of Lords*, ch.5.
19. The German court comprises 16 judges, elected for terms of up to 12 years. The Spanish court comprises 12 members, appointed for nine years, with one-third chosen every three years. The chambers therefore approve four members each, with two of the remaining four members appointed by government and the other two by the General Council of the Judiciary. The French Constitutional Council has nine members, appointed for nine years, with one-third chosen every three years. The presidents of the two parliamentary chambers each appoint three members, with the remaining three appointed by the President of the Republic. The Italian court comprises 15 members, appointed for nine years. Five are appointed by joint parliamentary session, five by the President of the Republic, and five by the ordinary and administrative courts.
20. See C.F. Juberías 'A House in Search of a Role', in S.C. Patterson and A. Mughan (eds.), *Senates: Bicameralism in the Contemporary World* (Columbus, OH: Ohio State University Press, 1999).
21. M.T. Newton, *Institutions of Modern Spain* (Cambridge: Cambridge University Press, 1997), pp.68–9.
22. G. Smith, 'The Nature of the Unified State', in G. Smith *et al.* (eds.), *Developments in German Politics* (Basingstoke: Macmillan, 1992), p.45.
23. See Sontheimer, 'The Federal Republic of Germany'.
24. See Jeffery, 'German Federalism in the 1990s'.
25. J. Mastias, 'A Problem of Identity: The French Sénat', in Patterson and Mughan (eds.), *Senates: Bicameralism in the Contemporary World*, p.172.
26. See W. Safran, *The French Polity* (New York: Addison Wesley Longman, 1998).
27. See Mastias, 'A Problem of Identity'.
28. Y. Mény, *The French Political System* (Paris: La Documentation Française, 1998), p.74.

29. J. Uhr, *Deliberative Democracy in Australia* (Cambridge: Cambridge University Press, 1998), p.122.
30. Uhr, *Deliberative Democrac in Australia.*
31. See R. Smith, 'Parliament', in J. Brett, J. Gillespie and M. Goot (eds.), *Developments in Australian Politics* (Melbourne: Macmillan, 1994).
32. See Russell, 'The Territorial Role of the Upper House', and Russell, *Reforming the House of Lords*, ch.10.
33. For a fuller discussion of these issues see Russell and Cornes, 'The Royal Commission on Reform of the House of Lords'.

Procedure: A Case Study of the House of Lords

SIR MICHAEL WHEELER-BOOTH

> 'Procedure is all the poor Briton has, now that any Government which commands 51% of the House [*of Commons*] can at any moment do anything they like'
>
> K. Pickthorn, MP, *Official Report*, 8 Feb. 1960

> 'law has at first the look of being gradually secreted in the interstices of procedure'
>
> H. Maine, *English Law and Custom*, p.389

The term 'parliamentary procedure', I have noted over a career in the service of parliament, is one which tends to bring a look of bemused indifference to the faces of students of the British parliament. But in a constitutional system which is not written or codified and which combines the sovereignity of parliament, the pre-eminence within the Parliamentary Trinity of the House of Commons, and the *de facto* domination by the executive over the House of Commons, the truth of the quotation from Pickthorn is evident and suggests that study of parliamentary procedure is not wasted time to those who wish to understand the working of our political system.

Since 1870 the procedures of the House of Commons have been streamlined and 'democratised' by, as a distinguished Clerk of the Commons reassuringly described it 'the converting of the comfortable old parliamentary coach into an up-to-date, streamlined legislative engine'. This procedural change was forced on the reluctant Commons in response to the determined filibustering and exploitation of the old rules by the Irish Nationalist MPs[1] and to enable governments to legislate to implement their programmes.

This study first describes briefly the procedure of the Lords in the reign of James I, as 1621 saw the writing down of the then procedures in the first

---

Sir Michael Wheeler-Booth was Clerk of the Parliaments 1991–97, Commissioner for the Welsh Assembly 1998–99, a member of the Royal Commission on House of Lords Reform 1999–2000 and is now Special Lecturer in Politcs at Magdalen College, Oxford.

edition of *Public Business Standing Orders* or *'Remembrances'*. Then, jumping briskly forward three and a half centuries to the period 1960–99, current Lords procedures are described in the later twentieth century before the passage of the House of Lords Act 1999 and the exclusion of the majority of hereditary peers by succession. Finally, we examine the procedural problems which the half reformed 'interim House' of Lords faces on several fronts. Firstly to react to the recommendations of the Royal Commission on the Reform of the House of Lords *A House for the Future*, Chairman Lord Wakeham (hereafter called the 'Wakeham Report').[2] Secondly, the 'interim House' has to decide whether it can preserve its old system of self-regulation in a situation where its composition is altering rapidly, and becoming more political and professional. Thirdly, can the present procedures on legislation in the Lords continue unchanged, where they contrast markedly with those in the Commons, and pose an increasing threat to the government 'business managers' and the government's programme of bills. In recent years governments of either complexion bring forward an ever increasing amount of legislation – much of it ill-prepared. Despite pledges to 'modernise parliament', the present government so far has failed to meet the rhetoric of its manifesto that 'the House of Commons is in need of modernisation'.[3] Finally, there is the problem of 'social hours'; both Houses sit longer hours in plenary than any other parliament, which discourages those with family responsibilities.

These factors suggest that the time may have come for reconsideration of the ancient Lords procedures. Such reconsideration will need to bear in mind popular support expressed in evidence to the Royal Commission for the existing open and self-regulating procedures, which led the Wakeham Commission to recommend that 'the second chamber should seek to continue the House of Lords' tradition of open procedures' (Recommendations 116–18).

This contribution considers in detail only the House of Lords, as it is only of that institution that the writer has sufficient detailed knowledge. But a recent comparative study of nine upper houses, suggests that the procedures of many second chambers are relatively free and leisured, with a lack of a guillotine and other draconian methods whereby the majority/government can have their way in first chambers.[4] A number of influential second chambers, including the United States Senate, which the begetters of the United States constitution believed 'should be as much like the House of Lords as possible',[5] Australia[6] and Canada[7] modelled themselves initially, and took many of their procedures from, the British Upper House. Latterly, in a number of second chambers there has been a development of detailed scrutiny of legislation, and it has been the more recent second chambers, notably in Australia, who have pioneered procedures which have been copied at Westminster. The Scrutiny of Bills Committee in the Australian Senate was the starting point – and the example which was followed in the House of Lords, where the widely praised Delegated Powers Committee is directly based on the Australian model.

Lords Procedure in 1621

Underlying the procedures of the House of Lords there has long been a broad philosophy, based on certain principles; many previously shared with the House of Commons. To write this is not to imply that parliamentary procedures were brought forth fully thought out from the womb of the Mother of Parliament, but rather that the parliamentary practice of the two Houses was evolved slowly by trial and error, to meet certain needs – for example, clarity in legislation and compatibility within the existing unwritten law and custom of the realm. The origins of our early parliamentary procedures have been much studied of late. This recent research has been facilitated by a flowering of antiquarian and procedural interest in the early seventeenth century in both Houses of Parliament, and by their clerks. Outside parliament the antiquarian studies of our institutions by notable students, like Selden and Coke, included some who laboured from a love of learning, while others had a more or less conscious political agenda, such as providing precedents for parliamentary opposition to royal 'despotism'. Or, as Maitland put it in his great Rede lecture 'the seventeenth century [saw] ... the struggle for the medieval, the Lancastrian, constitution in which Coke and Selden and Prynne and other ardent searchers of mouldering records won their right to be known to school-boys'.[8] The study of seventeenth century parliamentary procedure has been facilitated by the chance survival of a considerable corpus of source material – much of it preserved from incineration in the Jewel Tower across the road from the disastrous fire of the Palace of Westminster on 16 October 1834.

From early days, the practice – sometimes called more portentously the 'law and custom' of parliament – of the two Houses developed slowly. This still governs many essential aspects of procedure, including that of three readings of bills, with a committee and report stage, or that each House proceeds by way of debate on a motion and question put. The early seventeenth century was the time which saw the procedural rules of the House of Lords systematically set down, notably in the Standing Orders in 1621 – the year that Robert Bowyer's place as Clerk of the Parliaments was filled by Henry Elsynge. These distinguished clerks, as Elizabeth Reed Foster has vividly described,[9] shared an interest in parliamentary procedure and markedly improved the recording of parliamentary precedents; they were fortunate to coincide with a period in which there was a marked increase of interest in procedure, both by the members of the House, and by lawyers and antiquarians outside the House.

The preparation of the Standing Orders was carried out in February and March 1621, under the authority of the Committee of 'Lords named and appointed to take Consideration of the Customs and Orders of this House, and of the Privileges of the Peers of the Kingdom, and Lords of Parliament'.[10]

As Bond recognised in his edition of the 1621 Standing Orders, previously most procedure was customary, and largely unwritten, unregulated by a body of Standing Orders. Indeed, the House of Commons remained in this state of procedural innocence – a kind of parliamentary Garden of Eden – for many years, with a first solitary standing order agreed to in 1677,[11] when a member (Meres) called attention to the absence of 'records of your Standing Orders, whereas in the Lords House they have Standing Orders and Rules'. The first Commons Standing Orders of the 1670s were followed by a slow dribble of Standing Orders made during the eighteenth century. It was only in the nineteenth century, especially after 1870, that the Commons came to adopt a corpus of Standing Orders, aimed at the modification and restriction of the basic procedures 'so as to limit the occasions for, and in some cases, the duration of debate ... and give priority to the Government in organising the business of the House and in securing the passage of its own legislation'.[12]

In the Lords, at an earlier period, it was thought desirable to set down the 'Remembrances for order and decency to be kept in the Upper House of Parlyament' as a by-product of a committee set up to investigate a mistakenly worded Writ of Summons for Lord North – reflecting the strong interest then shown by the members of the House in matters of peerage, and their titles and privileges as peers. It also coincided with a revival of impeachment, as a method whereby both Houses could exercise criminal jurisdiction over unpopular Ministers of the Crown – copying fourteenth and fifteenth century practice.[13]

The coming together of interest by members in their privileges and precedence with that of clerks concerned to record the procedure and practice enables modern students to discern the underlying 'philosophy' based on certain principles of the Houses' practice in 1621, which, amazingly, have lasted to this day.

The first such principle was that of the equality of membership: The first meaning of 'Peer' given in Johnson's *Dictionary*[14] is 'equal: one of the same rank' although in a later definition this is qualified as 'a nobleman as distinct from a commoner; of nobility we have five degrees, who are nevertheless called *peers*, because their essential privileges are the same'. The proud Thomas (Howard) Earl of Arundel (1585–1646), who had cast reflection in the House of Lords on the newly enobled Lord Spencer was sent to the Tower by the House of Lords until he apologised – there were, it was said, 'no great Lordes' in the House.

Secondly, and closely dependent on the first, the House of Lords had no Speaker with powers of order, as in the Commons. As Standing Order 2 in the 'Remembrances for order and decency' put it:

> The Lord Chancellor, when he speakes to the House, is always to speake uncovered, and is not to adiourne the House or doe anything els, as mouth of the House, without the consent of the Lords first had, excepting the ordinarie things about Bills, which are of course [routine] wherein the Lords may likewise overrule, as for preferring one Bill before another, and such like.) And in case of difference among the Lords, it is to be put to the question, and if my Lord Chauncellor will speake to anything particularly, hee is to goe to his owne place as a Peere.

A third general consideration was the respect shown for all members of the House and their privileges, without differentiation of status according to rank or whether or not they were in royal favour. Hence the disputes with Charles I over the imprisonment of the Earl of Arundel and the withholding of a writ from the Earl of Bristol (1626), both of which cases resulted in victory by the House over the king, and strengthened the rights of what would now be called back-bench members.

Finally, an underlying factor was procedural freedom and flexibility, in which the majority would get their way in the long run, but would first give considerable licence to a minority to speak, move amendments and otherwise delay business. As now, members addressed the generality of the House, removing their hats to speak, and if several lords rose together, he who rose first spoke first, regardless of rank. Reference was not made to other members by name, but by a circumlocution. Speeches were typically informal and speaking from notes was deprecated. Voting was by name singly, in inverse order of rank, though tellers were appointed and divisions taken in cases of uncertainty only.

Modern Lords Procedure

If we jump 350 years to the present day, the extraordinary fact is that nothing essential has been changed since 1621 although the procedures of the House have evolved and become more complicated and above all written down.[15] But the same philosophy reigns, and there has been no great change in procedure as was witnessed in the Commons between 1870–1914. This resulted in part from the tactics employed by the Irish nationalist MPs, who, for understandable reasons in pursuit of Irish Home Rule used – or abused – the old procedures of the Commons – in an effort to make parliament and government unworkable.[16] Underlying the procedural changes in the Commons lay profound constitutional changes, whereby governments, supported by mass electorates and organised political parties, have come to control the Commons and its procedures, so as to legislate increasingly to give effect to their manifestos. A further factor in the shackling of the Commons has been the establishment of permanent government 'business managers', in particular the Private Secretaryship to the Government Chief Whip – a post which, since its inception at the end of the First World War, has been held by only three remarkable individuals.[17]

In contrast, the House of Lords remains – I believe uniquely in the world amongst legislative chambers – a self-regulatory body 'in which all its members are equal and ... there exist no powers of control by the Speaker. There are few standing orders and the House runs its own affairs according to good sense'[18] working on the basis of consensus, guided by the Leader of the House. As the *Companion to the Standing Order*[19] notes, the Leader 'advises the House on matters of procedure and order and has the responsibility of drawing attention to transgression or abuse of the rules of procedure'. The Leader has no formal authority and his or her advice should reflect the wishes of all sides. Responsibility for the maintenance of order therefore lies with the House itself, which imposes on each individual member a responsibility to act in accordance with the rules and the spirit underlying them.

The fact that the House is self regulating means that it has never delegated its powers to regulate its own proceedings to any other authority. The Lord Chancellor as Speaker, the Leader of the House, and the clerks all have some discretionary powers, but may be over-ruled either by any individual member, or by the House. Many of the practices in the Commons, which depend on a speakership with powers of order, such as the selection of amendments are therefore impossible in the Lords under current arrangements.

As described, the procedural freedoms are very old. They worked well in a relatively small House, in which the majority of its members knew each other, and accepted roughly similar patterns of behaviour; they also reflect a time when there was much less pressure of business than today. The freedom to participate in business has of late been under strain because of the pressure of business, and is now subject to certain constraints, for example the length of speech allowed in time-limited debate. Despite this, two essential points are that all members can initiate business, and all members can participate in business. Any member can ask a question, move a motion, or an amendment. It evokes a Rousseau-like sense of the self-regulating peer, without a Speaker with powers of order, and members acting in accordance with the rules and the spirit underlying them.

Legislative Procedures

The consideration of legislation is the 'jewel in the Crown' of Lords procedures – where most strikingly the restrictions applied in the Commons are absent in the Upper House. Legislation has priority over other business on Mondays, Tuesdays and Thursdays – but not on Wednesdays when debates take precedence. In practice this means that well over half the sitting time of the House is spent on legislation. Although most second reading debates are somewhat anodyne – as the Lords usually do not throw out public legislation at that stage – the later stages, committee, report and third reading, are normally taken on the floor of the House, where amendments can be moved by any member, without time limits or other constraints. These freedoms are more absolute than in other legislative chambers and enable members to revise legislation to their hearts' content, without procedural constraint. They are also open to abuse, for example the repetition of arguments on amendments at the various stages. Further, as most legislation is taken on the floor of the House, there is great strain in keeping up with the huge increase in the legislative load imposed in recent years – where the Commons may have six or more Standing Committees considering bills at a time, the Lords have usually only one channel through which the legislative river must flow.

Recently there have been experiments in taking legislation off the floor of the House, including the use of a Grand Committee which considers bills in the Moses Room, open to any member to attend, but without the power to divide on amendments. Such committees meet at the same time as the House, thus speeding the legislative process. This procedure has been copied from the Australian House of Representatives. Its use understandably remains the exception, because of the attitude of the opposition, who realise that taking bills off the floor helps the government to legislate more.

A further experiment has been in the use of Special Standing Committees, that is committees off the floor able to take evidence from experts and interested parties over a specified period, before considering the bill in question clause by clause: this procedure has enabled legal and technical bills, including some proposed by the Law Commission, to be included in the programme. This development allows parliamentarians to be able to speak directly to those who know, rather than having to pass through the cave darkly, as when ministers read out civil service briefs on the floor of the House. Such developments in legislative scrutiny were strongly supported by the Jellicoe Committee in 1990–91,[20] and by the Rippon Committee on Sittings of the House of 1992.[21] These Lords reports sought, so far with scant success, to encourage shortening the sitting time of the House of Lords, trying to copy the Commons Jopling Report on Sittings of the House 1992 – which has succeeded, despite the reservations of the Commons' Whips, in significantly shortening the hours of sitting, hence reducing the workload and the resulting disincentive to potential members, in particular women with families.

How Procedures are Changed

Although the House is self-governing, with equality of membership, and questions of order relating to the conduct of business being decided by the 'sense of the House', there are nevertheless rules. The present day *Standing Orders relating to Public Business*, the descendant of the 'Remembrance for order and decency to be kept in the Upper House of Parliament' of 1621, has been extended to cover the main procedures of the House on public business (there are comparable volumes on private bills and on judicial business). Since 1862, the bare bones of the Standing Orders have been supplemented by a printed *Companion to the Standing Orders*, first privately circulated but now a public document, authorised by the House, which has grown greatly in length as more and more procedure has had to be set down (30 pages in 1955 to 275 in 1994). The increasing length of the *Companion* has led to a demand for a shorter handbook, and a *Brief Guide to the Procedure and Practice of the House of Lords* has been published since 1975, particularly directed as an aid to new members.

Changes in procedure are now made at the prompting of the Procedure Committee which is appointed annually and which includes the leaders and whips. Its composition ensures that its recommendations are followed even if they do not always follow a government lead. Thus the House remains master of its own procedures, and whipping is not used to overturn the Committee's recommendations (as is the practice in the Commons). The recognition that the procedures of the House are a matter for the House alone to determine was followed in the Government White Paper and in the Royal Commission Report.[22]

Practice and Procedure Committee 1976–78

In 1976, following the decision by the Commons to set up a committee to consider public business, which eventually led in 1979 to the establishment of permanent departmental select committees (the St John Stevas reforms), the Lords set up a similar enquiry. In their report, reforms of the legislative procedure in the Lords were recommended where permanent subject committees to consider legislation would have been established. At the time difficulties between the two Houses were endemic and in the debate there was an equivocal response to the report. As a consequence, no action was then taken. But one possibility for allowing a greater flow of legislation through the Lords would be to go back to the Practice and Procedure Committees Report (appropriately updated) and to implement proposals on somewhat similar lines.

GROUPS

The Procedure Committee considers specific proposals for procedural change, but from time to time *ad hoc* groups have been set up, by the leadership, to stand back and examine the procedures and practice of the House as a whole. Up till now, the upshot of such enquiries has been against revolutionary change as the House has not wanted to become more like the Commons, but preferred to continue self-regulation. However, in debate on 10 May 2000 on a motion by Lord Peston to 'call attention to the case for a review of the workings of the House of Lords in the 21st century', considerable support was expressed for radical change in the procedures of the House. No action has yet been taken in response to this debate.

The 'Usual Channels'

The leaders and whips of the parties and sometimes the cross-bench convenor are called the 'usual channels' as if preserving their anonymity generated safety from attack. Together they provide the solvent which makes the House work. They work together closely, and should have a high degree of mutual trust and be able to repose confidence in each other with the certainty that their secrets will not be betrayed.

Chief of them is the Leader of the House[23] who is appointed by the prime minister, is in the Cabinet and is responsible for government business in the House. But, as the Speaker has no powers of order, it is the leader who advises the House on matters of procedure and order, expresses the 'sense of the House' and draws attention to transgressions of the rules. The dual role as spokesman for the government and for the House, as its 'shepherd' is delicate, and sometimes inevitably involves an element of make-believe. The government Chief Whip makes the detailed arrangements of government business.

The non-government parties also have leaders and chief whips, who act as channels for information and pressure, on behalf of their parties – to those who drew up the detailed plans for the business of the House – that is the Leader, Chief Whip, and their Private Secretary (who is a clerk on secondment for about three years). The cross-benches, which have increased notably in numbers and importance over the last 50 years (from 50 in 1945 to 173 in May 2001) have, since 1965, had an elected 'Convenor' who intermittently is a member of the 'usual channels'.

Recent Changes: Increase in Workload

The last 40 years have seen a remarkable increase in the level of business in the Lords: late night sittings are now commonplace, average daily attendance has more than trebled from 1960–99. The main increase has been in legislative work, especially the painstaking revision of public bills brought from the Commons, which takes more time than any other function: legislative work trebled between 1970 and 2000, and sitting hours have doubled over the same period. Governments of whatever party are introducing more and more legislation: the statute book grows larger and larger. The public demand that governments respond to the increased complexity of modern life by legislation. As the Lords' procedures remain 'unimproved' by the streamlining introduced in the Commons, the members of the House of Lords – although un-elected, unpaid and rather elderly – are in practice carrying out an increasing proportion of the work of scrutinising legislation – some of which is little considered in the Commons, because of a lack of time, the functioning of the Standing Committee system, the imposition of guillotines, and other procedures aimed at curtailing debate or a combination of all of these.[24]

More public legislation is being introduced into the Lords as first House, including controversial government bills such as the Criminal Justice (Mode of Trial) Bill 1999, subsequently defeated, and the Human Rights Bill 1997. The more technical Law Commission and Consolidation bills have long been introduced first into the Lords. Private members still possess an unfettered right to introduce bills, and the absence of constituency pressures have caused many bills on social issues to be pioneered in the Lords, including those on abortion, homosexuality, sexual discrimination and euthanasia (which did not pass).

Select Committee work, largely in abeyance from 1911 until 1972 has greatly increased since 1972 – especially on the European Community (since 1974), and Science and Technology (since 1978), while a series of *ad hoc* committees have been established on a wide range of subjects. The most recent of these is a select committee on the Monetary Policy Committee of the Bank of England and a new Constitutional Committee to examine the constitutional implications of all public bills and to review the operation of the Constitution.

Recent Changes in Composition

The passage of the House of Lords Act 1999 has radically altered the composition of the House by removing the majority of hereditary peers by succession (92 have been reprieved by virtue of the 'Weatherill' amendment) and thereby largely eliminating the previous political imbalance and permanent Conservative preponderance. It is too early to be precise about the effects of these changes, but to date a widespread perception has been that the House has become more 'political', there has been some weakening of previous practice whereby the Lords usually would not press their objections to government legislation to the limits. Since 11 November 1999 and Royal Assent to the House of Lords Bill, there have been a number of occasions when the Lords have defied the government, and used their powers to the uttermost. Some talk of a breakdown of the previous self-denying Lords' practice[25] but it is too early to say.

It is clear that the 'interim' House, that is the one in place since the passage of the House of Lords Act 1999, is assertive or, as the then Leader, Lady Jay, put it, 'more legitimate, more authoritative, more worthy of respect'. In the parliament from 1997 to July 2000, the government had been defeated 87 times, an increase of more than three times the average under the previous Conservative administrations – including the rejection of an important mandated government bill, the Criminal Justice (Mode of Trial) Bill, the vetoing of an important statutory instrument on Greater London Elections and disagreeing to the repeal of S.28 of the Local Government Act 1988.

Can Self-Regulation Last?

A number of factors have combined to pose the question whether the old system of self-regulation in the Lords can last or whether substantial, even radical procedural adjustments may be required to meet the new challenges. These challenges come from four sources, but they are all potential catalysts for change.

Firstly there are the compositional changes already made and the further changes envisaged in the Wakeham Report. The exclusion of the bulk of hereditary peers has inevitably changed the ethos of the House to a degree. The large creations made by Mr Blair – over 200 in four years compared with 205 by Lady Thatcher in 11 years – have brought so many new members into the House that its capacity to assimilate them and 'tame' them is questionable. The new members tend to be younger, there are more women, and the party appointees are expected – so it is said – to obey the party whip to a degree not customary in the Lords. What is clear is that there is a certain change in the practice of the House, with a certain 'assertiveness' and willingness to use its powers. The arrangement whereby the 'interim House' has been put in place has encouraged the opposition to exploit its numerical superiority to the government – while it lasts. The uncertain future of the 92 hereditaries reprieved by the Weatherill amendment is another factor encouraging resistance, perhaps with a certain feeling of *après moi le deluge.*

A second source of procedural change may come from the Wakeham Report itself. Although that report was careful to reserve decisions on the internal workings of a reformed House to that body itself, it did go on to recommend a continuance of open proceedings (para.16.6); that any restrictions on the rights of members should seek to preserve the essential character of what exists at present (para.16.10) and that the conduct of business should be seen to allow the chamber to remain self-regulatory. Perhaps because of these reassuringly traditional general sentiments, commentators – most of whom condemned the report for blandness in terms of compositional changes – failed to note how radical a report it is in terms of procedural and functional changes. Procedural innovations suggested included amongst others proposed Committees on the Constitution, Human Rights, Treaties and Devolution; improved procedures on subordinate legislation and better EU legislative scrutiny and EU ministerial statements and increased pre-legislative scrutiny of public bills.

Thirdly, there is the problem of processing legislation, which increases year by year. Despite cogent criticisms of the legislative process, particularly in the Commons, which have been made in recent years, to date no serious attempt has been made to improve the quality of draft legislation before it is presented to parliament, or to reform the system of parliamentary scrutiny of legislation in the Commons. By comparison, the Lords' procedures are leisurely and allow ample opportunity for lobbyists to deploy a case, in a House where party politics and government credit continues to play a less dominant role than in the Commons. The disparities between the Houses' treatment of legislation are becoming very marked, in circumstances where a heavy government programme makes it ever more desirable from the government business manager's viewpoint to lessen the differences between the Houses.

Finally there is the question of 'social hours': the House of Lords sits long hours (on average for 7 hours 29 minutes each sitting day in 2000 and second only to the Commons in the world). The Wakeham Report recommends that at least 30 per cent of the membership of the reformed second chamber should be women, with the 'aim of making steady progress towards gender balance in the chamber as a whole over time'. If the average sitting hours remain long, and if members are expected to attend to vote on legislation taken on the floor, an inevitable consequence will be that only older women or women without children, or women willing to place their children in childcare for the majority of the time will be eligible for membership.

There are ways of addressing these problems which would offer advantages both to the government and to the opposition by increased use of legislative committees off the floor of the House. One possibility would be to revert to the recommendations of the Practice and Procedure Committee of 1977, which suggested that there be a number of specialist select committees linked to specific policy areas which would scrutinise bills and other proposals within the relevant areas, taking evidence as requisite. An alternative would be to make pre-legislative scrutiny the rule, rather than the exception, as at first appeared to be the intention of the present government. Either of these suggestions would lead to a strengthening of the role of the House on legislation, but would also offer the government the bait of allowing more legislation to pass into law, without undue delay.

In conclusion it may be appropriate to recall a lecture given by Lord Moulton[26] (1844–1921), a law lord, who had been a Liberal MP between 1885 and 1906 (with interludes when he was unsuccessful at the polls). In his address 'Law and Manners' to the Author Club on 4 November 1912 – in the year which saw the major changes in the procedures of the House of Commons already alluded to – he spoke as follows:

> take Freedom of Debate in the Houses of Legislature such as our House of Commons. For centuries the members had unrestricted freedom of debate, and no inconvenience was felt. But in recent times, members of this House have said to themselves: 'We have unrestricted freedom of debate. We will use it so as to destroy debate. The absence of imposed restriction enables us to do it.' This obstruction was developed, and it had destroyed freedom of debate, and, indeed, all useful debate in practically every Legislature. The freedom due to absence of positive restriction has been treated by the individual members as leaving their use of debate a matter of Absolute Choice, fettered with no duty that they were bound to regard. They shut their eyes to the fact that the freedom was given to them in trust to help forward debate, and that it was incumbent on them to use it. Clumsy and even mischievous regulations have necessarily been introduced which fetter debate but prevent its being absolutely stifled. The old

> freedom cannot now be entrusted to the members, because when they possessed it they did not respond to it by the exercise of that moral sense which would have led them to treat it as a trust, and not as an absolute possession, unburdened by obligations which they should compel themselves to regard.

W.G. Gladstone, who strongly resisted the changes in Commons procedures, even though he was himself the victim as prime minister of the filibustering by the Irish Nationalists, made a similar point when he wrote about the British Constitution, which 'presumes more boldly than any other the good sense and good faith of those who work it … the assumption is that the depositaries of power will all respect one another… in the consciousness that they are working in the common interest for a common end … When these reasonable expectations fail, it must be admitted that the British Constitution will be in danger'.[27]

It remains to be seen whether the spirit of the ancient procedures of the House of Lords can be preserved, with appropriate changes to enable more legislation to be properly scrutinised without undue delay, or whether a more prescriptive system has become inevitable on the Commons model, with the consequence that the executive would control both Houses of Parliament, instead of just one.

NOTES

1. See Lord Campion *et al.*, *Parliament – A Survey* (London: Allen & Unwin 1952), ch.7; and E. Hughes, 'The Changes in Parliamentary Procedure (1880–1882)', in *Essays presented to Namier* (London: Macmillan, 1956), pp.289–320.
2. The author of this article was a member of the Royal Commission, and therefore objectivity on the Report is not claimed.
3. On the deficiencies of the legislative process in the two Houses, see *Making the Law* Report of the Hansard Commission on the legislative process (Chairman Lord Rippon of Hexham) 1992, and more recently, *Strengthening Parliament*, the report of the Commission to Strengthen Parliament (Chairman Lord Norton of Louth) 2000, the Modernisation Committee's Report of *Programming of Legislation and Timing of Votes* (H.C.589 of 1999–2000) and Constitution Unit *Parliamentary Scrutiny of Draft Legislation* by G. Power (2000).
4. S.C. Patterson and A. Mughan (eds.), *Senates: Bicameralism in the Contemporary World* (Columbus, OH: Ohio State University Press, 1999).
5. K. Bradshaw and D. Pring, *Parliament and Congress* (London: Quartet, 1973), p.203.
6. H. Evans (ed.), *Odgers' Australian Senate Practice* (Canberra: Senate, 9th edn. 1999).
7. F.A. Kunz, *The Modern Senate of Canada: A Re-Appraisal 1925–63* (Toronto: University of Toronto Press, 1965).
8. F.W. Maitland, *English Law and the Renaissance* (Cambridge: Cambridge University Press, 1901), p.31.
9. E.R. Foster, *The House of Lords 1603–1649* (Chapel Hill: University of North Carolina, 1983) see especially pp.45, 51–4. Robert Bowyer (1609–21 as Clerk), followed Sir Thomas Smith (1597–1609) and preceeded Henry Elsynge (1621–35).

10. M.F. Bond (ed.), *Manuscripts of the House of Lords* (New Series) vol.X (London: HMSO, 1965), especially pp.xxxix–xlvi and 1–27.
11. B. Kemp, *Votes and Standing Orders of the House of Commons: The Beginning* (London: HMSO, 1971), p.6.
12. J.A.G. Griffith and M. Ryle, *Parliament, Functions, Practice and Procedures* (1989), p.178
13. M.V. Clarke, 'The Origin of Impeachment', *Fourteenth Century Studies* (Oxford: Oxford University Press, 1937); and C.G. Tite, *Impeachment and Parliamentary Jurisdiction in Early Stuart England* (London: Athlone Press, 1974).
14. S. Johnson, *Dictionary* (London: 5th edn. 1784).
15. The chief differences since 1621 are that members of the Lords are no longer obsessed with their rank, privileges and procedure, as they were in the seventeenth century. Secondly, impeachment and attainder have fallen into desuetude as a means of punishing unpopular ministers. On the other hand, the appellate jurisdiction of the House, prolonged by the Appellate Jurisdiction Act 1876, has and is flourishing. Male peers no longer wear hats in the House – although they continued to do so until the early twentieth century.
16. Hughes 'The Changes in Parliamentary Procedure (1880–1882)', pp.289–319, and Josef Redlich, *The Procedures of the House of Commons*, pp.3, 5, and see a good modern evaluation in P. Norton, 'Parliamentary Procedure: The Hidden Power?' in D. Butler, V. Bogdanor and R. Summers (eds.), *The Law, Politics and the Constitution* (Oxford: Oxford University Press, 1999).
17. It was R.H.S. Crossman who first appreciated the great importance of the post, see *Diaries of a Cabinet Minister* vol.2 (London: Hamish Hamilton & Jonathan Cape, 1976), p.625. 'Freddie Warren' (the then Private Secretary) 'was one of the most important persons in British politics' and 'is still in control of the parliamentary timetable'. Unfortunately the Government Whips' Office has not as yet been studied in depth.
18. See Report by the Group on the Working of the House 1971 10th Report, Procedure Committee H L 227 of 1970–71.
19. *Companion to the Standing Order* (1994 edn.), p.15. See also Report of the Royal Commission on the Reform of the House of Lords *A House for the Future*, 2000 Cm 4534.
20. HL Paper 1991–92, 35–1.
21. HL Paper 1993–94, 88.
22. *Reforming the House of Lords* (Cm 4183) p.41, *A House for the Future* Cm 4524 ch.16, p.160.
23. J.C. Sainty, 'The Origin of the Leadership of the House of Lords', in C. Jones and D.L. Jones (eds.), *The House of Lords 1603–1911* (London & Ronceverte: Hambledon Press, 1986) which gives a masterly account of the origins: unfortunately there is no serious published work on the modern leadership.
24. D. Shell and D. Beamish, *The House of Lords at Work* (Oxford: Oxford University Press, 1993), esp. ch.12 'Conclusion' by D. Shell.
25. For Lords restraint on legislation before the passage of the House of Lords Act, see V. Bogdanor, *Power and the People* (London: Victor Gollancz, 1997), p.98 'The common perception of the House of Lords is that it has few powers. In fact, its powers are greater than is usually thought, but its peculiar composition means that it is rarely able to use these powers to threaten legislation'. No-one would write in these terms in 2000.
26. J.F. Moulton, Lord Moulton (1844–1921), son of a Wesleyan minister, educated at Kingswood School, and after a short spell as an assistant schoolmaster, went to London University where he read mathematics, and thereafter to St John's College Cambridge. He was Senior Wrangler in 1888 with the highest total marks ever obtained. Fellow of Christ's College Cambridge 1868. Attended Cambridge Union debates, speaking in favour of votes for women, university reform and Irish conciliation. Called to the bar 1874, QC 1885, specialised in patent law and made large income. 1885–86 Liberal MP Clapham, S. Hackney 1894–95, Lancaster 1898–1906, Lord Justice of Appeal 1906, Lord of Appeal in Ordinary

1912, created KCB 1915 and GBE 1917 for brilliant organisation of Explosive Supply Department, a branch of the War Department. Lord Birkenhead in tribute spoke of 'intellectual force and dynamic impulse of personality which had enabled a judge to play a supreme part in the European War'.

27. Quoted in W.E. Hearn, *The Government of England* (London: Longmans Green, 1887), p.190–91, from W.G. Gladstone, *Gleanings from Past Years* (London: John Murray, 1879).

Dealing with Big Brother: Relations with the First Chamber

ROGER SCULLY

Central to the contemporary debate over reform of the House of Lords in the United Kingdom has been not merely the issue of the *composition* of the second chamber (with discussion focusing around matters like the elimination of the hereditary element and the possibility of a wholly or partly elected house) but also the future relationship of the reformed chamber with the lower house, the House of Commons. It is virtually impossible to think in any sustained way about second chambers without considering the question of inter-cameral relations. How is the second chamber to stand in relation to 'Big Brother', the lower house? In its final report, and in response to much debate on the matter, the Wakeham Commission on reform of the British upper house stated its clear view that

> It should *not* be the role of the second chamber to substitute its own opinion for that of the House of Commons. The House of Commons should continue to be the pre-eminent Chamber of Parliament and should remain the principal forum for the resolution of political differences.[1]

The two issues of the composition of an upper house and the relative powers held by the two chambers are clearly related. The degree to which the first chamber is seen as *the* house of the people, and its bicameral partner is viewed as having a lesser or even negligible degree of democratic legitimation does have an impact on the structural relationship between the two.[2] Both in terms of formal prerogatives and in the legitimacy believed necessary to wield such powers, the general statement can be made that the closer the degree of equivalence in democratic legitimacy among the two chambers, the closer the equivalence of legislative authority that appears to be enjoyed by the two houses. This is not a precise correlation, but there are enough examples to validate this statement.

There is much more to be said, however, about how the composition of a second chamber might interact with the question of inter-cameral relations

---

Roger Scully is Lecturer in the Department of International Politics, University of Wales, Aberystwyth

TABLE 1
A COMPARISON OF THE POWERS AND SELECTION METHOD OF SECOND CHAMBERS FROM NINE COUNTRIES

	Directly Elected?	
	Yes	*No*
Powers of Chamber		
Strong	USA, Germany (indirectly elected), Australia, Italy (vast majority elected)	
Moderate	Spain (mostly elected)	Canada, France (very indirect
	election), UK	
Weak	Poland	

Source: Adapted from A. Mughan and S. Patterson (eds.), *Senates: Bicameralism in the Contemporary World* (Columbus, OH: Ohio State University Press, 1999), pp.24–6; also see the appendix to their chapter in this volume, pp.54–9.

than is captured in the above table. To understand this, we must remind ourselves that parliamentary chambers are not islands unto themselves, hermetically sealed from a broader political context, but rather exist as arenas within which political battles are fought. In particular, they are arenas for competition between political parties. Thus, when speaking of the relationship between two parliamentary chambers we are often talking in part about relationships within and between political parties – even if these relationships are significantly mediated by the institutional rules and formal prerogatives that govern much parliamentary behaviour.

The purpose of this article is to explore some potential patterns of inter-chamber relations within a bicameral system. The aim is to go beyond analyses that consider only the formal powers of the two chambers by also considering two further matters: the partisan composition of chambers, and the maintenance of party unity. The basic argument to be developed is that there will tend to be a significant inter-relationship between these factors that will shape inter-cameral relations in a more complex manner than one could deduce merely by examining the formal powers of the two chambers. In developing this argument, a middle course is steered between the very high levels of abstraction deployed in some formal modelling analyses of bicameralism and other work that, while very data-rich, may often be less useful for deducing general patterns. In short, much of what follows should be understood as being essentially a simplified 'pre-formal' analysis, which aims not at the final word on the topic, but rather at an exploration of some significant possibilities.

POWERS AND PARTIES: THE DRIVERS OF INTER-CHAMBER RELATIONS

As Michael Mezey has observed, 'most of the legislative literature is firmly rooted in time and place, and for much of the sub-field the place is Washington, D.C., and the time frames are usually current'.[3] Unlike American-centred work which assumes a separation-of-powers system, however, the analysis here is predicated on the assumption of a *parliamentary* system of government: that is, one in which the executive emerges from, and is dependent for its maintenance in office on continued majority support within, the lower house of the parliament.

The apparent simplicity of the parliamentary system can raise certain analytical problems with the usage of much commonplace terminology. For instance, it has long been understood that in parliamentary systems the relationship between the 'executive' and the 'legislature' is more complex than the simple dichotomy implied by traditional labels.[4] The presence within the chamber of the executive, and the highly influential role of the forces of *party* within the legislature, can make a simple distinction often highly misleading and at times extremely unhelpful.

Party, and the existence of the executive within parliament, can also intrude into the notion of inter-cameral relations to make them more complicated than they may, at first glance, appear. In their ground-breaking analysis of bicameralism, George Tsebelis and Jeanette Money suggest that 'the existence of a second chamber appears to have little effect on the relationship between the legislature and the executive'.[5] However, as it is developed, this argument seems to be based on an understanding of executive–legislative relations that is somewhat dubious – in particular, that the only salient consideration here is the maintenance of the executive in power. Considered more broadly – and in particular with reference to the issue of the impact of parliament on the policy agenda of the executive: what has sometimes been termed the 'viscosity' of the legislative process[6] – bicameralism and executive–legislative relations seem inextricably intertwined. In parliamentary systems of government the executive is also generally the chief legislator, using its majority in the lower house – which grants it the right to hold the executive levers of power – to drive through a legislative programme. The legislative dominance of the executive is only likely to be checked on any consistent basis by the existence of one or more of three conditions:

- The absence of a permanent majority supportive of the executive in the lower house. While not the normal situation in parliamentary systems of government, minority government is, as Kaare Strøm has conclusively demonstrated, far from unheard of.[7]

- Severe disunity among the party or parties that form the governing majority such that it fails to function as an effective unified force: this is, in many respects, the functional equivalent of the previous condition, in denying an executive a stable majority in the lower house.
- The existence of a *significant* second chamber – that is, one with the ability to impose some degree of 'viscosity' into the policy process. For this to occur, a second chamber must have both the formal powers to impede the passage of executive proposals and the willingness to deploy those powers. The most likely reason for a willingness to use powers on the part of a second chamber is a difference in the partisan composition of two houses, with the governing party or coalition being unable to count on majority support in the same way that it can in the lower house. Among the most famous examples of this sort of phenomenon are the three periods of *cohabitation* in the (semi-presidential) Fifth Republic France, and the fairly frequent control of the Bundesrat by parties not in the majority coalition in the Bundestag in the Federal Republic of Germany.

In short, the first and perhaps the most important point that must be understood with regard to relations between the first and second chamber in any parliamentary system of government is that they cannot be understood as separate from executive–legislative relations, but are closely interconnected. And in turn, executive–legislative relations are impossible to understand in practice without recourse to the concept of party.

One useful way of developing this point further is to consider that within a bicameral parliamentary system of governance, political divisions between parliamentarians can take three primary forms:

- Cleavages can operate along *institutional* lines, such that most members of one chamber, *regardless of party or other affiliation*, stand opposed to the other.
- Alternatively, the major line of division may come between the executive and the legislature such that non-governmental members of the parliament, *regardless of party or other affiliation*, stand opposed to those holding executive office.
- Divisions can operate across the lines of party, where *regardless of institutional position or incumbency* (or lack thereof) of executive office, those of one or more party grouping stand opposed to those of other party group(s).

Of these alternatives, it seems clear that the 'party' mode of division is the most common, and indeed is often dominant, in the activity of many parliamentary chambers. While party divisions have generally been thought to be particularly stark in the British context, considerable research on other chambers, through enquiry into factors like the voting cohesion levels of parliamentary party groups, illustrate that party loyalty is a dominating feature of the landscape across a wide variety of settings. The most common line of cleavage in parliamentary divisions is that of party;[8] dissent by parliamentarians of the same party is generally rare on issues where party leaderships indicate a favoured position (although that position may often be the outcome of intensive negotiation within the party grouping beforehand); and divisions between opposing parties are very common. Such patterns are frequent even in the more 'consensual' chambers of continental Europe.[9] It is also true that even in areas where parliaments are supposed to act in a more 'non-party' mode (such as in many committee sessions), the influence of party is often far from absent – perhaps simply because those in different parties have fundamentally different views of the world, or because they find it difficult to resist the temptation to cohere even when such behaviour is not necessarily required.

At the same time, it may often be misleading to make absolute party unity an *assumption* in analysis. Some work in the formal theory tradition starts from this position; while this may occasionally be helpful as a simplifying heuristic, to do this is to make absolute what is generally somewhat less than so.[10] Party division may follow from any number of causes – internal ideological cleavages, personal rivalries, differing strategic visions, or indeed along the lines of different institutional positions. When present in either or both of the chambers of a parliamentary system, party divisions have the potential to complicate matters considerably.

Relations between a first and a second chamber can be understood, then, as being driven primarily by two factors. The first is the formal prerogatives granted to a second chamber. These can vary considerably, but where the upper house is invested with substantial formal powers, it has at least greater potential to make a significant difference to the policy process. That potential will only be realised, however, if the upper house is willing to use its formal powers. This is where the second factor, party, becomes of crucial importance. The existence of party organisations that claim the loyalty, and shape the behaviour, of parliamentarians, is something that cannot be ignored. Party may matter simply because a different party balance exists across two chambers; a second possibility is that divisions may exist within parties across or between two chambers. In the next section, I explore how these three factors – powers, party balance and party unity – can influence patterns of inter-cameral relations and, indeed, the broader political environment.

EXPLORING INTER-CHAMBER RELATIONS

The aim of this section is to explore possible patterns of relations between the two chambers in a bicameral system by sketching out some broad, hypothetical examples, supplemented with the occasional illustration from the real world. I will consider how variations in the powers of the second chamber may interact with some of the other factors highlighted previously to shape the nature of bicameral relations: how the upper house stands in relation to the lower one. I begin with probably the easiest example, that of the virtually powerless upper house, and then go on to explore more complicated (not to say more interesting) alternatives.

The Powerless Upper House

It is far from unknown for there to be second chambers which are virtually devoid of significant prerogatives. Although the situation is, in practice, often complicated by the presence of certain chambers that have some nominal powers but are loath to use them, one can still identify examples of upper houses that appear to fit reasonably neatly into this category.[11]

A lack of formal powers may condemn the upper house to a fair degree of political impotence. This does not necessarily mean, however, that the chamber will be completely insignificant. An alternative role to that of the powerful legislator may evolve, in which the upper chamber seeks to use its status as part of the parliament to exercise a 'Voice' function.[12] That is, the chamber, or at least some of its membership, may seek to act as something of a lobbying group for particular viewpoints, and perhaps attempt to embarrass those in authority by raising particular issues. One of the classic examples of a chamber adopting this role is the European Parliament (EP) in the early 1980s. The EP was at that time (although matters have changed substantially in subsequent years) virtually powerless to influence major policy developments, with most legislation and other policy development going through the other 'chamber' of the EU's quasi-legislature, the Council of Ministers. The EP was able to carve out a moderately effective role for itself, however, as a lobby for further measures of closer integration. Led by the veteran Italian Euro-federalist Altiero Spinelli, the chamber passed a far-reaching Draft Treaty on European Union (1984), much of which has actually been enacted by national governments over the following period.

The party composition of a powerless upper house is fairly unimportant, except in as much that if the chamber is dominated by opponents of the government, it is more likely to wish to act as a voice for alternative political positions. Party unity, however, may well be fairly lax in such chambers. Given that the body has little substantive impact, there is little incentive for party organisations to expend the necessary time and effort in maintaining complex 'whipping' systems.

The Moderately Powerful Upper House

Many, indeed perhaps the majority, of upper houses are neither totally powerless nor the full legislative co-equals of the lower house. The precise forms of the limitations on the powers of second chambers vary widely. They include restrictions on the policy scope of what the upper house may adjudicate over (such as the well-known limitations on the role of the British House of Lords in the British budgetary process) and more direct constraints on the ability of the upper chamber to block the passage of matters agreed by the lower house. Such restrictions may mean that the power of the upper chamber is limited to 'asking the lower house to think again'; that is, requiring another vote to confirm the will of the first chamber; alternatively, there may be *de jure* or *de facto* time limits on the blocking powers of the upper house.[13]

Even if the powers of the upper chamber are limited, however, the fact that they exist offers the potential for the house to become a significant player in policy-making. Just as a skilful poker player may on occasion be able to achieve success with a poor hand of cards, even limited powers offer the potential for real political influence. For instance, an ability to delay legislation might be used to wring concessions out of an executive that cannot afford, for one reason or another, to sustain a substantial delay in the passage of its proposals through parliament. This therefore raises the question of under what circumstance the lower house will be willing to exploit its powers to the full.

Bearing in mind what was stated in the previous section, the most likely general cause of an upper house being willing to deploy its full powers to inhibit the will of an executive-dominated lower house must be a difference in the party balance across the two chambers. If a majority in the second chamber are from parties other than those in the governing majority, they would seem to have little incentive to refrain from utilising the prerogative granted to the second chamber. A good example of this process is given by Franks, who documents how the Canadian Senate, long regarded as among the weaker second chambers in the world, showed itself suddenly willing to use its limited powers to considerable effect in the mid-1980s. This occurred when the radical new Progressive Conservative government of Brian Mulroney, supported by an overwhelming majority in the House of Commons, had to face a second chamber dominated by the opposition Liberals.[14] Even though the non-elected status of Canadian senators has traditionally been viewed as requiring them to exercise the powers of the chamber with discretion, and not to challenge the ultimate will of the democratic house, Liberal senators became a significant thorn in the side of the Mulroney administration.

The likelihood of such 'opposing majorities' existing in the two chambers depends, of course, to a great extent on the method by which the membership of the second chamber is arrived at. Mulroney found himself in difficulty because the Canadian system of appointment to the Senate did not allow him to immediately replace his Liberal foes with more like-minded senators; he had to wait until almost the close of his premiership before acquiring a Senate more to his liking. Subject to the constraints of what is seen to be 'fair', and a government's ability to sustain a certain degree of public embarrassment over charges of 'packing' the chamber, a system of appointment by the governing majority does, of course, give those parties considerable leverage to mould the upper house to a partisan balance probably quite similar to that in the lower one. The greater the proportion of members that can be appointed by the government in a given time-period, the more quickly the upper house can be made compliant. This is, of course, to many eyes a central argument for removing the power of appointment from the hands of the government, something the government of Tony Blair in Britain has indicated it will seek to do – at least to some extent – at some unspecified stage in the future.

An elected upper house is a very different creature from an appointed one. For one thing, the legitimacy supposedly conferred by democratic election tends to make parliamentarians less abashed about utilising the powers available to them. But, in addition, elections provide the public with an opportunity to send political messages that are often uncomfortable for those in power. The phenomenon of the 'mid-term protest vote' is well known across many political contexts: voters appearing to take the opportunity to deliver a warning shot to a government at a less important poll. Recent work has significantly advanced our understanding of voting in 'second-order' elections, where voters perceive less to be at stake than in the election that decides a national government. In such polls, of which elections to an only moderately powerful upper house would certainly constitute one example, the public are significantly less inclined to vote with the 'head' (that is, cast a ballot for their most preferred among those parties that have a realistic chance of winning) compared with 'first-order' national polls, and much more willing to vote with the 'heart' (for parties whose policies are liked but who are perceived as having no realistic chance of success at a national election) or even with the 'boot' (deliberately voting in a manner which registers a protest).[15] The result of such different voting processes is generally that opposition and smaller parties, including extreme and other types of 'fringe' parties, tend to do better in second order contests than they would in national general elections held under similar circumstances. Thus, an elected upper house possessing modest powers might look very different from the lower one simply because of the manner in which voters would view the elections. This could then, in turn, have fairly obvious consequences for the relations between the first and second chambers.

Unity of action across the two chambers begins to matter more for a party as the powers of the second chamber grow. With a moderately important upper house in place, a party will no longer be able simply to neglect party management there. At the same time, given that the lower house retains a clear superiority, the party leadership is likely to be concentrated in the lower house. The possibility of tension then exists between the 'principal' (the party leadership in the lower house) and their 'agents' in its bicameral partner. The party must work out a means of managing its affairs in the upper house while acknowledging that the lower house must remain the primary focus of attention.

The Strong Upper House

The upper house that is more or less the co-equal partner of the lower house is a relative rarity in the democratic world, but it is far from unheard of. Perhaps the most obvious example is the US Senate – a chamber which, indeed, is in some senses the superior of the House of Representatives, possessing as it does a greater role in executive appointments, and also has a stronger voice in foreign policy through its prerogative of ratifying treaties. Most US states closely follow the national example, in not only having two chambers but by making them roughly equal partners.[16] But some parliamentary systems also have strong upper houses. Perhaps the most celebrated major example is the Bundesrat in the Federal Republic of Germany, which has equal rights with the Bundestag in a vast range of legislation impacting on the provinces that Bundesrat members – delegates from the provincial governments – are there to represent. But even some unitary states, like Italy, have upper houses more or less co-equal with the lower one.

A strong second chamber makes for a different political system to one where the lower house is 'the only show in town'. If the upper house is invested with significant responsibilities, and further if it possesses the legitimacy granted by democratic election, then it can offer considerable resistance to the will of the majority in the other chamber. Thus, the partisan composition of the chamber becomes crucial. If there are 'opposing majorities' in the two houses, then the executive will be likely to be far more constrained in its ability to push forward a policy agenda than it would minus such a chamber. It was, of course, the ability of the Conservative/Unionist-dominated House of Lords to resist the will of the

Liberal government in the early part of the twentieth century that led to the first substantial limitations in the powers of the Lords. The Liberals, however, had the considerable advantage of being the majority in an elected chamber, opposing a chamber that was then – with the exception of a small number of bishops – a purely hereditary upper house. An *elected* second chamber is far more able to maintain a defiant stance, even if the result can be legislative 'gridlock'.

How likely is it, then, that a powerful upper house will possess a different majority from the lower one? Again, the method of selection of the membership will obviously be crucial. If the chamber is elected, the importance of the chamber may mean that voters are less liable to view the ballot as a virtually costless 'second-order' poll. The timing of the election may then be crucial: opposing majorities will be more likely if the vote occurs during periods of mid-term unpopularity for the government. But another pertinent factor is that, whatever time the poll is conducted, at least some voters may deliberately choose to aim for a 'balance-of-power' between the chambers; in a similar way as voters in presidential systems like the USA often indulge in 'split ticket' voting, casting their ballot for one party in Congress and another for the presidency, in parliamentary systems when the parties are not particularly trusted, the public may actually wish to build in checks and balances between the parties. That such things actually transpire quite often – see, for example, the large swing to the Christian Democrats in provincial elections, giving them control over the Bundesrat, that occurred very swiftly after the decisive victory for the Social Democrats in the 1998 German national elections – suggests that voters are often alive to these possibilities.

Whatever the partisan balance between the chambers, party unity will be of the utmost importance when both chambers are politically significant. Indeed, unity assumes a dual dimension; parties will need to aim for both *intra-* and *inter*-chamber cohesion. How that unity is achieved, however, can become progressively more complicated as the upper house becomes more important. With both chambers counting, parties will need a rather bifurcated focus for their campaigning attentions and indeed in terms of the presence of the party leadership. Parties thus need to work out a means of managing their affairs that accounts for the concerns of their membership in both chambers and their relative strength in both.

CONCLUSION

This essay has sought to analyse relations between the first and the second chamber in a bicameral political system, basing the analyses on bicameralism in parliamentary systems of government as exist in much of (particularly western) Europe. The topic of inter-chamber relations is more far-reaching and important than it may at first appear. One reason for this is that second chambers vary considerably in the powers they possess, and thus in their potential impact on the policy-making process. A second factor that must be considered, however, is the involvement of political parties in both chambers of the legislature. The balance of parties in the two houses, as well as the degree of unity that the parties are able to sustain, will do a lot to shape the manner of relations between the first and second houses.

A key development in contemporary political science has been the 'new institutionalism': a re-assertion of the importance of institutions in political life. This general theme has found specific articulation in work on parliaments – perhaps most notably in the work of Judge, who has demonstrated how parliament in the UK has shaped the entire political system, even though parliament is not generally the powerful decision-maker implied by the 'parliamentary sovereignty' doctrine.[17] Similar sentiments can be applied more generally to the study of bicameralism. Though the force of party may mean that 'inter-chamber relations' is often a misnomer, or at least a proxy for conflicts between political parties, the existence of two chambers, and the formal prerogatives granted them, can have a wide and lasting impact on the whole of a political system.

NOTES

1. Royal Commission on Reform of the House of Lords, *A House for the Future* (London: HMSO, 2000), p.26.
2. For elaborations of this point, see many of the chapters in A. Mughan and S. Patterson (eds.), *Senates: Bicameralism in the Contemporary World* (Columbus, OH: Ohio State University Press, 1999).
3. M. Mezey, 'Legislatures: Individual Purpose and Institutional Performance', in A. Finifter (ed), *The State of the Discipline II* (Washington, DC: American Political Science Association), p.356.
4. The most insightful and encompassing conceptual analysis of executive–legislative relations remains that of A. King, 'Modes of Executive–Legislative Relations: Great Britain, France and Germany', *Legislative Studies Quarterly*, 1 (1976), pp.11–34.
5. G. Tsebelis and J. Money, *Bicameralism* (Cambridge: Cambridge University Press, 1997), p.1.
6. See J. Blondel, 'Legislative Behaviour: Some Steps Towards a Comparative Measurement', *Government and Opposition*, 5, pp.67–85.
7. Kaare Strøm, *Minority Governments and Majority Rule* (Cambridge: Cambridge University Press, 1990).
8. As research on 'free votes' shows, party is the dominant feature even when voting is conducted on an apparently non-party basis without pressure from whips to follow line of party leadership. For research in the British context on this phenomenon, see A. Mughan and R. Scully, 'Accounting for Change in Free Vote Outcomes in the House of Commons', *British Journal of Political Science*, 27 (1997), pp.640–47; and P. Cowley (ed.), *Conscience and Parliament* (London & Portland, OR: Frank Cass, 1998).
9. This is true even for perhaps the ultimate consensual chamber, the European Parliament (EP). Despite the fact that parties in the EP are multi-national groupings composed of individuals

elected from many countries, and originally as representatives of numerous national political parties, voting cohesion among the multi-national party groups is considerable, and divisions between the groups are the dominant line of cleavage in the chamber. For further details, see T. Raunio, *The European Perspective: Transnational Party Groups in the 1989–1994 European Parliament* (London: Ashgate, 1997).

10. For a number of perspectives on this theme, see S. Bowler, D. Farrell and R. Katz (eds.), *Party Discipline and Parliamentary Government* (Columbus, OH: Ohio State University Press, 1999).
11. The closest example in a major contemporary European democracy is probably the Senat of post-Communist Poland which, with only fairly minor exceptions, is subordinate to the lower house, the Sejm; see D.M. Olson, 'From Electoral Symbol to Legislative Puzzle: The Polish Senat', in Mughan and Patterson (eds.), *Senates: Bicameralism in the Contemporary World.*
12. A. Hirschmann, *Exit, Voice and Loyalty: Responses to Decline in Firms, Organizations and States* (Cambridge: Harvard University Press, 1970).
13. For an overview of several examples, developed elsewhere in their book, see Mughan and Patterson (eds.), *Senates: Bicameralism in the Contemporary World*, pp.24–6.
14. C.E.S. Franks, 'Not Dead Yet, But Should it be Resurrected?', in Mughan and Patterson (eds.), *Senates: Bicameralism in the Contemporary World.*
15. See C. van der Eijk and M. Franklin, *Choosing Europe? The European Electorate and National Politics in the Face of Union* (Ann Arbor, MI: University of Michigan Press, 1996).
16. The one state to which this comment certainly does not apply is Nebraska, which alone among the 50 has a unicameral state legislature.
17. D. Judge, *The Parliamentary State* (London: Sage, 1993).

The Territorial Role of Second Chambers

MEG RUSSELL

Upper houses of parliament classically perform scrutiny and revising functions with respect to government policy and legislation. In this they are generally the junior parliamentary partner, shadowing the work of the lower house, and often possessing considerably lesser powers. However, many also have a unique function, not shared by the lower house, of representing the territorial interests of provinces, regions or states at the national level. The origins of this territorial role of upper houses, the extent to which it is a feature today, and whether such chambers in practice fulfil a territorial role are investigated. Finally, the future, and the extent to which the territorial model may be becoming the standard one for upper house design is discussed.

THE ORIGINS OF THE TERRITORIAL ROLE

The territorial function of upper houses may be traced back to the establishment of early federal states.[1] Where a federation was formed by a group of self-governing territorial units (for example, provinces or states), it was natural to create an institution in which representatives of each of the units met together. Hence the thirteenth-century Swiss Confederation, for example, started out with one legislative body comprising ambassadors from the states, and a similar model was followed by the German Confederation in the nineteenth century. In both of these cases it was only later that a popularly elected chamber was added, to represent the citizens of the federation directly.[2]

When the federations of the US, Canada and Australia were formed (in 1787, 1867 and 1901 respectively), national parliaments were created with first chambers largely modelled on Westminster. These chambers were all directly elected, with elections based on single member constituencies, using the 'first past the post' system. Seats were distributed on a population basis in order that all citizens had roughly equal representation in parliament. But such a situation left smaller and less populous states or

---

Meg Russell is a Senior Research Fellow at the Constitution Unit, University College London.

provinces fearing that their interests would be swamped in parliament. In the making of the US constitution, the form of representation in the Senate was 'the most highly contentious issue the Founders faced'.[3] The final design was a compromise between large and small states, whereby the lower house was balanced with a Senate giving two seats to each state, irrespective of population. The upper house was also given co-equal powers. Thus no law could be agreed without the backing of the majority of the people's representatives and the majority of the states' representatives.

In Australia, as in the US, 'The single most contentious issue of the Australian founders, and the one that took up the most space in the convention debates and almost caused the break-up of both the 1891 and 1897–98 conventions, was the design of the Senate'.[4] The four smaller Australian states demanded equal state representation in a powerful upper house as a condition for their involvement in the federation. This demand was grudgingly accepted by larger states as a price worth paying, although some concessions were made by smaller states over the upper house's powers.[5] The result is a hybrid system built on the Westminster and US models, where the constitution demands that all states have an equal number of representatives in the Senate. Thus each state now has 12 Senators, although the population of the largest, New South Wales, is more than ten times that of the smallest, Tasmania.

In Canada similar arguments were made, but the large provinces were successful in resisting pressure for equal representation of each province in the Senate. However, the Canadian federation was founded on the principle of equal representation for three geographical 'divisions', where two of the divisions comprised the two largest provinces, and the third comprised the two smaller.[6] Subsequent additions to the Canadian federation have, however, resulted in this principle being broken.

In all of these cases state interests were protected by the upper house being given considerable powers. The US, Australian and Canadian Senates retain the power to veto any government bill. However, in the US and Australia states were further protected, not only through equal representation but also by the method of selecting upper house members. The upper house and lower house had a similar status, as both were elected. The Canadian Senate used a more traditional composition method – appointment – which was truer to the Westminster model. As a result the Canadian Senate has not played the central role in government enjoyed by its Australian and US counterparts.

Today, second chambers remain most common in federal states. The Inter-Parliamentary Union recognises 178 parliamentary democracies worldwide, of which 67 are bicameral. However, amongst the 22 states which are federations, 18 have upper houses. In all of these cases the upper house represents the sub-national units of the federation. However, the popularity of the territorial model has now spread well beyond federal states, to become the commonest form of representation in upper houses world-wide.[7] This is the case in particular in states where there has been some degree of devolution to regional government. For example the post-war constitution of Italy states that 'the Senate of the Republic is elected on a regional basis', whilst the post-Franco constitution of Spain states that 'the Senate is the chamber of territorial representation'. The means by which this territorial representation is achieved in different second chambers are diverse, as discussed below.

TERRITORIAL REPRESENTATION

The territorial model has the advantage that it gives the upper house a distinct representational basis to that of the lower house. Whilst the latter is elected on a popular basis to represent the citizens, the former represents territorial units. This can help ensure that the two chambers are distinct, with different perspectives and types of members.

The way seats are distributed between territorial units remains an important difference between the chambers in many bicameral parliaments. The US Congress, where the Senate gives equal representation to each state, is still the classic example. Like Australia, many other states – not all of them federal – have followed this model. Thus in South Africa and Russia, for example, the upper house gives equal representation to each province. Even in unitary Poland the upper house is elected largely on the basis of 47 constituencies each electing two members, irrespective of population.

Although this is the classic territorial model, the majority of federal states allocate seats in the upper house giving some consideration to population. However, less populous areas are still generally over-represented.[8] For example, in Germany a compromise principle is used, which neither gives equal representation to states nor is strictly population-based. Each state has between three and six seats in the upper house, depending on its number of inhabitants. This is despite the largest state having almost 30 times the population of the smallest. The express purpose of this arrangement was to ensure that neither large states nor small states could dominate the legislature.[9] In Spain, representation in the upper house is primarily on the basis of sub-regional provinces, which each have equal representation. This is supplemented by additional representatives from regions, with seats distributed on a population-weighted basis similar to that used in Germany. This results in the region of Madrid, which comprises just one province, having nine seats in the Senate, whilst the region of Castilla-León, with half the number of inhabitants, is represented by 39 senators.[10]

TABLE 1
TERRITORIAL REPRESENTATION IN SELECTED UPPER HOUSES

	Upper House Represents	Selection Method	Distribution of Seats
Australia	states	direct election	equal
Austria	Länder	indirect election	weighted
Canada	provinces	appointment	weighted
Germany	Länder	indirect election	weighted
India	states	indirect election	population-based
Italy	regions	direct election	population-based
Poland	voivodships	direct election	equal
Russia	republics and regions	indirect election	equal
South Africa	provinces	indirect election	equal
Spain	provinces	direct election	equal
	regions	indirect election	weighted
Switzerland	cantons	direct election	weighted
US	states	direct election	equal

In many cases the composition of the upper house differs from that of the lower house not only in distribution of seats, but also in method of selection. The territorial model offers the opportunity to represent three distinct interests within each geographical unit: its assembly, its government, or its people. Where the territorial assemblies or governments are represented this creates an indirect form of accountability between the upper house and the people, through elections at sub-national level. It also creates a direct connection between sub-national institutions and the national parliament. Where the people are represented directly, the link with territorial institutions is more likely to be weak, although the upper house may enjoy democratic legitimacy and popular support.

A common form of indirect representation in upper houses is election by state or provincial legislatures. This method was used for election to the US Senate prior to 1913, when direct elections were introduced.[11] The same method is now used for elections to the upper houses of Austria, India and the Netherlands, for example, and for regional members of the upper house in Spain. Those elected may or may not be members of the assemblies which elect them – a matter which may either be stipulated nationally or devolved for decision to individual territories.

Less common is the representation of sub-national governments in the upper house. The classic example of this model is the German Bundesrat, whose members comprise state (Länder) ministers. This is a legacy of the original 'federal council' (Bundesrat) which met during the first German federation. Although members of the upper house effectively sit on an *ex officio* basis, they may be considered to be 'indirectly elected' due to the link between government, legislature and electorate in their states. Similarly in South Africa, where upper house members are elected by provincial assemblies, provincial premiers are automatically given one of these seats. In Russia upper house seats are shared between the governments and parliaments, with each republic or region represented by two representatives, one chosen by each.

The alternative is for the upper house to represent the people of the territorial areas, rather than their institutions. In most cases this is achieved through election. Hence in Australia, the US and Switzerland, and at least notionally in Italy, members of the upper house are elected by the people to represent their state or region respectively. In Spain the majority of upper house members are directly elected to represent the provinces, with a minority indirectly elected by members of regional assemblies. Where both chambers are directly elected, the systems of composition are generally made distinct through different electoral boundaries, terms of office and electoral systems. Thus in Australia and the US senators are elected on a state-wide basis, for twice or three times the term length, respectively, of lower house members. In Australia proportional representation is used for the upper house, while the lower house is elected by the majoritarian alternative vote.[12] In Canada the upper house could also be said to represent the people, since its appointed members have no connection with either provincial governments or parliaments. However, since members are appointed from the centre to represent the provinces, with no provincial involvement at all, the public feel little ownership of their upper house representatives.

TERRITORIAL ROLES

In a country with devolved tiers of government, there may be many benefits from using the second chamber to provide links from the territories to the national parliament. Such an arrangement has the potential to bind the nation together, minimise the dangers of fragmented decision-making and encourage common positions to be found which are to the benefit of both the nation and its component territories. The territorial roles played by an upper chamber may be broken into three categories:

- representing the territories and their interests at the national level;
- providing a forum for the different territorial units to debate policies and agree common positions;
- linking the national parliament to territorial assemblies or governments.

Different territorial second chambers address these roles in many different ways, with varying levels of success. A territorial function may be built into the upper house through special powers over legislation which affects the territories, special procedures for voting along territorial lines, additional debates in the upper house on territorial matters, committees with territorial responsibilities, providing access for members of sub-national assemblies to speak in the national parliament, or providing reporting routes for upper house members to sub-national assemblies. Each of these roles is discussed below.

Powers over Territorial Legislation

One of the clearest signals that the upper house represents the sub-national units of the state is to give its members extended powers over legislation which is deemed to affect these units particularly. The classic example of this system is found in Germany. Here the Bundesrat has only a delaying power over 'ordinary' bills, but an absolute veto over bills affecting the work of the Länder. However, in most policy areas the federal government has the power to legislate whilst the Länder have responsibility for implementation.[13] Hence the Bundesrat's veto extends in practice to around 60 per cent of all legislation. Similarly, the upper house has a veto over any constitutional amendments, ensuring that any constitutional change has broad support, including the support of a majority of state governments and legislatures. The federal parliament therefore provides upper house members – themselves members of state governments – with an effective means to represent territorial interests and influence federal government policy. In doing so the upper house also provides a forum for states to come together and act collectively.

Seating and Voting Arrangements

The territorial nature of the German Bundesrat is reinforced by the seating and voting arrangements in the chamber. Unlike most parliamentary chambers members do not sit in party groups, but in delegations representing each state. Each delegation has a single weighted vote, equivalent to its number of seats, which is cast by the delegation leader. These arrangements are a natural result of the Bundesrat's membership, where members work together in their role in state governments. However, since these governments tend to be coalitions, block voting requires agreement between members of the coalition on the attitude to be taken on every aspect of federal policy. Coalition agreements made before state governments take office thus often extend to how the delegation will vote in the upper house.[14] Unlike most parliamentary chambers the federal government cannot predict the outcome of votes on the basis of party strengths in the chamber, but instead must appeal to a number of coalitions controlled by different combinations of parties.

In South Africa the upper house, the National Council of Provinces, has some features inspired by the German system. Here there are also two categories of legislation, based on which bills affect the provinces. Ordinary legislation is decided by a simple majority vote in the upper house, where members of provincial delegations may break up and vote in party groups. However, bills affecting the provinces, and constitutional amendments, must be decided by each provincial delegation voting as a block. Approval requires the consent of five of the nine provinces. Unlike in Germany, upper house delegations have been elected by provincial legislatures in proportion to party strengths, so include members of the opposition party at provincial level. Thus opposition positions may be voiced in the upper house. However, provincial delegations are mandated by their assemblies, and their positions are thus determined by the majority party, or parties, as in Germany.[15]

Debates and Committees

In Spain around 20 per cent of upper house members are, like members in South Africa, elected by regional ('autonomous community') assemblies. However, there is no requirement on these members to operate in regional blocks, and in practice they join the other members (elected by the sub-regional provinces) in forming party groups. There is also no requirement for legislation of particular interest to the regions to be treated differently in the upper house, with some very limited exceptions.[16]

The Spanish Senate has made efforts in recent years to try and develop a role as a more territorial chamber. One initiative was the establishment in 1994 of a 'General Committee for the Autonomous Communities'. This 50-member committee is open to all of those senators who are elected by regional assemblies. The most innovative feature is that the committee is also open to representatives of autonomous community governments, who have the right to request that the committee be convened and propose issues for discussion.[17] The committee has a long list of responsibilities, which include debating territorial issues, scrutinising legislation from a territorial perspective, and scrutinising bills with a particular territorial content. Although its overall impact is still unclear, it has amended many bills from the perspective of the regions, and carried out inquiries into issues such as the regions' relationship with the EU.[18]

The committee is also charged with hosting an annual debate on the state of the Spanish regions and decentralisation. On the occasions when the debate has been held it has been a high-profile event, attended by many members of regional governments, national government, the Senate and the lower house. All regional presidents are entitled to give a speech in their regional language and the prime minister also makes a keynote address. However, whilst the committee has been given the role of hosting this debate – since Senate standing orders would prevent this happening in the chamber itself – it is the government, not the committee, which has the power to call it. Hence although the debate was intended to be annual, it took place only twice between 1994 and 1999.

Initiation of Legislation

The Spanish constitution allows regional assemblies to propose bills to the national parliament. These bills may be introduced by representatives of the relevant regional assembly. However, despite the Senate's constitutional status as the 'chamber of territorial representation', these introductions take place in the lower house. In Germany, in contrast, state bills may be introduced in the Bundesrat directly by members of state governments, in their capacity as upper house members. If such bills are accepted by the Bundesrat, the federal government has a duty to respond. The bill is then debated in the lower house, and will be proposed there by a representative of the sponsoring state government (who is also a Bundesrat member). Thus, unlike in Spain, state government members have speaking rights in both chambers of the national parliament. This constitutional right extends to allow them to attend and be heard in the lower house and its committees at any time.[19]

Accountability to Territorial Institutions

Whilst a territorial upper house may offer access for representatives of the provinces, regions or states to the national level, it should also ensure that these representatives are accountable to those they represent. Ideally this accountability would include some form of linkage to the sub-national institutions, to create two-way communication and help bind policy-making at different levels of government together.

Where members of the upper house are elected by sub-national assemblies, the accountability of members to these assemblies could potentially fulfil both roles. However, unless mechanisms are put in place for formal reporting to assemblies, this may not happen. Once again Spain is an example. Here the majority of members elected to the upper house by regional assemblies perform dual roles, also holding seats in the assemblies which elect them. However, there is no mechanism for these senators to report to their assemblies on their activities in the upper house.

In Germany, Bundesrat members also play dual roles – as members of the upper house and of state governments. In both roles they are accountable to members of state assemblies, and their activities are scrutinised. Although accountability for the two roles may frequently be blurred, there are occasions when activity in the Bundesrat is the clear focus of attention. Some state assemblies have Bundesrat committees, specifically to monitor the activities of ministers in the upper house. On matters of particular significance – such as constitutional amendments – there may be debates in state assemblies before the Bundesrat votes.[20]

THE EFFECTIVENESS OF UPPER HOUSES AS TERRITORIAL CHAMBERS

The preceding section proposed that there are three broad roles which territorial upper houses may play. It also began to indicate, however, that the extent to which these roles are fulfilled varies greatly between different 'territorial' second chambers.

In some cases it is difficult to find evidence of any territorial role being played by the, nominally territorial, upper house. The chambers in Australia and Canada are examples. Here members represent their state or province, respectively, but there is no requirement of them to reflect this representation in the activities which they carry out in the chamber. Members sit and vote in party groups, have no particular powers over 'territorial' legislation, and do not take part in territorial debates or committees. Neither is there any formal mechanism for senators to report back to state or provincial legislatures. Senators have no speaking rights in these assemblies, and in Australia it is forbidden to hold office in both the Senate and a state assembly.

In Australia evidence suggests that the Senate is far from a champion of states' rights in general. In 1995 Wayne Goss, the premier of the state of Queensland, commented that 'none of us any longer pretend that the Senate continues to perform its political and constitutional function on behalf of the States. In fact there have been many cases in which the Senate has actively worked against the interests of the States'.[21] This hypothesis has been exhaustively tested by David Hamer, who concludes that:

> By any measure of public performance – amendments to Government bills, initiation of private members' bills, motions, questions to Ministers – there is no evidence that Senators have been any more diligent in protecting State interests (real or supposed) than have the [members of the House of] Representatives: if anything, they have been slightly less diligent.[22]

It is therefore questionable whether the Senate is properly carrying out its originally intended function as a states' house. It could, however, be more accurately described as a 'house of state parties', an institution which does have some benefits. The proportional electoral system ensures that voters in each of the states have representatives in the upper house from each of the main parties – something which may not be the case in the lower house. As a result, the main parliamentary party groups include members from each of the states. The Senate therefore does provide a voice for the states in parliament, albeit primarily in party caucus rather than through the formal business of the house.

In Canada the role of the Senate in representing the interests of the provinces is more questionable still. Here there is no guarantee that provinces will enjoy representation by each of the parties, as there is no tradition of prime ministers appointing senators from the opposition. Thus parties which have never held federal government office – such as the Bloc Québécois – have no seats in the upper house. Many senators do have roles in provincial parties, so may provide informal connections to provincial politics. They have also traditionally been used to balance Canadian cabinets, where the governing party is not represented in key provinces in the lower house. However, the lack of provincial involvement in selecting members of the Senate has seriously damaged its credibility as a territorial chamber, and for many decades there have been calls for reform. Proposals have ranged from provincial involvement in appointments to an 'elected and equal' Senate on the US or Australian model.[23]

In some cases, such as Spain, the second chamber is struggling to take on its territorial role.[24] There the chamber was not given clear territorial responsibilities, despite its constitutional duty of territorial representation. Over time this weakness has become clear and there have been some attempts to rectify it. However, the chamber is also damaged by the fact that only one-fifth of its members represent the regions, which are now the dominant territorial force. Even these members have no clear accountability to the assemblies which elect them, and the Senate functions largely as a chamber of national parties. The chamber has not played an effective role in binding the regions together and diffusing territorial tensions. There have been many calls for reform, to bind the upper house more closely to the regions. However, nationalist and separatist forces are now firmly opposed to a more federal-style parliamentary chamber.[25]

The 'very federal house' is the German Bundesrat, which has been described as the 'single most important institution' of the German federal state.[26] There is no doubt that the chamber acts to bring state concerns to the national table, facilitate debates between states and also provide accountability mechanisms to state legislatures. However, the central role of the chamber is very much the result of its unique membership – comprising blocks drawn from state executives – as well as of its powers. The role that state ministers have in the upper house, and their potential power to block federal legislation, helps create a system of federal – state relations which is described as *politkverflechtung* – literally an 'entanglement'.[27]

The Bundesrat is, however, quite unlike other parliamentary chambers. The status of its members means that there are few plenary sittings – the chamber works to a rigid timetable of three-weekly meetings, which each last just half a day. The main work of the chamber is carried out through its committees, which are attended by state civil servants and rarely by ministers. Even plenary sessions are attended by officials, alongside whichever state ministers are most relevant to the legislation under discussion. The backing of officials and other state resources makes upper house members potentially far more influential than MPs, and the influence of the states in parliament extends beyond the upper house and into the Bundestag and its committees.[28]

THE FUTURE

Despite what may be limited success in operating truly territorial upper chambers, the territorial model is growing in popularity worldwide. Nations which are reforming their upper houses are increasingly looking to this model, and some which nominally use it are attempting to improve its operation.

Examples of new territorial upper houses are those of Russia (1993) and South Africa (1994), which both use forms of indirect election with seats distributed equally amongst geographical units. The latter has attempted to take some of the best elements of the German model and adapted these to create a uniquely South African variant. Reform is being sought in countries such as Canada, Spain and Italy where the upper house is failing adequately to fulfil its territorial role. In the former, difficulties within the federation in reconciling the demands of large and small states, and the particular needs of Quebec, have helped leave the chamber unreformed after more than a century of debate. In Spain there are similar difficulties, despite a consensus amongst the main parties that the chamber should play a more territorial role, probably including giving more seats to the regions.[29]

One of the important lessons from Spain is that a territorial upper house must keep pace with devolution. If new devolved arrangements are not reflected in the upper house immediately, it may prove impossible to build these in later. This lesson is reflected in Italy. Here regional government was finally established throughout the country in 1970, and the reform of the upper house has since been considered necessary, within a review of the entire constitution. The most recent proposals, in 1997, would have given the Senate greater powers over regional legislation than over ordinary bills, and provided seats for representatives of regional and local government in the upper house or its committees.[30] However, there is little sign that these proposals will be acted upon.

The recent proposals of the Royal Commission on Reform of the House of Lords in Britain also included an element of territorial representation.[31] The Commission's terms of reference required it to take account of the recent devolution reforms in the UK, including the establishment of an elected Scottish Parliament and Welsh Assembly. Its response was to propose that a minority of elected members be included in the reformed upper house, to represent the nations and regions of the UK. However, there was no suggestion by the Commission that the new chamber might play a territorial role, apart from the proposed establishment of a new 'Devolution Committee'. This falls short of even the minimalist measures taken recently in the Spanish upper house to boost its territorial role. The Royal Commission's proposal that 'regional members' of the upper house would make up only a minority risks falling into another trap encountered in Spain. The remainder of members would – like those in the unpopular Canadian Senate – be appointed from the centre. As devolution progresses, Britain is in danger of joining the group of nations where debate is raging on how the territorial role of the upper house can be boosted.

CONCLUSIONS

The territorial upper house model is growing in popularity, and coming into use in increasing numbers of states. However, whilst territorial representation may mark upper chambers out from their respective lower chambers, distinct territorial roles have been harder to establish.

In analysing the effectiveness of upper houses to perform their territorial functions it is notable that directly elected chambers such as those in Australia and Italy fare less well than their indirectly elected counterparts. Accountability to the public, and enhanced electoral legitimacy, may be substituted in these cases for meaningful links with territorial institutions. However, indirect election does not guarantee that such links will be forged. For example in Spain indirectly elected upper house members behave like their directly elected colleagues, creating a party-dominated house with few territorial traces. This is the result of an institutional design which did not sufficiently allow for the progressively greater devolution which followed.

The German Bundesrat may truly be described as a territorial chamber, in both representational and functional terms. But its status is dependent to a large extent on its unique membership and the particular nature of German federalism, in which it plays a central part. However, there are aspects of the Bundesrat's design which may potentially be exported to enhance the territorial nature of other second chambers. For example, the chamber's seating and voting arrangements are not dependent on its composition, and neither is its enhanced power over territorial bills. The links between the

Bundesrat and state assemblies are genuine, through the requirement for accountability by state ministers. Similar reporting mechanisms could be adopted for members of both indirectly and directly elected second chambers. Indeed, some of these features have been included in the new Constitution of South Africa.

There is growing pressure in many states for upper chambers to be reformed in order to take on more effective territorial roles. This is particularly the case in countries where devolution has overtaken the design of the upper house, or where there are territorial tensions. However, once these tensions arise, reform is difficult to negotiate successfully. Other states, such as the UK, which are at the early stages of the devolution process, should therefore give careful consideration to the connections between territorial constitutional reform and upper house reform.

NOTES

1. See Donald Shell's contribution to this volume.
2. G. Tsebelis and J. Money, *Bicameralism* (Cambridge: Cambridge University Press, 1997).
3. B. Sinclair, 'Coequal Partner: The US Senate', in S.C. Patterson and A. Mughan (eds.), *Senates: Bicameralism in the Contemporary World* (Columbus, OH: Ohio State University Press, 1999).
4. B. Galligan, *A Federal Republic: Australia's Constitutional System of Government* (Cambridge: Cambridge University Press, 1995), p.75.
5. A. Cumming Thom, 'The Powers of an Upper Chamber over Legislation', *Constitutional and Parliamentary Information*, 153 (1988), pp.3–17.
6. C.E.S. Franks, 'Not Dead Yet, But Should It Be Resurrected? The Canadian Senate', in Patterson and Mughan (eds.), *Senates: Bicameralism in the Contemporary World.*
7. J. Coakley and M. Laver, 'Options for the Future of Seanad Éireann', in *The All-Party Oireachtas Committee on the Constitution, Second Progress Report: Seanad Éireann* (Dublin: Government of Ireland, 1997).
8. R. Watts, *Comparing Federal Systems* (Montreal: McGill-Queen's University Press).
9. R. Sturm, 'The Changing Territorial Balance', in G. Smith *et al.* (eds.), *Developments in German Politics* (Basingstoke: Macmillan, 1992).
10. C.F. Juberías, 'A House in Search of a Role', in Patterson and Mughan (eds.), *Senates: Bicameralism in the Contemporary World.*
11. Sinclair, 'Coequal Partner'.
12. Italy is an exception, where the electoral system for the two chambers is very similar, and both are elected on the same day for the same term of office. Here the link between upper house members and regions was also weakened in 1993 by the electoral system change from regional lists to a form of additional member system.
13. C. Jeffery, 'German Federalism in the 1990s: On the Road to a "Divided Polity"?', in K. Larres (ed.), *Germany Since Unification* (Basingstoke: Macmillan, 1998).
14. W.J. Patzelt, 'The Very Federal House: The German Bundesrat', in Patterson and Mughan (eds.), *Senates: Bicameralism in the Contemporary World.*
15. C. Murray, *Designing Parliament for Co-operative Federalism: South Africa's National Council of Provinces* (Cape Town: University of Cape Town, 1999).
16. The upper house formally has greater powers over legislation implementing agreements between the autonomous communities, and concerning the 'autonomous communities clearing fund'. But the additional powers are minimal, simply giving the Senado the right to refer such bills to a joint committee of both chambers in the event of a dispute, rather than

being immediately overridden by the lower house. The Senate also has exclusive power to take action against an autonomous community which is 'acting against the interests of Spain'. However, this extreme sanction has never needed to be used (Juberías, 'A House in Search of a Role').

17. M.R. Ripollés, 'The Spanish Senate', in *Dossier Prepared with Information of the Seminar, Spanish Senate* (Madrid: Senado, 1999).
18. M. Russell, *Reforming the House of Lords: Lessons from Overseas* (Oxford: Oxford University Press, 2000).
19. Patzelt, 'The Very Federal House'.
20. B. de Villiers, *National-Provincial Co-operation – the Potential Role of Provincial Interest Offices: The German Experience* (Johannesburg: Konrad-Adenauer-Stiftung Occasional Papers, 1999).
21. *Australian*, 11 July 1995.
22. D. Hamer, 'Towards a Valuable Senate', in M. James (ed.), *The Constitutional Challenge* (St. Leonard's, NSW: Centre for Independent Studies, 1982).
23. Russell, *Reforming the House of Lords*; Franks, 'Not Dead Yet, But Should It Be Resurrected?'
24. Juberías, 'A House in Search of a Role'.
25. Russell, *Reforming the House of Lords.*
26. Patzelt, 'The Very Federal House', p.60.
27. P. James, 'The Federal Framework', in P. James (ed.), *Modern Germany* (London: Routledge, 1998).
28. Russell, *Reforming the House of Lords.*
29. Juberías, 'A House in Search of a Role'.
30. *Progetto di Legge Costituzionale: Revisione della Parte Seconda della Costituzione*, Commissione Parlamentare per le Riforme Costituzionali, ref. 2583-A (Rome: Senato della Repubblica, 1997).
31. *A House for the Future*, Royal Commission on the Reform of the House of Lords, Cm 4534, 2000.

The Politics of Second Chamber Reform: A Case Study of the House of Lords and the Passage of the House of Lords Act 1999

MICHAEL COCKERELL

In July 1998 Margaret Jay was appointed Leader of the House of Lords and given an historic task by Tony Blair: to abolish the rights of hereditary peers. She was up against hundreds of Tory Lords, most of them hereditary. Baroness Jay declared: 'It is my belief that the most thoughtful among the hereditary peers of all political persuasions know that the time has come to say thank you and goodbye.'

Speaking at the Labour Party conference in 1998 the Prime Minister, Tony Blair, had made his view clear: 'People say there's no Tory opposition any more. Well there is, it's alive and well and unelected and in the House of Lords with a three to one majority over us. Not a vote to their name, but able to vote down the plans that the people voted for in our manifesto. I call that arrogance.'

Blair had appointed Jay as Labour's first woman Leader of the Lords – not least because she shared his view of the hereditaries. She told me: 'The fact of the matter is that it's their collective presence which is unacceptable, the fact that they are there because they inherited their seats as a birthright in a modern democracy.'

Although New Labour had come to power promising to abolish hereditary peers, Baroness Jay knew that for 100 years governments had come to grief on the issue. The inside story of what happened this time vividly illustrates the difficulty of turning election rhetoric into reality.

The Lord Chancellor, Lord Irvine of Lairg, was one of a high-powered team of ministers and civil servants brought in to help Lady Jay with the abolition Bill. Against them were the Conservative lords, a mixture of appointed life peers and the hereditaries, who together outnumbered the Labour peers by nearly three to one. They were led by Viscount Cranborne and Lord Strathclyde, both of whom had views as to why Tony Blair wanted to end the right of hereditary peers to sit and vote in the Lords. Lord Strathclyde observed:

Michael Cockerell is a political documentaries film-maker with the BBC.
This contribution is adapted from the transcript of the author's television documentary 'The Lady and the Lords' transmitted on BBC 2 television on Sunday 6 February 2000

> This is not about balance this is about control. This is about power. This is about crushing dissent. What the House of Lords has done over the last two years, in fact what it has done over the last twenty years, is to provide dissent against the Government of the day. That is a great role. We should relish that role. It is about to be done away with.

Baroness Jay took a rather different view: 'They [the Conservatives] have had forty five years in Government since 1911 to do it their way if they had wanted to. They never did, and they didn't because it involved losing their Conservative majority in the Upper House. So the real change is a massive political one.'

The battle to abolish the hereditaries would claim many casualties, including two party leaders in the Lords. The man Tony Blair appointed to lead the Lords when he won power in 1997 was Lord Richard, a former European Commissioner, and self-proclaimed Old Labour figure. He was up against the Tory Leader Lord Cranborne and his Chief Whip Lord Strathclyde. Lord Cranborne was a scion of the House of Cecil whose family had been involved in statecraft and high intrigue for 400 years. Now he had a cunning plan to force Lord Richard to negotiate. As he explained:

> I don't think it's proper for the House of Lords to disrupt the legislative programme of a popular recently elected Government, but what is on is to kid the Government into thinking that we would. And in order to do that what I want to do is to pick very carefully the issues on which we defeat them and to ratchet up the number of defeats and the importance of the defeats to make them believe that that is our intention, and that it's going to completely destroy their legislative programme.

Lord Richard said that he had been given instructions by Tony Blair to 'flush out' the Tories, and find out whether there could be a bipartisan approach to abolishing the hereditaries.

> MICHAEL COCKERELL: Who initiated the contacts with Lord Cranborne?
> LORD RICHARD: Well we knew they wanted to talk.
> MICHAEL COCKERELL: How did you know that?
> LORD RICHARD: Oh, well various sort of subterranean channels, told us that the Tories really wanted to talk.

As a result Lord Cranborne's home in Chelsea was deemed to be a suitably safe house for the two leaders and their chief whips to meet for lunch.

> VISCOUNT CRANBORNE: Ivor [Lord Richard] quite rightly thought that our initial contacts ought to be made rather discreetly. My house is reasonably discreet and it seemed to be a rather convenient venue

> which he was happy to come to. And we had a very agreeable time.
> LORD RICHARD: Very agreeable as far as I remember. I don't remember what the food was. But it was very pleasant, and I think if it had been left to the four of us there we could probably have produced a package.

But it was not to be. In July 1998, Tony Blair sacked Lord Richard, and promoted his deputy Lady Jay to replace him. In the words of Viscount Cranborne: 'They shafted Ivor. And the reason he was shafted is clear. He was sacked because he genuinely wanted an effective reformed second chamber, he and I agreed about that.' Lord Richard's version:

> Well I'm more old Labour then New Labour. My views on the Lords are perhaps more radical than some other members of the Government. I think that – I've forgotten who said it now, but I think Ken Livingstone said it actually just after I was sacked. He said 'oh it's very simple why Ivor was sacked, Margaret Jay looks better in a short skirt'.

It was Lady Jay's job to pilot the abolition Bill through parliament and into law. Unlike those born to the ermine, Baroness Jay was not attracted by what she saw as the old-fashioned flummery of the Lords. The daughter of the former Labour Prime Minister, James – now Lord – Callaghan, her role was a far cry from her earlier careers as a television producer and running an Aids trust. Initially, Lord Strathclyde believed that this move was 'a substantial stroke of genius by Tony Blair' because Lady Jay 'would bring a certain amount of her femininity to bear upon the backbenches of all parties', while Viscount Cranborne declared that: 'I thought that she would be rather a good Leader of the House. She had a very good, rather olympian manner, but nice manner and people found her elegant and persuasive. And she had authority. She was of course de facto also a hereditary peer which made a number of us rather sympathetic to her.'

The government's chosen tactic was to introduce a short bill to abolish the hereditaries, leaving the second stage until later, not least of all because of what had happened to the attempt at Lords reform in the House of Commons 30 years before. As Lord Callaghan of Cardiff put it in the Lords:

> I support the way in which the Government's carrying this out, and I do so because of my own experience as Home Secretary in 1968. We introduced a bill of twenty clauses. Thirty one new clauses were added, two hundred and fifty nine amendments were put down. Several new schedules were tacked on. We staggered through after eleven days, including morning sittings, to clause five. When then we threw in the towel.

At the beginning of the 1998–99 Parliamentary Session it was announced that a bill was to be introduced to remove the right of hereditary peers to sit and vote in the House of Lords. It was said to be the first stage in a process of a reform designed to make the House of Lords more democratic and representative. Baroness Jay explained how her approach differed from previous atttempts at reform:

> By trying to do the whole package at once, by saying we will get rid of the hereditary peers and then do the long term reform of the House, the short term reform, getting rid of the hereditary peers, would have got bogged down because nobody could agree about the long term. So what we said right from the start on this occasion was, we get rid of the hereditary peers, we clear the ground. We get rid of that vested interest of people who while they're there will always vote for nothing to change, and then we can have a sensible debate and sensible proposals and sensible action on the long term solutions.

It was not an approach that went down well with the Conservatives. As Viscount Cranborne saw it: 'This argument about a two stage reform is rubbish. And what it really shows of course is the reality, which is Blair was frightened of an independent House of Lords and he wanted to emasculate it with a nominated House. That's the truth.' On the contrary, Baroness Jay insisted to the House:

> The Government believes that modernising the Constitution is vital to modernising our democracy. Legislating to stop hereditary peers being members of Parliament removed a profoundly undemocratic element. And it is my belief that the most thoughtful among the hereditary peers of all political persuasions know that the time has come to say thank you and goodbye.

The government did, however, face criticism from amongst their own supporters, criticism based upon why it was that a directly elected second chamber was not a good idea. Baroness Jay and her political strategy team of ministers, senior MPs and party officials realised that it was an argument that they would have to confront, that they would need to spell out why it wasn't, and then more importantly say why the alternatives were better. As Baroness Jay explained to her team at the time:

> I think you want to start with the positive picture, saying that what we want from the second chamber is this, that, and other characteristics. Now how do you achieve that? Not by having the democratic direct elections which will simply replicate the Commons and not get the kind of second chamber that you want to fulfil these functions. Starting from that positive end makes it much easier because you're

> not put immediately on the defensive. Because the question is always phrased in terms of 'how can you at the end of the twentieth century justify any House of Parliament which isn't at least mainly directly elected'. So we've just got to turn that round.

Tory hereditaries soon turned against Baroness Jay. They disliked what they saw as a bossy manner and a dismissive attitude towards them. Baroness Jay responded by declaring that 'Some of them are pretty hopeless. They may not be pretty hopeless gardeners, they may not be pretty hopeless husbands or pretty hopeless huntsmen, but certainly pretty hopeless as parliamentarians and democrats', and asking: 'Do we want to be the only country in the world that has a hereditary element in one of its chambers of Parliament except for Lesotho?'

However, behind the scenes a new, ultra secret set of talks over the possibility of a deal had begun. They involved the Lord Chancellor, Lord Irvine of Lairg and Viscount Cranborne. As Lord Irvine of Lairg explained:

> Robert Cranborne said that he believed that if we cleared the hereditaries out, all seven hundred and fifty or whatever the number was of them, that that would be the last that the country would ever hear of House of Lords reform. That it just wouldn't take place. That stage two would not in fact happen. I assured him it would. We both treated one another as honourable people and I believe that he acted one hundred percent honourably with me throughout.

While Viscount Cranborne declared that: 'In all my dealings with Derry [Irvine] he's been completely straight. He kept his word, kept quiet about what he said he'd keep quiet about and I've never had any problem with him at all.' Indeed, Lord Irvine went on to point out that: 'One of the most amazing parts of this story is that radio silence was maintained. It must've been the best kept secret for a very long time in British Politics.'

Before Tony Blair made him Lord Chancellor, Derry Irvine was a commercial lawyer, well used to cutting a deal. He decided to make Viscount Cranborne an offer, namely that a few hereditary peers could be reprieved in exchange for Tory co-operation over the abolition Bill. As Viscount Cranborne himself explained:

> Sure as eggs is eggs Derry gets in touch and says, all right what about fifteen self elected hereditaries in the transitional house. So I said, don't be so ridiculous, I'm not in the business of bargaining. Derry said I'm not in the business of bargaining either. So I said well I'll tell you what we want is a hundred. It's the minimum I think I can get away with. He laughed and said don't be so silly. So I said, well fine, battle of the Somme and Paschendale, we'll ruin your legislative programme next year and the whole thing will be deeply embarrassing and ghastly.

Lord Irvine took up the story: ‘He was describing the uncontrollable conduct of the hosts of backbench Tory hereditaries on his benches. He wasn’t issuing a formal threat he was just describing what he no doubt genuinely believed would have occurred.’ Both men had weapons of last resort that they preferred not to use. Viscount Cranborne did not want to draw further fire on the Tory peers by defying a popular Labour government, and Lord Irvine knew that the government could bulldoze its legislation through, but it would cause chaos. So they both had an interest in reaching agreement. Lord Cranborne continues the story:

> Anyway he rang me up and he said what about fifty. This was some days later. So I said well I’m not in the business of bargaining, and I reported this to William Hague (Conservative Party Leader) who was amused. He was the only one who knew about this at this stage. And by July we’d got as far as seventy five. There was a certain rationale that it was one in ten roughly of the hereditary peers.

As Lord Irvine put it: ‘It was a formula. One in ten didn’t seem to be so unacceptable. The Labour Party is getting rid of nine tenths of the hereditary peers.’

Viscount Cranborne then came up with a new ploy to up the numbers. He suggested that a further 15 hereditary peers who hold official positions in the house should also be reprieved:

> I could hear Derry’s sigh of relief and he said ‘well I’ll ask the Prime Minister’, and by return I got, ‘done’. Which gets us up to ninety. So I say, fine, well it’s not very elegant and we’re going to get into a certain amount of ridicule about all this because it was obviously just a rather inelegant way of bridging a negotiating gap, which it was. And I said well you will of course give me the Earl Marshall and the Lord Chamberlain. ‘Done’ he says.

As Lord Irvine concludes: ‘So he got the figure up from seventy five to ninety two. And good luck to him. He didn’t get a hundred.’

However, Viscount Cranborne now ran into trouble with his own side, when the Shadow Cabinet vetoed the plan. But he was not to be put off. He was later to be called the Oskar Schindler of the hereditary peers. For, without telling his own leader, William Hague, he smuggled himself into Number 10, to discuss the deal directly with Tony Blair. Viscount Cranborne takes up the story:

> Blair was a little late, he was very agreeable, offered me whisky. We sat down in one of the sitting rooms upstairs, he suggested that it would be sensible to let this out sooner rather than later, at least one would have some sort of control over it, and I saw the force of that. We talked about the details of how that might be done. And he said ‘well that all

> sounds perfectly possible, but I'd better ask Alastair [Campbell – the Prime Minister's press secretary] to see whether he thinks this is all right.' And so I said well I'd be perfectly happy to talk to Campbell.

Consequently, Viscount Cranborne met Alastair Campbell to discuss how best to make the deal public. He was still keeping William Hague in the dark. As Lord Irvine observed: 'I do think at that time Lord Cranborne had an awareness that he was skating on very thin ice. I think it must be the case that he saw a real risk that he would be dismissed, because he did say that from one point of view perhaps what he was doing was committing high treason.'

Viscount Cranborne at last told William Hague what he had agreed with Tony Blair. As Lord Cranborne explained: 'He was extremely upset. And I said well please don't raise it at Prime Minister's Question time, which was his initial reaction, because it'll make you look an awful fool and Blair will make mincemeat of you. Anyway he said "no, I must".' And raise it he did:

> WILLIAM HAGUE: It's no good Honourable Members opposite shaking their heads. What they don't know is the Prime Minister does propose to keep hereditary peers in a stage one reform of the House of Lords. Where does that leave his principles now?
> TONY BLAIR: Madam Speaker, I take it from that that he opposes the deal that has been agreed by the Leader of the Conservative Party in the House of Lords. Now Madam Speaker as a result of this we will indeed remove hereditary peers.
> WILLIAM HAGUE: No, no deal has been made with the Conservative Party. What we know Madam Speaker is that the Prime Minister intends to turn the House of Lords into a house of cronies.
> TONY BLAIR: Well Madam Speaker, look I can't credit the Right Honourable gentleman engaging in what is a kamikaze mission on his side. All I can say to him is that even his cronies in the House of Lords agree with me that it's better to try and get this reform through with the minimum of difficulty – that is in the interests of the Country.

Viscount Cranborne apologised to William Hague for behaving like 'an ill-trained spaniel', and leaving his leader to clear up the mess. At an impromptu press conference in the Lords, he said: 'I said I'm extremely sorry that I behaved outrageously but I'd do it again.'

> REPORTER: Did you offer your resignation at any point?
> LORD CRANBORNE: 'Yes, but he said he'd rather sack me. So I said I think in his place I'd have done the same.'

Lord Irvine explained the events from the government's standpoint:

> The Tory Party was at such ludicrous sixes and sevens that the Labour Party thought well this is absolutely marvellous for us, this must be a

> very good deal for us. I believe that it was a very good deal for us, but the misjudgement of William Hague made it very much easier for us to demonstrate to the Labour Party that this really was a good deal for us. So William Hague played into our hands.

Viscount Cranborne's political friend Lord Strathclyde was appointed leader by William Hague after the whole Tory front bench had threatened to resign in protest at Cranborne's sacking. Baroness Jay takes up the story:

> Although we were told what Lord Strathclyde's understandings with William Hague were about – which were that he continued on the same basis that Lord Cranborne had – which of course made a complete nonsense of sacking Cranborne, but given that we were told that, we assumed his bona fides. But we didn't know that that was what he had actually agreed, because it seemed so extraordinary that William Hague should sign on to such a deal. I mean say to somebody you're fired because you've done this but you can have the job as long as you stick to the deal which I've just fired him for agreeing. But we had to take that on trust a bit.'

By now Baroness Jay had approached new players to take the Cranborne–Irvine deal forward. The former Commons speaker Lord Weatherill led the crossbench, or independent, group of peers, the second largest in the Lords. Lord Weatherill had been working on his own formula, and now agreed to propose in his own name an amendment to the abolition Bill that would reprieve the 92 hereditary peers.

The stage was now set for peers to debate the Bill, including the new amendment. But although the original Bill was unusually short – just five clauses – peers had tabled hundreds of new amendments. Baroness Jay explained the government's approach:

> We used to play it different ways different days. Some days we would say, well this is the day on which we say nothing. I see restraint is the mood today. And other days we would say well this is clearly a day in which we have to be rather heavy. And other days we would take another tactic. It was really honestly dependent slightly on our mood of either irritation or whatever it might be as we rehearsed the same arguments yet again.

The Government had appointed a Royal Commission to recommend what a fully reformed House of Lords should look like. It was headed by the former Tory Chief Whip Lord Wakeham. Baroness Jay was therefore able to answer critics who asked what would happen after the abolition of the hereditaries with the mantra 'we're waiting for Wakeham'. Debate in the Chamber itself continued, with the government still resisting – as Baroness Jay explained during one exchange:

> My Lords I shall attempt to reply to the Noble Lord's amendment with great animation in order not to invite the Noble Lord Earl Ferrers to suggest that I am either exhausted or bored with the proceedings of this house. I'm certainly not. And I would say to the Noble Lord that his amendment is in fact another valiant attempt to find a combination of circumstances in which hereditary peers may remain in your Lordship's House with certain rights. And I am sure the Committee will not be surprised to hear me say that it is frankly no more acceptable to the Government than the others.

As Lord Irvine saw it: 'The hereditary peers felt deeply hurt and deeply offended and not valued for what they were, as they saw it the only truly independent members of the House. I mean they have been around for hundreds and hundreds of years. So it was very very fraught.' Indeed, as one hereditary peer, Lord Montagu of Bealulieu, put it: 'I think there's a slightly mean streak in the way that people who have been here for over fifty years remortgage the House. I think there could be a little bit more generosity of spirit.' While another, Lord Carrington, declared: 'As a result of this there's a good deal of ill will and things have been said about hereditary peers by various Members on the Labour front bench which I think are both unnecessary and not particularly helpful.'

The criticism did not come as a surprise to Baroness Jay: 'We always thought that it was going to be a tremendous amount of fire and thunder and general drama all round the House of Lords, because so obviously it was a major issue of self interest for vast numbers of the Members of it.'

The Bill team frequently met to discuss how to counter what they saw as obstructive tactics employed by hereditary peers who were masters of parliamentary procedure. As Baroness Jay explained:

> It was very fortunate that three absolutely top class lawyers (Lord Irvine, Lord Falconer and Lord Williams of Mostyn) were assigned as it were in Ministerial terms to this Bill, because that gave us firepower which was more than adequate frankly to knock down most of the things which were dreamt up by the hereditary peers.

Lord Falconer takes up the story:

> The way the opposition went in the Bill, unlike any other Bill I'd ever seen, was it became an incredibly sort of intense legal debate, with frankly mad legal propositions being advanced. When I was a barrister whenever you didn't really know what you were talking about you'd focus very much on the procedure rather than the subject.

The Bill team met to discuss how to deal with proposed amendments – for example, Earl Ferrers raised a small but scholarly point, namely to delete the word 'a' when it appeared before hereditary and replace it by the word 'an'. The discussion at the meeting went as follows:

> MEMBER OF MEETING: Well that is correct. What is party correctness?
> MEMBER OF MEETING: I suspect that although he was not educated at a State School he is right in that.
> LORD IRVINE: I have a great deal of sympathy with that proposition and I do not really quite understand why the Parliamentary draughtsman is so hostile to it.
> MEMBER OF MEETING: Are you an an or an a?
> BARONESS JAY: I'm an an. I'm an an, I was brought up to say an hotel.
> MEMBER OF MEETING: I think you should drop the 'H'. It's an 'ereditary or a hereditary.
> MEMBER OF MEETING: An hereditary.
> MEMBER OF MEETING: If you're a cockney it's an, and you should drop the aitch.
> LORD IRVINE: I agree.
> BARONESS JAY: Well I want to know why the Parliamentary draughtsman doesn't agree.
> MEMBER OF MEETING: Precedents apparently are in favour.
> MEMBER OF MEETING: But they're bad precedents.
> MEMBER OF MEETING: Precedents are in favour of a .
> MEMBER OF MEETING: Yes, without the N.
> BARONESS JAY: Well the only thing is when I saw [the draughtsman] yesterday he said to me in a slightly worried tone "you're not accepting any of these amendments are you, I think the whole Bill may fall apart".
> LORD ACTON: Well I'm a hereditary peer but apparently Earl Ferrers thinks he's an hereditary peer. The Ferrers are a very ancient Norman family and maybe he's thinking in French I don't know.

The debate continued in the Chamber:

> THE EARL FERRERS: For instance an historian, an hotel, an hysterical scene, an hereditary title, an habitual offender. My Lords that comes from Fowler's Modern English Usage. My Lords I defy even the Government to beat that, and I suggest that that is a more appropriate word to use rather than a. I beg to move.
> LORD WILLIAMS OF MOSTYN: An was formerly usual before an unaccented syllalble beginning with aitch, and is still often seen and heard. An historian, an hereditary title. I read on. But – Now the aitch in such words is pronounced the distinction has become anomalous. I think we ought to stick to a on this occasion. But I think it's something we probably ought to return to in Third Reading.

Other amendments also had to be considered – for example, an arcane amendment dealing with the two senior hereditary positions due to be reprieved in the Bill, namely the Earl Marshal and the Lord Great Chamberlain. The question was should the words 'of England' be added to their titles as stated in the Bill? Lord Irvine explained at one of the Bill Team meetings:

> The one thing I wanted to take your view on is the one against which officials have marked consider. And that's group fourteen clause two. Now in fact the Earl Marshall and the Lord Great Chamberlain are of England. So we could add the words of England to the Bill without losing anything. There are presently no holders of the Scottish Offices. The Offices have not been abolished, they could be revived, and it's probably pure theory that they would be. If they were revived then you could have in theory confusion. And apparently the Duke of whoever he is has got Lord Lion King of Arms of Scotland on his side about this. But quite honestly the amount of my life that I am willing to devote to this question is severely limited and I rather think we should just give it to them. And it's a dead easy thing to give – why not give it.
> BARONESS JAY: Right. Well my only worry about it is, and I don't care about it – but my only worry is that if we appear to give away things about which we don't care tuppence we shall find ourselves giving away things which are actually quite significant – just because we are uninterested in them.
> LORD IRVINE: 'Well I see the force of that too. Let me tell you, and this I think is positively my last word on this subject, the Duke of Montrose must this morning have rung my office about a dozen times to find out what our attitude to this is. Now I'm quite honestly willing to agree or to resist, as I say in the name of consistency we can resist.
> LORD WILLIAMS OF MOSTYN: I think we should approach it with an open mind and resist it. [Laughter]

Baroness Jay explained later what it had been like on the floor of the House: 'We have been so patient, we have sat there for hour after hour. We have dealt with every amendment with courtesy, with calm, with attention to detail. But there really does come a point when you begin to feel that it is simply self indulgence.' This of course was not how the Conservative Peers saw it:

> LORD STRATHCLYDE: I wondered whether she had any interest in the mechanics of constitutional change rather than just the brutal politics of it. I've come to the conclusion that what she's really interested in is the brutal politics of it.

But to temper the brutal politics, Lady Jay and Lord Strathclyde would meet in less confrontational surroundings for example over lunch – following the civilised traditions of their predecessors. As the summer recess approached, on the agenda for the lunch between the two leaders was the Bill's very slow progress, and the problems both leaders were having with their own supporters. Baroness Jay had to consider whether there was anything she might offer Lord Strathclyde to help him with his Tory peers, without alienating her own side. As she explained at one of the meetings of the Bill Team:

> There is a sense in which Strathclyde would like another piece of a victory in quotes to take back to the Commons. And we haven't had that follow up meeting with him to address that.
> LORD CARTER [Government Chief Whip]: I've always felt that as they've said it's a bad Bill they would need for their own purposes to have some defeats to show that they were trying.
> LADY SYMONDS [Government Minister]: You know what we've got to think about is our own backbenchers getting very grumpy. Because they are quite tense about this. They feel we've already given a lot in Weatherill – and now there's more to give? They'll get pretty cross about it.
> LORD CARTER: We're in danger of having to sit a long way into August which will create complications even with our own people.
> BARONESS JAY: There's no point in us simply being defeated at Report stage on amendments which we could avoid, if we were to do things round the edges, not necessarily agree to, but take other positions which might meet their concerns – and then be able to extract something from them. But I think the overall perspective is that we don't need politically to give any more.

At the start of the summer recess the abolition Bill was on schedule, but all sides knew that the hardest part was still to come. Consequently, come the autumn, as Lord Strathclyde and the Conservatives returned to the fray, there were still many uncertainties surrounding the Bill. Two of his peers had mounted complex legal challenges, claiming that the whole Bill was unconstitutional and should be thrown out. And Lord Strathclyde had warned Baroness Jay that there was still a chance that a combination of Tory and crossbench hereditary and life peers might defeat the Bill:

> I think Margaret Jay knows enough about the way the House works that there is a real possibility that enough people would think that this is the wrong thing to do. Because the other thing I've said to her is that under no circumstances would I or anybody else in the Conservative Party vote for this Bill.

After learning the result of the two legal challenges to the Bill, Lord Strathclyde addressed his frontbench troops:

> The two legal challenges that we had brought to the Privileges Committee failed, but I don't think we should be overly despondent about that. We did the right thing bringing them forward. There was clearly a doubt at the very heart of the legislation and the Government should be extremely grateful that we have clarified that doubt.

Under the terms of the Bill, the hereditary peers were able to vote for which of their fellow hereditaries they wished to preserve as members. As Lord Strathclyde explained to his troops: 'Whether or not this Bill gets to Royal Assent, we still have a process to get through and those of you who are hereditary peers here must register. If you have not registered either to vote or to be a candidate you will lose that right forever. So it's very serious.

Lord Strathclyde knew that if the Bill was voted down, the government would use its powers to throw out all the hereditaries. He decided that the Tory peers should abstain. As he explained:

> I've spent a long time – many weeks and months – thinking about this and I toyed with plan B – that we should throw it out. But I think this is the right decision. But there are certain very vocal opponents to this. They think that we should throw the Bill out and take the consequences – whatever they might be.

There was however uncertainty about how many hereditaries would join the so-called last-ditchers, and go down fighting. Consequently, the final debate would require careful co-ordination between the two frontbenches. Lord Strathclyde explained the approach: 'I think that Margaret [Jay] ought to pop up and give her five minute speech as to why the Bill should be now passed, I will immediately then make my contribution, which will explain why we are abstaining on this, but also explaining why it is such a terrible Bill. Then that will set the tone of the debate.'

Baroness Jay later paid tribute to Lord Strathclyde and the way he controlled his members: 'Having been a little rough about some of the hereditary peers I would certainly give credit to Thomas Strathclyde for the way in which he held his troops together, which was extremely difficult.' When asked if he did indeed control his own peers Lord Strathclyde observed:

> As the scaffold has been built outside the House of Lords, the guillotine has been sharpened and the Labour Party tricoteurs are gathering, I think increasingly that has concentrated the minds of a great deal of back bench peers in the House of Lords, hereditary peers who are about to be booted out. And inevitably an element of control disappears. And

> of course there's always been a long tradition in the House of Lords that peers don't do what the party whips want them to do.

In the third reading debate Lord Strathclyde declared:

> My Lords, like so many Noble Lords crowded anxiously here tonight I honour those on all sides – people who I am proud to claim as friends – who soon will be driven from us by this Bill. A long chapter of history is being closed tonight. But my Lords the tale is now told, the past is done, the glass is shattered and it cannot be remade. The Prime Minister has taken a knife and scored a giant gash across the face of history. But the past is no longer the point.

The Abolition Bill was passed on its third reading by a majority of 140, with most hereditaries following Lord Strathclyde, and abstaining. As the Bill went back to the Commons, the hereditaries held their own election. One-tenth of the 750 hereditaries were to survive. It was an elaborately complex voting procedure. The Tories, as the largest party, had to select 42 of their candidates, and place them in order of preference. The crossbench, Labour and Liberal Democrat hereditaries had to go through the same procedures with their proportionately fewer candidates.

The Tories waited nervously to find out how popular they really were with their colleagues. When the results came, Earl Ferrers was top of the Tory poll, ahead of his young leader, Lord Strathclyde. And in a surprise twist, Lord Cranborne, who had unexpectedly withdrawn from the ballot, was one of seven former leaders of the Lords to receive a life peerage from Tony Blair. Tony Benn, the veteran Labour MP who had long ago renounced his own hereditary peerage, observed: 'Cranborne has been rewarded with a life peerage – the Cecils always end up on top'.

In the final Commons debate on the Bill, Benn offered his analysis of what Baroness Jay had achieved:

> This is a total breach of the election manifesto upon which we're elected. I have to say that, because there was no provision in it whatever that we would not only allow hereditary peers to remain but allow them to elect each other in perpetuity. And I think that parties should take their manifestos seriously – particularly as we had an overwhelming majority. And by now we could have had what I would like to have seen – a wholly elected second chamber.

Lord Irvine responded to Benn's charge of not delivering on the manifesto commitment:

> But that is self evident, we did not deliver on our manifesto commitment. We delivered nine tenths of our manifesto commitment

> with the whole of our legislative programme unscathed and it was added to by further useful legislation. And the thing about deals is that they never give complete satisfaction to everyone. In fact the nature of a good deal probably is almost by definition that it doesn't giver complete satisfaction to both sides.

Now it really was the end of the peer show. The end of an 800-year tradition was in sight. When the hereditary peers arrived for the last day that any of them could attend by right of birth, Baroness Jay marked the occasion by declaring:

> My Lords, my earlier words which some said were a little brusque at third reading were to say 'thank you and goodbye'. Let me say this afternoon that gratitude was sincere, genuinely meant and properly merited. And the friendly goodbyes we offer are also simply meant. We wish you all very well.

Lord Strathclyde was not convinced:

> I don't think that Margaret wrote those words herself, I think she had to get somebody else to do it, and I think she said it with slightly gritted teeth. And I don't think anybody believed that she meant what she said. But the fact that she did say it I think meant that she had learnt a valuable lesson of the process. And I suppose we should all be grateful for that.

When asked if lessons had been learnt, if something might have been handled and done in a different way in getting the Bill through, Baroness Jay declared:

> No, because all of the things that some members of the Tory Party say 'oh if they'd been nicer about it, if they'd been more charming, if they'd been this, that and the other', are complete nonsense. Those people who were determined to oppose this Bill, were determined to oppose it, they just weren't sufficiently well organised to achieve any major victories. And the people who were making the political decisions in the front of the Tory Party were sufficiently politically sophisticated and sufficiently politically in touch to know how far and how little they could go with their own backbenchers and with the wider Conservative Party and with us.

The Royal Commission report on the future of the House of Lords was published in January 2000. It recommended a mainly appointed house, with an elected element, but no hereditaries; and that the power of patronage should be taken away from the Prime Minister and given to an independent appointments commission.

Baroness Jay promised to give the report 'proper consideration' and said that she hoped it might provide a basis for the next stage of reform. But the Tories suspect that Tony Blair wants to lose Wakeham in a Whitehall pigeonhole. They feel he is now very happy with the patronage he can exercise in a House of Lords that he's largely stripped of its hereditary element. It is a view strongly rejected by Lord Irvine: 'The Prime Minister emphatically does not want a House of Tony's cronies. And this is the first Prime Minister who has indicated absolutely clearly that he goes along with a significant diminution in the traditional powers of the Prime Minister in relation to a fully reformed House.'

At the farewell party held for the small band of Labour's 19 hereditary peers – the first turkeys in history known to have voted for Christmas – there was a strong sense of guilt among the few who survived the cull; as one of them, Lord Rea, explained: 'I feel very much as if I've been on an aeroplane or a train that's had a major disaster. And I'm a survivor. I'm feeling a bit guilty about it, as survivors do'. He went on to observe: 'The only thing that's good about having a continuation of a hereditary peerage rather than accepting a life peerage, should it have been offered, is that one is more of a free agent – a free spirit if you like' – the classic argument used by the hereditary peers and their supporters in defence of their presence in the House of Lords.

At the farewell party the Earl of Longford – himself a reprieved hereditary, having been created a life peer as a former leader of the House – declared: 'I hope that all hereditary Labour peers will eventually in one way or another reappear. We're told we are going to have a lot of life peers made, well the first choice should fall on the existing hereditary labour peers who've made such a great contribution. Otherwise it's all humbug.' On this, it should perhaps be noted that five of the ousted Labour hereditary peers (and two of the ousted Liberal Democrat hereditary peers) were created life peers in a special creation of 33 working peers announced in March 2000; in short, a total of 17 hereditary peers have been given life peerages enabling them to continue as members of the House of Lords.

The whole abolition process had been a case study in the problems of moving from the easy certainties of opposition into the reality of government. The Governer of New York, Mario Cuomo, once said: 'We campaign in poetry, we govern in prose.' Lord Irvine's final verdict was: 'The other side would have liked a lot more than a hundred hereditaries to stay. We would have liked fewer. But against a century of failure to reform the hereditary peerage I claim a huge success in having nine tenths go in legislative peace.'

From One Chamber to Two: The Case of Morocco

JAMES P. KETTERER

Despite years of scholarly neglect of the role of legislatures in the developing world, it is now well understood that an effective and representative legislature is critical to the long-term success of any democratisation process. Among other things, a state in transition to a pluralistic democratic system must develop a legislature that is active in discharging its various constitutional powers and representative functions without causing an impasse with the executive (which often gives cause for the executive or military to hijack the democratisation process).[1] To do so, the legislature must provide the incentive for a wide range of political groups to participate constructively in the policymaking process. At the same time, however, the legislature must ensure that minorities are represented and their rights protected, and that elite interests are represented to the extent that they do not seek a patron outside the democratic system (often the military) – which can quickly destabilise a state. In short, the legislature in a state in transition must strike a difficult balance between simultaneously offering mass representation and maintaining stability through elite and minority interests. As the case of Morocco demonstrates, a bicameral legislature can provide structure for this balance.

The Moroccan electorate in 1996 ratified a new constitution that, among other things, replaced a unicameral parliament with a bicameral body. Although the 1996 Constitution generated considerable scholarly interest, little attention has focused on the bicameral aspect of the new parliament and its intended effect on the political dynamics of Morocco. This cameral change, however, represents an important step for the Moroccan political system in both the structuring of a key governmental institution, allowing for an opposition-led coalition to form a government, thereby strengthening

---

James P. Ketterer is a Senior Associate of the International Development Group, State University of New York.

A substantially earlier version of this paper was presented at the Third Annual Workshop for Parliamentary Scholars and Parliamentarians, Wroxton College, August 1998. Subsequent fieldwork for this study was supported by a grant from the American Institute of Maghrib Studies. The author would like to thank I. William Zarman, Abdo I. Baaklini, Lisa Angerame, Catherine Sweet and Karim Mezran for their comments on various versions of this article.

Morocco's political party system. As we shall examine, these changes in the Moroccan political system were made possible through the shift from unicameralism to bicameralism.

In short, Moroccan citizens directly elect members to the lower house of the new parliament. At the same time, members of the upper house are elected via regional assemblies and professional organisations. The upper house ensures that the parliament will represent local and elite interests and also control the power to dissolve the government. At best, this new parliament can serve to strike a balance between increased representation and protection of interests. At worst, as some claim, it can maintain an authoritarian system with democratic window-dressing. Clearly, however, Morocco's new bicameral parliament specifically seeks to address two key items neglected by previous unicameral parliaments: representation and stability.

This article seeks to contribute to the democratisation and legislative studies literature by offering a critical analysis of Morocco's new bicameral legislature and its role in Morocco's self-declared democratisation process. Specifically, the article examines the ways in which Morocco's previous experiments with parliaments left many political forces outside the political process. This left the Moroccan system unable to catalyze its democratisation process because of the persistence of weak political parties, low levels of participation, and the resistance of entrenched forces seeking to maintain their interests. The article does not attempt to address the nature of bicameral legislatures *vis-à-vis* legislative efficiency or internal legislative processes.

Rather than a comparative study examining various cases of unicameral to bicameral shifts as part of a democratisation programme, this article employs the plausibility probe approach and analyses the single case of Morocco. This is an initial test of a hypothesis that can be used to determine if more cases should be examined and different methodologies employed at a later date.[2] Morocco was chosen as a single case for theoretical purposes as it represents the only example of a cameral shift in the midst of a democratisation process. While other states are contemplating such a cameral shift, including Zambia's proposed House of Chiefs and Zimbabwe's upper house that was rejected in the most recent constitutional referendum, these cases are not yet at a comparable stage. The creation of the Polish Senate and other similar cases in eastern Europe are perhaps the closest examples, but they came about as part of a regime change and the end of Soviet domination.[3] Morocco, on the other hand, is a case of institutional re-design with no regime change – an attempt to design a legislative institution to cushion the regime from the inevitable shocks of the democratisation process. In that regard, then, it is quite different from the Polish case. The comparative element of this study is between Morocco's 1992 and 1996 constitutions and their respective unicameral and bicameral parliaments.

WHY BICAMERALISM?

> Bicameralism ... originated in the essentially pre-democratic view that the representation of the nation required both an upper and lower house, in the class-conscious sense of 'upper' and 'lower'.[4]

The above quote crystallises much of the general thought on bicameralism, specifically the notion that upper houses tend to be a relic of a pre-democratic era. How, then, does Morocco's bicameral experiment fit into the historical context and evolution of bicameral legislatures? And, more importantly, how does a shift from unicameralism to bicameralism fit into the context of a process of political liberalisation?

Most changes in the number of legislative chambers are from two to one. Yet some states have shifted from unicameral to bicameral legislatures (Poland, China, Hungary, the USSR), while Canada has examined ways to empower its relatively impotent Senate.[5] As noted above, some maintain that:

> In Western democracies, bicameralism is most often the inheritance of a predemocratic past. Either a second chamber is, like the British House of Lords, derived from earlier aristocratic or other non-democratic origins, or it is a compromise invention like the American Senate, designed to protect specific values other than specified democratic ones, such as federalism.[6]

Neither is the case in Morocco. Why then, in the name of democratisation, would Morocco buck the modern trend towards unicameralism?

Tsebelis and Money note that '[b]icameral institutions have been used to maintain the status quo, to amalgamate the preferences of different constituencies, and to improve legislation, and have been justified in all of these terms'.[7] The majority of scholarly works on bicameralism focus upon the effect of two chambers on the law-making process and various intra-parliamentary institutions (committees, for example). In states in transition, bicameral legislatures seek to touch upon each of these roles. More immediately, however, bicameral legislatures can serve the institutional role of bringing diverse constituencies into the democratisation process while at the same time maintaining state stability; this role of bicameralism has not been fully developed in either the legislative studies or democratisation literature.

The role of bicameralism in democratic transitions is not limited to the most recent wave of democratisation following the cold war. It is well grounded in the evolution of legislative institutions. Tsebelis and Money detail the intellectual evolution of bicameralism, noting that the ancient Greeks elaborated the virtues of mixed government over simple government:

> Simple government encompassed the interests of only one social class – the one (monarchy), the few (aristocracy), or the many (republic) – while the mixed government included representatives of two or three of these constituent interests. According to this line of reasoning, the various interests serve to balance each other, to prevent the degeneration of the political system into either tyranny or anarchy.[8]

Aristotle and Plato spoke about the need to achieve a balance of power through representation of different social classes and argued that the downfall of both oligarchies and democracies is caused by a failure to combine corresponding components. Tsebelis and Money note that this balance of power is achieved specifically through 'multiple interest representation', in which '[n]o single element in society is able to employ the instruments of government to exploit the remainder of society, thereby avoiding the explosion of discontent and the ultimate overthrow of the political order'.[9] Indeed, one of the key modern justifications for bicameralism is the ability of two chambers to represent class or other interests that would otherwise be left out of the political arena. In this case, the development of the British House of Lords and the emergence of the House of Commons serve as classic examples. In addition, early American colonial legislatures and the post-Revolutionary War Congress also split into two landed interests (the Senate) and populist concerns (the House).

Another argument that supports the notion that bicameralism is beneficial rests on the notion that two chambers allow for the 'simultaneous representation of aggregate national views as well as the special outlook of geographical components such as regions or states'.[10] In this case, bicameralism is a function of federalism. While Morocco could not be classified as having a strong federalist structure, there has been an increasing emphasis on the regional level of government and that is clearly reflected in the composition of the new upper house. Bicameralism is also often justified as an institutional 'check on each other's actions' and mechanism for avoiding 'legislative excess and ill-conceived or hasty decisions'.[11] Here again, the importance placed on stability in the Moroccan system and the preference for a gradualist approach to democratisation fit well with this justification of bicameralism. In addition, but related to the previous justification, bicameralism is argued to offer a diversity of 'legislative outlook and response'.[12] As I shall discuss below in greater detail, the Moroccan monarchy and other political actors have used these justifications for bicameralism, in one form or another, to address perceived inadequacies in the unicameral parliament's role in the democratisation process.

THE STAGNATION OF MOROCCAN POLITICS: SEEKING A WAY OUT

In the late 1980s and early 1990s, Morocco appeared to be making serious attempts to open its political system. These openings, however, were limited. The previous unicameral parliaments offered limited mechanisms for the representation of mass interests since those parliaments were dominated by indirectly elected political actors aligned with the monarchy. In addition, because the unicameral parliament was either seen as making hasty and provocative decisions (thereby incurring the monarchy's wrath), or making no decision at all (thereby appearing to be entirely co-opted by the monarchy), the previous unicameral parliament did not engender popular support. Let us examine this stagnation of Morocco's democratisation efforts in more detail.

While at first glance Morocco appears to have a relatively thriving political system, and the formal opposition seems to have made strides in the last decade compared to the rest of the Arab world, it is clear that Morocco has had substantial difficulties in finding mechanisms to represent large components of the population. This is no small problem: as institutions have failed to bring diverse components of Moroccan society into the democratisation process, more and more of the poor and working class are attracted to criminal networks and informal opposition groups related to those networks. Islamist groups also attract a wide array of adherents; many of them discontented by limited opportunities for economic advancement or political participation. These various groups pose a clear threat to the monarchy and seek to undermine not only the democratisation process, but also the very sovereignty of the state. Unlike many Arab states, political parties have long been seen as the primary answer to problems of representation in Morocco, and Morocco boasts a multiparty system. As we shall see, however, parties without corresponding institutions failed to offer avenues of representation for a wide array of interests in Morocco. By the 1990s, this was creating problems for the parties and the monarchy itself.

In the 1950s, much attention was given to the development of political parties in the Middle East, and political scientists saw the parties as important components of broader political development. These hopes were based on the Western experience, in which parties had supported polities as they organised citizens, helped them formulate their demands and gave an order to elections and the making of public policy. Those hopes have been largely unmet in the Middle East and North Africa; Morocco is no exception. Morocco's opposition parties have long been seen as ineffective agents of political change. While there are many parties in Morocco, they have rarely truly contested elections, sought to represent large constituencies, or challenged the monarchy. Many see the parties in Morocco as suffering from narrow bases of support, unclear platforms and vulnerability to manipulation from the palace. The result is a weak political party system and a polity in which decisions regarding reform emanate nearly exclusively from the palace. Unless Morocco can peacefully generate politically representative institutions, the democratisation process is likely to remain in the hands of predatory rulers whose commitment to the process is tenuous, or fall prey to violent opponents of the state.

Participation in and the structuring of a representative parliament are important links between civil and political society – in cases in which the parties are credible and viable. Civil society, as conceptualised so often in recent works, does not alone supply the answers for a sustained transition to democracy. It is only when the social and political forces of a polity are institutionalised that a consolidation can have a real chance of developing. The development of a sustainable democracy is difficult without the emergence of political society as an arena in which the system specifically arranges itself for political contestation in order to gain control over public power and the state apparatus. As Stepan notes:

> A full democratic transition must involve political society, and the composition and consolidation of a democratic polity must entail serious thought and action about those core institutions of a democratic political society – political parties, elections, electoral rules, political leadership, intra party alliances, and legislatures – through which civil society can constitute itself politically to select and monitor democratic government.[13]

In addition, Robert Fatton says:

> unless civil society can generate – especially from 'below' – an effective political society, extrication from dictatorial rule can easily degenerate into a 'sham democracy', or a new dictatorship. Should subordinate classes fail to create their own political organisations, the balance of power will inevitably favor predatory rulers and middle-sectors whose commitment to democracy is always ambiguous and tenuous.[14]

A lower house of parliament often serves this role for the subordinate classes.

The creation of institutions capable of representing the interests of the subordinate classes is clearly a requirement for the establishment of a balance of power of societal forces from which democracy can emerge. Africa, for instance, in this age of democratisation has given birth to social movements rather than institutions, and the political groupings that have crystallised have tended to be based on clientelistic, ethnic and personalistic criteria.[15] The representation of the subordinate classes alone, however, will leave other critical elements out of the process – possibly with destabilising consequences. Politics, and the political institutions of state, must be seen as viable and credible means by which multiple interests are represented.

Although attitudinal surveys in Morocco indicate a reasonably high degree of political knowledge, the statement that 'no man with a brain in his head gets involved in politics in Morocco' has long epitomised formal political participation in Morocco.[16] In the 1980s, Eickelman noted that there is a 'silent majority' in Morocco 'who do not actively participate in formal politics'.[17] The parties, too, have been seen as moribund. Twenty-five years ago, John Waterbury deemed Moroccan political parties to be nothing more than 'open-ended receptacles devoid of ideological content'.[18] With the opposition parties venting their frustration and in obvious disarray following the 1993 elections, it was clear that if democratisation was to continue, then the structure and opportunity for representation in Morocco would have to change. What is less acknowledged, however, is that the stability of the monarchy itself is predicated on maintaining the legitimacy of all of Morocco's recognised parties – and finding a place for them within government.

Formal Moroccan political parties have long been a key to the monarchy's continued rule, as the king simultaneously perpetuates their existence and fragments them. King Hassan II has skilfully played off ten major political parties against one another as they competed for patronage and power, and manipulates rivalries between them and the military. Because of this fragmentation and manipulation, the parties under Hassan were not successful at attracting a wide base of support. Consequently, party activity was confined to a small minority of the populace. In addition, parties were more susceptible to internal squabbling, personal rivalries and poorly articulated platforms. While these weaknesses have prohibited the parties from mounting any credible position to the monarchy's rule, the monarchy does not want to weaken them to the point that they disappear. The parties play an important role in deflecting criticism of the monarchy's policies and in drawing away support for more radical elements and the military. In addition, active and viable parties are required to legitimise the parliament more fully as a credible democratic institution. Since the parties are often perceived as having been thoroughly co-opted and manipulated by the monarchy, using them to develop the legitimacy of the parliament is a difficult task. And, because the parliament does not appear to be legitimate, the parties running for seats in the parliament seem all the more to be lackeys of the monarchy. This process simultaneously eats away at the legitimacy and appeal of both the political parties and the parliament. Without creating a parliament in which all the major parties could aspire to leadership and parties capable of leadership, it was becoming clear in the early 1990s that King Hassan's strategy of multi-party rule would falter.

The bicameral experiment of the mid-1990s sought to break that cycle of political de-legitimisation by creating a political institution (the lower house) that could be openly contested in free elections and even ruled by the opposition. This would potentially bolster the image of the parliament and the viability of the political party system in Morocco.

MOROCCO'S PARLIAMENTS IN HISTORICAL CONTEXT

Upon achieving independence in 1956, Morocco established a constitutional monarchy with the king as head of state. Several parties were inherited from the independence movement, so a version of a multiparty system was included in the new state. As we shall examine, however, the credibility and viability of this multi-party system has been tenuous at times. In 1962, King Hassan II drafted a Constitution, and a national referendum approved it overwhelmingly. The Constitution gave extensive powers to the king and established a unicameral parliamentary system based on competitive elections. The first national elections were held in May 1963. The opposition did well in the elections, but the king had many opposition deputies arrested on accusations of electoral fraud, and in November 1963 the Supreme Court annulled many other races won by opposition members. Replacement elections were held in January 1964, giving the pro-monarchy coalition (the Front for the Defence of Constitutional Institutions) control of the parliament. The parliament was meant to legitimise the monarchy, but not to threaten it in any way. The strong showing by the opposition in the parliamentary elections threatened a king who saw himself as synonymous with the state, and he was therefore unwilling to place himself in competition with another state institution.

The next two years saw extensive social and political unrest in Morocco, and riots in March 1965 led the king to suspend parliament, ban all party activity, and appoint a new government with himself as prime minister. He thus assumed both legislative and executive power. For the next five years, Morocco remained without a parliament. In July 1970, the king and his advisers prepared a new Constitution and it was approved by another national referendum. A second round of parliamentary elections followed in August of that year, and a boycott by a coalition of opposition parties allowed pro-monarchy candidates to win 220 of the 240 seats. Many saw these elections as rigged in favour of the pro-monarchy parties, and the opposition boycott merely ensured their victory.[19] This time, instead of arresting the opposition, the king apparently guaranteed that the parliament would pose no threat by guaranteeing the election results. Following attempted military coups against him in 1971 and 1972, the king submitted yet another Constitution for a popular referendum in 1972. This time, it gave additional powers to the parliament and provided for regular elections every six years. Two-thirds of the deputies were to be directly elected and one-third selected by an electoral college of local officials.

Legislative elections that had been postponed twice due to the conflict in the Western Sahara were eventually held in 1984. Deeb maintains that these elections were 'more representative than the previous elections and relatively free of manipulation'.[20] Nine political parties and two trade unions participated, with 1,366 candidates competing for the 199 seats elected by direct vote. (Note that the party participation increased dramatically when the powers of the parliament were increased.) Five seats were reserved for candidates representing the 450,000 Moroccans living abroad. The opposition, however, won relatively few seats in the new, larger parliament of 306 deputies.

In 1992 the major opposition parties formed the National Front (al-Koutla) to contest government policies and demand electoral reforms, guarantees for fair elections, lowering the minimum age for voting, and greater powers for the legislature. In response, the king proposed amendments to the Constitution to meet some of these demands. The 1992 Constitution made changes in key areas for more accountable government. It empowers the prime minister to select his or her own ministers and places the cabinet under the prime minister's authority. Previously, the king both chose and ruled the cabinet directly. In addition, the parliament's oversight power over the cabinet was enhanced, and the prime minister and cabinet were held increasingly accountable for policy decisions.[21]

The parliament's powers also increased in other areas:

- Unlike all the previous constitutions, a royal decree of a state of emergency does not automatically dissolve the parliament (although the king did still retain the power to dismiss the parliament in this Constitution);
- The king must act on bills passed by the parliament within 30 days after they have been forwarded to him. Previously, the king could avoid acting on a bill indefinitely, thereby entirely ignoring the will of the parliament;
- The 1992 Constitution empowered the parliament to create investigative commissions, thereby enhancing parliamentary oversight;
- Under this Constitution, ministers were mandated to respond to MPs' questions raised during official question period within 20 days. Previously, ministers often ignored questions raised in the parliament;

- The 1992 Constitution requires that parliament endorse a new cabinet and the programme submitted by the government. If the vote on the government's programme is negative, the entire cabinet must resign.

Denoeux and Maghraoui note that these changes were an attempt by the monarchy to respond to the political aspirations of the urban middle classes. These classes in Morocco were not well integrated into the channels of the monarchy and are more likely to press their interests through formal organisations and institutions such as political parties, interest groups, NGOs, syndicates, trade unions and parliament.[22]

Despite these areas of legislative empowerment, the king retained considerable legislative authority. For example, the parliament's area of legislation is limited to certain areas, while the king can legislate in any area. Article 27 of the 1992 Constitution also allowed the king to dissolve the parliament by decree, and the king could set and change the date of parliamentary elections. While the 1992 Constitution substantially enhanced the powers of the Moroccan parliament, the king still clearly reserved his prerogatives: 'Islam forbids me from implementing a constitutional monarchy in which I, the King, delegate all my powers and reign without governing ... I can delegate power, but I do not have the right, on my own initiative, to abstain from my prerogatives, because they are also spiritual.'[23] Many opposition activists saw this statement as evidence that King Hassan II had absolutely no inclination towards creating a parliament with independent powers. In the context of past Moroccan parliamentary experiments, however, it is far more likely that the king was merely confirming his position as Amir al-Mu'minin (Commander of the Faithful). But this statement sends a message to both his supporters and the opposition alike that he will not allow any radical programmes to threaten the stability of the state or the interests of his supporters. What is problematic in all of this, however, is that it undermines the credibility of the opposition and leaves them no political space or institution in which to operate.

Elections were held in June 1993, the fairest and most representative in Morocco since independence. The parliament of 1993 had 333 deputies, 222 of whom were elected by popular vote, and 111 of whom were indirectly elected by electoral colleges of local officials. Twelve parties and two trade unions participated. The ballot system for the parliament caused vociferous protest by the opposition parties, as a high number of the indirectly elected seats went to pro-government parties (79 per cent), while the pro-government forces could only garner 54 per cent in the direct elections. The king, who had said many times that he wanted to provide a mechanism for *alternance* in the political system offered the opposition the opportunity to form a government, but refused to grant them the portfolios of the Interior, Foreign Relations, Justice or Finance ministries. The opposition balked at this proposal. While seeking to find a way to put the opposition into leadership positions, the king was also seeking to maintain the support of those elite forces in control of those key ministries. In addition, he was seeking to prevent those powerful political forces that might feel threatened by the democratisation process from abandoning or hijacking the process altogether and searching for other, non-democratic patrons to protect their interests (remember, King Hassan II survived at least two coup attempts carried out by elements of his own military).

THE 1996 CONSTITUTION

By 1996, a familiar pattern was in place in Morocco: for 35 years, King Hassan had periodically used popular referenda to support new formulae for ruling, and the precise powers and size of the parliament were adjusted to both meet the demands for greater openness and maintain the stability of the state. It is in the context of this formula – and to address those previous parliamentary experiments that had not succeeded – that Morocco's new bicameral parliament was created.

The most significant aspect of the 1996 Constitution is its establishment of a directly elected lower chamber, the 325-member Chamber of Representatives (Majlis an-Nawab). An upper Chamber of Councillors (Majlis al-Mustachareen) of 270 members is appointed by local councils, professional organisations and labour syndicates. White notes, that '[i]n contrast to the previous system, the new bicameral system should have less of a structural bias in favor of the palace than the unicameral Majlis'.[24]

The Constitution creating the new parliament was drafted between 1994 and 1996, with the assistance of three French constitutional scholars – Georges Vedel, Yves Gaudemet and Michel Rousset.[25] The Constitution provides that the lower house be elected for five-year terms by direct suffrage, and the upper house be elected for nine years with one-third of the chamber up for re-election every third year. The upper house is additionally complex because three-fifths of its members are elected by a regional electoral college consisting of local bodies known as *collectivites locales*. The remaining two-fifths are chosen by electoral colleges composed of representatives from professional associations. This arrangement is part of a larger government initiative to decentralise state functions to local authorities. White notes that King Hassan has, at times, invoked the German model in his vision of Morocco's 'need to move to a more federal system'.[26]

Both chambers can initiate laws and propose amendments. Moreover, both chambers must examine a law successively so that it can be adopted in identical terms. Article 50 of the Constitution, however, accords pre-eminence to the lower house. That chamber possesses greater powers with regard to the composition of the ministerial cabinet, and it alone can vote after the cabinet submits a programme. Like Italy and South Africa, Morocco is the third country in the world to give its upper house the power to censure the government (Article 70).

The ability of the upper house to act as a check on the lower house allows the lower house to be more fully representative while it defends the interests of those threatened by a rapid democratisation process. In addition, the creation of two houses allows the king to continue to open up the political system within the context of the lower house, defend his own interests in the upper house, and remove himself as a direct political actor. In essence, the upper house is designed to represent a different constituency than the lower house in an attempt to keep as many political actors within the scope of formal politics as possible, thereby bolstering the democratisation process. As we shall discuss below, such manipulations in the past were having a cumulative negative effect on the legitimacy of both the monarchy and the array of Moroccan political parties.

The creation of a new bicameral parliament, according to White, was the result of several forces at work, with a particular emphasis on the frustration of the opposition following the 1993 elections.[27] The king was faced with the difficulty of finding a way to revive the interest in Morocco's political parties, which had been manipulated and co-opted so often since independence that they had become merely empty vessels for legitimate political opposition. As one observer noted, 'time may be running out for the parties'.[28] Without viable political parties, Morocco would be in danger of having opposition sentiments channelled into areas that would be destabilising to the state: some Islamist groups (contrary to standard Western opinion, not every Islamist group seeks to overthrow the state), criminal networks and other radical organisations. In addition, Morocco has been under considerable pressure from Western financial donors and the European Union (which the king is negotiating with for association status) to show real progress in the area of democratisation.

We will now examine the political context in which Morocco's new parliament was created, and those factors leading to its being structured as a bicameral parliament. More specifically, we will examine how the creation of the new parliament addressed two key areas in Morocco's democratisation process: (1) bolstering the viability of political parties through *alternance* and (2) offering a semblance of political protection of interests to those elites, minorities and others perceiving that the democratisation process threatens their interests.

A HOUSE OF THEIR OWN

The constitutional amendment of 1996 and the elections of 1997 were supported by a considerable majority of the major political forces in Morocco, including the main opposition parties that had so strongly protested against the 1993 elections. The fact that the opposition USFP (Socialist) party participated, along with the old-guard Istiqlal (the old Independence Party), indicates that those forces on the left were supportive of the new parliament as a function of the democratisation of Moroccan political life. The tenor of politics in Morocco changed substantially between the 1993 and 1997 elections. For example, 'Abd al-Rahman Yusufi, the leader of the socialist USFP who had fled after the 1993 elections, returned to active political life, ran for office, and is now the prime minister. The control of the lower house by the USFP-led coalition finally allowed the opposition to take control of many of the key ministries and bring to fruition the king's plan for robust political parties alternating power.

At the same time, the strong showing of the rightist parties in the local councils and their domination of the upper house indicates that entrenched elites have not abandoned the democratisation project as they do not see their interests wholly vulnerable to a perceived tyranny of the majority as represented by the lower house. Business interests also voiced their support for the new parliament through the General Confederation of Moroccan Businesses. Those forces that dominated the 1993 parliament now control the upper house and serve as a check on the directly elected lower house. The zero-sum game of the 1993 unicameral parliament has become a power-sharing arrangement made possible by the new bicameral

TABLE 1
CHAMBER OF REPRESENTATIVES: SEATS WON IN THE GENERAL ELECTION, 25 JUNE 1993 (17 SEPTEMBER FOR THE THIRD OF REPRESENTATIVES ELECTED BY INDIRECT VOTE)

Party	Seats
Union socialiste des Forces Populaires	56
Union Constitutionnelle	54
Istiqlal party	52
Mouvement Populaire	51
Rassemblement National des Indépendants	41
Mouvement National Populaire	25
Parti National Démocrate	24
Parti du Progrès et du Socialisme	10
Parti Démocratique pour l'Indépendance	9
Union Marocaine du Travail	3
Organisation de l'Action Démocratique et Populaire	2
Parti de l'Action	2
Independents	2
Total	**333**

TABLE 2
PARLIAMENTARY ELECTIONS, 1997

		Majlis al-Nuwab Seats	Share	Majlis al-Mustasharin Seats	Share
Bloc Démocratique (al-Kutla)					
Union Socialiste des Forces Populaires	USFP	57	18%	16	6%
Istiqlal/Parti d'Independence	PI	32	10%	21	8%
Parti du Renouveau et du Progrès	PRP	9	3%	7	3%
Organisation de l'Action pour Démocratie et Peuple	OADP	4	1%	0	0%
Sub-total (al-Kutla)		**102**	**31%**	**44**	**16%**
Entente Nationale (al-Wifaq)					
Mouvement Populaire	MP	40	12%	27	10%
Union Constitutionelle	UC	50	15%	28	10%
Parti National-Démocrate	PND	10	3%	21	8%
Sub-total (al-Wifaq)		**100**	**31%**	**76**	**28%**
Centre					
Rassemblement National des Indépendents	RNI	46	14%	42	16%
Mouvement Démocratique et Social	MDS	32	10%	33	12%
Mouvement Nationale Populaire	MNP	19	6%	15	6%
Mouvement Populaire Constitutionel et Démocratique	MPCD	9	3%	0	0%
Sub-total Centre		**106**	**33%**	**90**	**33%**
Other					
Front des Forces Démocratiques	FFD	9	3%	12	4%
Parti Social et Démocratique	PSD	5	2%	4	1%
Parti de l'Action	PA	2	1%	13	5%
Parti Démocratique pour l'Independence	PDI	1	0%	4	1%
Trade unionists		0	0%	27	10%
SUB-TOTAL OTHER		17	5%	60	22%
GRAND TOTAL		**325**		**270**	

Source: Compiled from Moroccan Government Sources

arrangement. This is illustrated in the 1993 and 1997 election results shown in Tables 1 and 2.

There were also significant gains in the effort to bring previously disenfranchised groups into the political process through the parliament. Unlike 1993, for example, the new parliament brought political forces into the game that had been entirely excluded previously; Islamists, for example, won ten seats. Nevertheless, formidable political forces remain outside the sphere of Moroccan political institutions. One of the key Islamist groups, for example, has not been brought into the mainstream of Moroccan politics with the new parliament. Al-'Adl wa al'Ihsan (Justice and Charity), led by 'Abd al-Salam Yasin, was not allowed publicly to state its position on the new Constitution.

Yasin remains under house arrest and research in Northern Morocco indicates that his many followers among the urban poor are not at all supportive of the political process. Drawing upon the same reservoir of supporters, many of those in Morocco involved in vast networks of smuggling and drug trafficking place their loyalty with drug barons with extreme anti-state positions (except to the extent that they can corrupt or coerce the state for their benefit). The exclusion of these two groups does not spell disaster for the Moroccan political system, but it is important to note that the new parliament is not a panacea for participation and stability. Each of these forces has substantial potential for creating instability and their sheer numbers of anti-state followers represent an obstacle to increased participation in electoral politics.

The ability of the monarchy, however, to both maintain the stability of the system and continue to open it up to previously excluded forces is a testament, in part, to the new bicameral parliament. The wide support for the referendum process, the heavy participation in the 1997 legislative elections, the formation of an opposition government, and the control of the upper house by pro-monarchy forces all bode well for Morocco's new bicameral parliament as a function of the democratisation process. With each house having nearly equal powers and controlled by competing forces, the bicameral system enhances 'the king's position as the ultimate referee'.[29] This allows the monarch to deflect the rough-and-tumble aspects of politics and avoid the sort of electoral and institutional manipulations that underscored much of Moroccan politics in the past.[30]

Only time will tell if the forces left out of the new game, or those entrenched anti-democratic forces, will have the desire and/or the wherewithal to upend this component of Morocco's democratisation process. But with many of the major political forces brought into the realm of legitimate politics, it is clear that King Hassan II, who died in 1999, created a potentially key institution when the bicameral parliament was ratified. It is now left to Hassan's successor, King Muhammad VI, to build upon that initial work. If the Moroccan system is to continue its incremental democratisation programme – and it has been one of the most successful so far in the Arab world – the parliament will have to move beyond merely representing a wide array of constituencies. Now that the long-time opposition has been leading the government for over three years, there is concern and frustration that they have been unable to deliver any substantive programmes dealing with Morocco's profound social and economic problems. The next stage of Morocco's democratisation programme will require, then, a parliament with the political will and the institutional capacity to carry out the lawmaking and oversight roles required of a democratic parliament more effectively. In the meantime, however, the seemingly anti-democratic concept of bicameralism has furthered Morocco's incremental democratisation.

NOTES

1. A. Baaklini, 'Legislative Structure and Constitutional Viability in Societies Undergoing Democratic Transition', in A.I. Baaklini and H. Desfosses (eds.), *Designs for Democratic Stability: Studies in Viable Constitutionalism* (Armonk, NY: M.E. Sharpe, 1997), p.127.
2. H. Eckstein, 'Case Study and Theory in Political Science', in F.I. Grenstein and N.W. Polsby (eds.), *Handbook of Political Science* (Reading, MA: Addison-Wesley, 1975), pp.108–13. See also B. Seaver, 'The Regional Sources of Power-Sharing Failure: The Case of Lebanon', *Political Science Quarterly*, 15/2 (Summer 2000), pp.247–71.
3. See D. Olson, 'From Electoral Symbol to Legislative Puzzle: The Polish Senat', in S. Patterson and A. Mughan (eds.), *Senates: Bicameralism in the Contemporary World* (Columbus, OH: Ohio University Press, 1999), pp.301–32.
4. G. Loewenberg and S. Patterson, *Comparing Legislatures* (Boston, MA: Little, Brown, 1979), p.121.
5. D. Olson and L. Longley, 'Conclusions: Cameral Change Politics and Processes in Three Nations and Beyond', in L. Longley and D. Olson (eds.), *Two Into One* (Boulder, CO: Westview Press, 1991), p.204.
6. Olson and Longley, 'Conclusions: Cameral Change Politics and Processes in Three Nations and Beyond', p.204.
7. G. Tsebelis and J. Money, *Bicameralism* (New York: Cambridge University Press, 1997), p.13.
8. Tsebelis and Money, *Bicameralism*, pp.18–19.
9. Tsebelis and Money, *Bicameralism*, p.19.
10. Longley and Olson, *Two Into One*, p.2.
11. Longley and Olson, *Two Into One*, p.3.
12. Longley and Olson, *Two Into One*, p.4.
13. A. Stepan, *Rethinking Military Politics: Brazil and the Southern Cone* (Princeton, NJ: Princeton University Press, 1988), p.4.
14. R. Fatton, 'Africa in the Age of Democratization: The Civic Limits of Civil Society', *African Studies Review*, 38 (1995), pp.89–90.
15. R. Fatton, 'Africa in the Age of Democratization: The Civic Limits of Civil Society', p.90.
16. H. Munson, *The House of Si Abd Allah: The Oral History of a Moroccan Family* (New Haven, CT: Yale University Press, 1984), p.13.
17. D. Eickelman, 'Royal Authority and Religious Legitimacy', in M. Arnoff (ed.), *The Frailty of Authority* (New Brunswick: Transaction Books, 1986), p.182.
18. J. Waterbury, *The Commander of the Faithful: The Moroccan Political Elite – A Study in Segmented Politics* (New York: Columbia University Press, 1970), p.118.
19. I.W. Zartman, 'Opposition as a Support of the State', in A. Dawisha and I.W. Zartman (eds.), *Beyond Coercion: The Durability of the Arab State* (London: Croom Helm, 1988), p.87.
20. M. Deeb, 'Morocco', in *World Encyclopedia of Parliaments and Legislatures* (Washington, DC: Congressional Quarterly Publications, 1998), pp.467–8.
21. G. Denoeux and A. Mahgraoui, 'King Hassan's Strategy of Political Dualism', *Middle East Policy*, 4/4 (Jan. 1998), p.108.
22. Denoeux and Mahgraoui, 'King Hassan's Strategy of Political Dualism', p.110.
23. 'Un entritrien avec le roi du Maroc', *Le Monde* (Paris), 2 Sept. 1992.
24. G. White, 'The Advent of Electoral Democracy in Morocco? The Referendum of 1996', *Middle East Journal*, 51/3 (Summer 1997), p.393.
25. T. Brehier, 'Des Francais specilialistes d'"ingenierie" constitutionelle', *Le Monde* (Paris), 13 Sept. 1996.
26. White, 'The Advent of Electoral Democracy in Morocco? The Referendum of 1996', p.395.
27. White, 'The Advent of Electoral Democracy in Morocco? The Referendum of 1996', p.395.
28. C.H. Moore, 'Political Parties', in I.W. Zartman and W.M. Habeeb (eds.), *Polity and Society in Contemporary North Africa* (Boulder, CO: Westview Press, 1993), p.44.
29. A. Baaklini, G. Denoeux and R. Springborg, *Legislative Politics in the Arab World* (Boulder, CO: Lynne Reiner, 1999), p.127.
30. Baaklini *et al.*, *Legislative Politics in the Arab World*, p.128.

Legislative Unicameralism: A Global Survey and a Few Case Studies

LOUIS MASSICOTTE

Talking about unicameralism in a special issue devoted to second chambers may look odd, but there is at least one good reason for doing so: at present, among the 178 countries belonging to the Inter-Parliamentary Union, bicameral legislatures are vastly outnumbered by unicameral ones (some 64 per cent of the total).

Further, second chambers, as 'upper' chambers are now called, are often true to their name and most of the time play the role of a junior partner in the legislative arena, rather than pretending to be an equal partner – a feature which has led some scholars to argue that many countries have formally bicameral, but in practice single-chamber, parliaments.[1]

Even among federations, the almost universal acknowledgement that second chambers are appropriate, indeed indispensable, at the national level often obscures the fact that at the subnational level of federal countries, only 73 state legislatures are bicameral out of over 450. Bicameralism prevails only in the United States and in Australia (except for a single state in each case) and survives in a minority of units in Argentina (nine provinces out of 23), in India (five states out of 25), in Russia[2] (four units out of 89) and in Micronesia (one state out of 4), while unicameral state legislatures are the rule in all other existing federations, including Germany, Austria, Belgium, Switzerland and Canada. We might add that the Scottish Parliament and the Welsh National Assembly,[3] as well as the legislatures of all Spanish Autonomous Communities, are unicameral.

Finally, the European Parliament is also unicameral.[4] The need of smaller countries for a louder voice has been met by granting them more seats than their population warrants, rather than by creating a second legislative body for that purpose.

Louis Massicotte is Associate Professor in the Department of Political Science, University of Montreal, Canada

EXPLAINING UNICAMERALISM

Can unicameralism be correlated with some features of countries, and to some extent be explained by their presence or absence? It can.

1. *The absence of federalism* or devolutionary arrangements is the first independent variable that is connected with unicameralism.[5] In federal countries, it is largely accepted that citizens must be represented on a state basis as well as on a strict population basis. The creation of a second chamber where the weight of smaller units is inflated has often been a precondition for the birth of the federations. This correlation is quite close: out of some 20 existing federations with a working legislature, all but three have second chambers. Only St. Kitts & Nevis (population 41,000), Micronesia (109,000) and Venezuela have a unicameral legislature.[6] On the other hand, unicameralism exists in over two-thirds of unitary countries.

2. *Population* is a second independent variable.[7] The rationale is that in countries with small populations, second chambers are often viewed as expensive and redundant bodies. Out of 77 countries with a population of less than five million, 55 have unicameral legislatures.

3. *Size* is often, though not always, a variable correlated with population.[8] In small countries, the necessity of having a second chamber is less obvious because the population is not scattered over large areas.

4. Unicameralism is also negatively correlated with a country being a *stable democracy* (defined here as a country having been continuously democratic since 1981).[9] This may sound paradoxical, because historically second chambers have often exhibited undemocratic features and been branded as brakes against the advance of democracy. Yet the correlation is strong enough to warrant this generalisation. Throughout their recent history, stable democratic countries have been spared breakdowns, revolutions or military coups, all factors that contributed elsewhere to the demise of many second chambers.

Of course, such correlations are indicative only. China, despite its size and population, has a single-chamber legislature, while small subnational jurisdictions like Wyoming and Tasmania remain bicameral. No one maintains that a second chamber made the former Soviet Union any more democratic, nor would anyone challenge the democratic credentials of Sweden or Denmark on the grounds of their legislative unicameralism.

These correlations do not pretend, either, to reflect the full range of factors that lead a country to opt for a single-chamber parliament. Whether second chambers have survived results from the interplay of a multitude of variables. For example, has the second chamber been reformed in its composition, so as not to appear hopelessly undemocratic? Has it behaved in a way that did not invite calls for its own abolition? The importance of historical accidents or catastrophes should not be underestimated either. This author's view is that once established, second chambers may outlive their usefulness for a long period of time in countries that are fortunate enough to avoid a regime breakdown due to a foreign invasion or a revolution.

THE HISTORICAL TREND TOWARDS UNICAMERALISM

Supporters of unicameralism contend it is the 'wave of the future'.[10] This is indeed supported by an examination of historical trends, though recent developments warrant some qualifications.

There is obviously a secular trend towards unicameralism. '*Securus iudicat orbis terrarum*', Sir John Marriott could intone in 1910. 'With rare unanimity, the civilized world has decided in favour of a bicameral legislature ... No modern State, whatever its form of government ... is willing to dispense with a second chamber.'[11] Among the then existing 50-odd sovereign countries with parliaments and British dominions, unicameralism prevailed only in a dozen Balkan, Central American, or decidedly smallish countries (Luxembourg, Liechtenstein and Monaco), all of which presumably lay outside the civilised world as defined by Marriott. Even around 1950, after the political upheavals generated by two world wars and the advance of communism, unicameralism could still be found in less than two-fifths (29 out of 80) of the sovereign countries then existing.[12] Today, as noted above, more than three-fifths of the IPU countries have unicameral legislatures.

This trend has been felt within federations as well. While second chambers are still standard in American and Australian states, Nebraska (in 1937) and Queensland (1922) opted for unicameralism, as have all Canadian provinces,[13] Brazilian states[14] and Nigerian regions[15] where second chambers once existed. In Germany, upper chambers existed in nine of the 25 states of the Wilhelmian Empire,[16] but under the Weimar Republic bicameralism survived only in Prussia.[17] After 1949, Bavaria was the only German state to have a Senate,[18] which was abolished in 1998. Among the states of the Indian Union, bicameralism prevailed in ten states out of 15 in the early 1960s, but exists in only five states out of 25 today.[19] Ten of the 14 provincial legislatures of Argentina were bicameral before Peron, while today only nine out of 23 are.[20] Cantonal legislatures in Switzerland have been unicameral 'from times immemorial'.[21]

Yet, over the last 20 years, bicameralism has thrived far more than during the previous three decades. Between 1950 and 1979, more countries abolished their second chamber (19) than created one or restored it (17), with nine countries creating a second chamber but abolishing it within the period. However, from 1980 to 1999, only six second chambers were abolished, while 11 were restored and 14 created anew, for a total of 25.[22] Among countries with working parliaments, the proportion having unicameral legislatures has decreased from 67.5 per cent in 1980 to 64 per cent today.

EXPLAINING THE RISE OF UNICAMERALISM

How can we explain the long-term rise of unicameralism? A look at the historical record reveals that there are two distinct pathways to unicameralism. Some countries simply never had a second chamber, others had one but abolished it.

Out of 114 countries with unicameral legislatures, no less than 79 apparently *never* had a second chamber throughout their parliamentary history (see list in Appendix 1). Unicameralism is not prevalent because bicameral countries have acknowledged that a second chamber was inappropriate. Rather, its huge lead stems primarily from the fact that since the 1950s the number of sovereign countries has jumped from about 80 to around 190, with dozens of African, Asian, Caribbean and Pacific countries becoming independent and generally opting for unicameral legislatures.

Why did they do so? Only tentative generalisations can be offered at this stage.

- Most of these countries adopted a unitary form of government, and many were small in size or population, all factors which even among Western democracies normally favour unicameralism.

- For many of these countries, the issue was not whether there was a need for a second chamber, but whether they needed a multi-party legislature at all! Until a decade ago, it was fashionable in some circles to dismiss pluralist democracy at best as a luxury only wealthy Western countries could afford, and at worst as a worthless façade camouflaging the dominance of the capitalist class.

- Most of these countries devised their early constitutions during the 1960s and 1970s, a period when second chambers had become less fashionable in Western democracies and were frequently indicted in progressive circles as redundant, reactionary or undemocratic.[23] This was also an era when it was commonly assumed that government could solve all problems, provided it was endowed with the means to do so. Unicameralism fitted with the ideological temper of these times far better than bicameralism, as the latter is consonant with a view of government as a standing threat against the liberties of the individual that needs to be checked.[24]

- Further, most of these countries were poor. In this context, the argument often heard in the West that second chambers are expensive, carried even greater weight.

- Some of these countries were controlled for a long time by the Communist Party, which objected as a matter of principle to bicameralism except in a federal context.[25]

- The fact that many of these countries were heterogeneous in ethno-linguistic terms might in theory have induced some of them to opt for bicameralism in order to ensure a better representation of a complex society. However, many may have been concerned that a formal acknowledgement of the existence of ethno-linguistic or regional cleavages through the creation of a second chamber might stimulate rather than alleviate fissiparous pressures within already fragile polities with arbitrary boundaries inherited from the colonial past.

A second group of unicameral countries formerly had a second chamber, but abolished it. Looking again at the record, we find that 34 countries once had a second chamber, but no longer do (see list in Appendix 2). This is an important finding. Countries where bicameralism was tried, found wanting and abolished are numerous, but constitute only a minority among the 114 unicameral countries. Most countries (about two-thirds) that once had a bicameral legislature still do.

Among the 34 countries where the second chamber was abolished, we find two distinct clusters:

- By far, the most frequent scenario for the disappearance of second chambers is that of developing countries with authoritarian right-wing regimes. These regimes set up façade constitutions that mimicked liberal democratic structures, including appointed or elected second chambers. Such legislative bodies were not deeply rooted, and often served as a camouflage for unpopular or corrupt regimes. Typical examples are senates in Cuba before Castro, in Nicaragua under the Somozas, in Egypt under King Faruk, in Iraq under Nuri Said, in Libya under King Idriss, in Iran under the Shah, in Hungary under Admiral Horthy, or the Portuguese corporative chamber under Salazar and Caetano. As far as we know, those senates hardly lived up to the theoretical ideal of bicameralism and did not play a significant autonomous role in the political process. When those regimes were felled by a revolution, a military invasion, an army coup or otherwise, second chambers, like all other ornaments of the façade, crumbled, never to re-appear. The abolition of the second chamber in these countries was a minute dimension of a major political shake-up which sometimes did away with any semblance of constitutional government. There was no in-depth public discussion focused on the relevance of the second chamber, which was deemed guilty by association.

- In a few constitutional and democratic polities, second chambers worked properly over a relatively long period of time, but over the years were found redundant, obtrusive, costly or anti-democratic and were therefore abolished either in isolation or as part of a new constitutional package. The list includes New Zealand (1951), Denmark (1953), Sweden (1970) and Iceland (1991), to which countries with a more chequered constitutional history like Sri Lanka[26] (1971), Ecuador (1979), Peru (1992) and Venezuela (1999) might be added. In most of these cases, unicameralism was the outcome of an orderly process and careful debate.

It is often assumed that second chambers have better prospects for survival if they are being directly elected by the people, because then they cannot be branded as illegitimate or undemocratic. There may be some truth in that. However, direct election *per se* certainly does not make second chambers invulnerable, as many bodies so constituted have been eliminated. Examples are the upper houses of Nebraska (1937), Cuba (1960), Ecuador (1979), Nicaragua (1979), Turkey (1980), Peru (1992) and Venezuela (1999). Provided the franchise is wide, direct election preserves senates against the accusation of not being genuinely democratic, but does not inoculate them against the charge of being redundant and expensive, and even less against a breakdown of the whole constitutional regime.

MOVING BACK FROM UNICAMERALISM

Did any of the countries that abolished their second chamber decide afterwards to restore it, thus acknowledging to some extent that a 'mistake' had been made? There are indeed some cases (I found 17) which can provide comfort to those who believe second chambers are indispensable. No example has been found of a mature democratic country restoring a senate that had been abolished in normal circumstances following full debate. Most cases of restoration we found occurred in countries where the second chamber had been swept away following the advent of an authoritarian regime (either a right-wing or a communist dictatorship), and was revived later when the country moved towards democracy.

A typical example is Spain, where the Senate of the liberal era disappeared with parliamentary government in 1923 when General Primo de Rivera assumed office. Both the Republic (1931–39) and Franco's regime later dispensed with a second chamber. However, in 1976, at a time when the country was moving towards democracy and devolving power to the regions, it was found fitting to restore the Senate.

Senates being revived, like the proverbial phoenix from its ashes, can also be found today in France (since 1852), Mexico (1874), the Dominican Republic (1924), Germany (1949), Paraguay (1967), Grenada (1983), Haiti (1987), Poland (1989), Romania (1991), Ethiopia (1995), Morocco (1996) and Cambodia (1998). In the Philippines, the Senate was abolished by the 1935 Constitution but revived five years later by way of a constitutional amendment, disappeared under Marcos' dictatorship in 1972 and reappeared again with democracy in 1986. In Thailand, the Senate has kept disappearing and resurfacing almost with every military coup since 1946. South Africa moved from bi- to unicameralism in 1980, then to a racially based tricameralism in 1983, and back to bicameralism in 1994. Interwar Czechoslovakia had a directly elected Senate. The Communists opted for unicameralism when they took power, but re-established a second chamber in 1969 when the country was recast as a federation. One of its successor states, the Czech Republic, also has a directly elected Senate.

Another interesting trend is the case of countries that had never had a second chamber, but decided to create one. This occurred in former Communist states like Croatia (1990), Russia (1993), Kyrgyzstan (1994), Kazakhstan (1995), Belarus (1996), Bosnia-Herzegovina (1998), Tajikistan (1999) as well as on the African continent: Namibia (1989), Burkina Faso, Gabon and Mauretania (1991), Congo-Brazzaville (1992),[27] Algeria (1996), Senegal (1998), and in the Asia-Pacific area: Pakistan (1973), Palau (1981) and Nepal (1990).

On the other hand, second chambers seem to have left few regrets in those democratic countries or subnational jurisdictions that abolished them following careful public discussion and consideration. The following cases have been well documented and will be considered in a more detailed way.

ABOLISHING THE SECOND CHAMBER: SIX CASE STUDIES

The Legislative Council of New Zealand[28] *(1951)*

Members of New Zealand's Legislative Council were appointed by the Crown, initially for life, and after 1891 for renewable seven-year terms. A major reform was adopted in 1914, which would have transformed the Council into a chamber elected by proportional representation (PR). However, the outbreak of the war led to the postponement of the reform, which was never implemented. As there was no fixed size, successive governments routinely swamped the Council, which acquired the unflattering reputation of a 'patronage dumping ground' and an 'institutional cipher'.

The circumstances that led New Zealand to become the first country in the Commonwealth to opt for unicameralism for its national legislature owe little to the tireless efforts of reformers, and much to a single individual, National Party leader Sidney G. Holland. While leading the opposition to a Labour administration, Holland introduced an abolition bill in 1947 in order to embarrass the government. The bill was defeated, but in the same year, two developments cleared the way for a change. First, New Zealand formally adopted the Statute of Westminster and acquired full power to amend its own Constitution without referring to Britain. Second, a pension scheme for parliamentarians was adopted, thus removing one of the last practical uses of the Council. Abolition was a minor item in National's platform at the 1949 election, which it won.

Holland thereupon secured the passage by the House of Representatives of an abolition bill. The bill did not include any compensation for incumbent councillors, and Holland had to pack the Council with 18 new appointees committed to abolition. Wavering among some members of this 'suicide squad' led to the subsequent appointment of other councillors (there were 25 in total) in order to obtain the expected result. The bill passed 26 to 16 in the Council, effective from 1 January 1951.

The debate still continues, fed not by any regret for the old Council, but by a widespread feeling that some counterweight is needed to the 'unbridled power' of the government. Parliamentary committees studied the issue in 1952, 1961 and 1964.[29] The Royal Commission on the Electoral System concluded in 1986 that no second chamber was necessary. Before they became prime ministers, Sir Geoffrey Palmer and Jim Bolger expressed sympathy for an elected second chamber, but the public was sceptical and nothing has been undertaken.[30] A survey conducted in 1990 found 21 per cent supporting the establishment of an upper house of parliament, 43 per cent against and 36 per cent with no opinion.[31] Those who believed the Prime Minister was too powerful focused instead, successfully, on the introduction of proportional representation in the House of Representatives, an achievement whose unpopularity so far may have cooled the reformist passion of many.

The Danish Landsting[32] *(1953)*

Denmark's second chamber, as reformed in 1915, included three-quarters of members indirectly elected by electors aged over 35, plus one-quarter selected by the Landsting itself on the basis of existing party membership. Unicameralism had been advocated since their origins by the Social Democrats, who from 1929 onwards formed a lasting coalition cabinet with the Radicals, and who did not change their position even after the ruling coalition secured a majority in the upper house in 1936.

In order to secure the consent of the Conservatives, the coalition devised a modified Norwegian-style arrangement, whereby 175 members would be directly elected by the people. The second chamber would be composed of two categories of members: 35 elected by the directly elected members of parliament from among themselves, 34 chosen from national party lists from among persons who had not stood as candidates for parliament (as a concession to the dreams of Conservatives for a corporative chamber) and one member representing the legislature of the Faroe Islands, for a total of 70. The remaining 140 members would constitute the first chamber. Both houses were to enjoy similar powers.

This reform was endorsed by both Houses and, after a general election, was put to a referendum in 1939. It secured the support of 91 per cent of voters, but failed! Indeed, in order to win, the YES votes had to be higher than the NO votes, and also to constitute 45 per cent of the *total electorate*. As a result of a low turnout, they failed to reach that benchmark by half of one per cent (11,812 votes).

After the war, the issue was raised again. Following years of discussion, a compromise was reached in January 1953 between the Liberal, Conservative, Radical, Social Democratic and Justice parties, only the Communists remaining outside the consensus. The essence of the compromise was that the parties of the right now accepted straight unicameralism, in exchange for safeguards against an abusive left-wing majority in parliament. The chief ones were a provision allowing one-third of parliamentarians to demand a referendum on important laws of a non-financial nature to which they objected, and the institution of an ombudsman.

Again, after a general election, the reform package was put to a referendum held on 28 May 1953. The measure was approved by 77.5 per cent of the voters (not as good a performance as in 1939), but passed because this time an increased turnout meant that the YES votes constituted 45.8 per cent of the total electorate.

Experience has revealed that the compromise worked a bit more to the advantage of the Social Democrats, as they got rid of a potentially embarrassing obstacle, while the referendum safeguard remained mostly inoperative (it has been used only once in over 40 years). On the other hand, the absence of a government majority in subsequent parliaments, as well as stronger parliamentary committees, have provided the kind of counterweight that had disappeared with the second chamber.

The Swedish First Chamber of the Riksdag[33] *(1970)*

While it had been designed in 1867 as a brake on radical majorities in the directly elected 'second chamber', Sweden's first chamber, as it was styled, had paradoxically become, through successive reforms, more amenable to Social Democratic control than its counterpart. As it stood prior to its abolition, the first chamber was indirectly elected by the municipal councils (themselves directly elected by PR) for an eight-year term, with powers equal to those of the second. Politically, the first chamber was originally dominated by the non-Socialist parties, but fell under Social Democratic control in 1941 and so remained until its abolition. Indeed, after the 1957 election, the Social Democrats remained in office with a majority in the first chamber, but only a strong plurality of seats in the second (directly elected) chamber.

Unicameralism was driven by the problem of conflicting majorities in both houses, and by the fact that the proportional electoral system used for the second chamber provided a slight advantage for the Social Democrats against a fragmented opposition, often resulting in a majority for the Left (Social Democrats and Communists) even while non-Socialist parties had a majority of the popular vote. Between 1963 and 1966, the Conservatives, the Centre and the Social Democrats came to share the preference of the Liberals for a single-chamber elected by a PR system that reflected more closely the support for each party. In 1967, those parties concluded an agreement that evolved into a constitutional amendment in 1970, which provided for a single chamber but enlarged unicameral Riksdag. In the early 1990s, a Swedish political scientist wrote that 'practically no criticism of the unicameral system was expressed in government studies and public debate in the 1970s and 1980s, although the Conservatives suggested some reduction in the number of seats in the Riksdag'.[34]

Nebraska (1937)

The abolition of the directly elected second chamber in this midwest state of the United States (population: 1.6 million) did not come swiftly or easily.[35] The idea was first raised in 1915 by a joint committee of the legislature, and failed by one vote (indeed, the vote was a tie) at the

1919–20 constitutional convention. Proposals for unicameralism were introduced in the legislature in 1917, 1925 and 1933, to no avail. Following a popular initiative, unicameralism was carried at a referendum in November 1934 with 286,086 votes (59.7 per cent) to 193,152, and became effective in January 1937. Ironically, the single chamber is styled 'the Senate'.

An important factor leading to that outcome was the tireless campaign waged by Senator George W. Norris. Among the chief arguments raised against bicameralism were the secrecy of the proceedings of the conference committee that mediated the conflicts between both houses; a tendency for members of one house to shift the responsibility of unpopular decisions to the other house (a practice known as 'buckpassing'); and that it was easier to hide corruption in a bicameral legislature. Unicameralism was also defended by pointing out that it would reduce the number of legislators, and that judicial review, gubernatorial vetoes and referendums already provided all the checks needed against abuses of power. Other factors allegedly contributing to the success of the proposal were the economic context, as the Depression struck particularly hard in this part of the continent, and the poor performance of state legislators at the previous session.

The Nebraska move has remained unique, as all attempts at emulation in other states failed.[36] An author has claimed that 'one would be hard pressed to prove the Nebraska legislature is more effective than bicameral bodies in other states',[37] another has concluded that 'forty years of experience has proved little, if anything, about the merits of unicameralism'.[38]

Yet most other sources are far more positive. Writing on the basis of numerous studies on this topic, Clyde Snider concluded that 'the one-house system appears, on the whole, to be enjoying marked success', citing the centralisation of legislative responsibility and a rise in the level of education and experience of legislators. Another author noted that 'the normal end-of-the-session rush to pass compromise legislation – so notable in Harrisburg and in Albany, for instance – has been eliminated because conference committees of two houses no longer exist'.[39] Commenting on a comparative study of legislative efficiency, a recent source concluded that 'where the Nebraska legislature rates highly it is largely because of its unicameral feature and its small size. A unicameral legislature is simpler and theoretically more comprehensible to the typical voter'.[40]

The fact that Nebraska combines the dual distinction of being the only unicameral and also the only non-partisan legislature in the country obviously makes it more difficult to distinguish the effects of the former from those of the latter. Certainly no one claims that, compared with the *status quo ante*, unicameralism has lessened the performance of the legislature or generated dissatisfaction. Perhaps the most telling fact is not that unicameralism has endured, but that over 65 years there has apparently been no serious attempt to undo it.[41]

The Legislative Council of Québec (1969)

Québec (population: 7.3 million) was the last Canadian province to abolish its Legislative Council. An upper house had been a feature of all constitutions that had been in force in the province since the introduction of a legislature in 1792. Since its early origins, the Council had been appointed for life by the Crown (which after the advent of responsible government in 1848 meant the government of the day), except for a brief period (1856–67) when most legislative councillors were elected for eight-year terms by the same electors as the Assembly. The latter experience was found unsatisfactory by most politicians, who in 1867 reverted to life appointments for the 24-seat Legislative Council of the newly created Province of Québec. From 1963, councillors appointed after that date were obliged to retire at the age of 75.

Under the Constitution, the Council had an absolute veto over all bills, including those providing for its own abolition or reform, and could not be swamped because of its fixed size. Abolition bills adopted by the Assembly in 1878 and 1900 were killed by the Council, which also thwarted an attempt in 1965 to reduce its powers to the same as those enjoyed by the British House of Lords. Finally, in late 1968, Premier Bertrand, with the support of the opposition party, was able to convince legislative councillors of his own party, being a majority in the Council, to agree to abolition, provided councillors would be paid until their death a pension equal to their annual salary as MLCs. 'It was a high price', later commented Premier Levesque, 'but fully worth it.' The measure became effective on 1 January 1969, and coincided with a thorough overhaul of the Assembly's procedures, including a revitalised standing committee system.

The Council had sunk into irrelevance well before its abolition, and had become largely discredited by the 1960s. Its heyday was the years between 1878 and 1900, when it frequently opposed measures presented by Liberal administrations. The Council brought down Joly's administration in 1879 by holding up supply until a split within the ruling party in the Assembly led to a change of government. In 1898, it voted down a bill providing for the creation of a department of education. In 1964–65, it killed an attempt to patriate the Canadian Constitution.

No regret has been expressed for the demise of the old Council ever since, and no attempt has been made in the legislature to restore it. However, former Premier Pierre Marc Johnson, while in opposition in 1986, toyed with the concept of a second chamber directly elected by PR; his idea was derided, did not evolve into a comprehensive plan, and was forgotten after he left politics one year later. Whether Québec's stringent linguistic laws of the 1970s and 1980s would have been passed unamended by the Council is a matter for speculation. In any instance, the courts provided a much more effective and credible check on the most agressively nationalist moves of successive Parti Québecois governments. Numerous observers have expressed concern over executive dominance of the legislature, but the relaxation of party discipline and the introduction of a proportional electoral system, rather than a new second chamber, seem to be the favourite panaceas of reformers.

The Legislative Council of Queensland[42] *(1922)*

Queensland (population: 3.4 million) is the sole Australian state with no second chamber. Its former Legislative Council was similar in many ways to Québec's. Its members were appointed for life. They numbered 15 but additional appointments could be made, with the result that membership had increased to 56 when the Council was abolished. Their powers were equal to those of the Assembly, except that after 1908 a measure sent up by the Assembly and rejected by the Council in two successive sessions could be put to the people in a referendum.

According to one source, 'the Council was always unpopular'.[43] Its fate was sealed with the advent in office in 1915 of Labour, which was committed to its abolition. Over the next two years, the Council twice rejected its own abolition, leading to a referendum in 1917. The referendum was negative (179,105 to 116,196), but Premier Theodore was determined to have his way and did not let the issue vanish. Abolition bills died again in the Council in 1918 and in 1919. Theodore made the future of the Council a central issue of the 1920 election campaign, which he won. He felt that there was no need for an upper house of any kind, and adopted Sieyès' rationale that an unelected one was destructive of parliamentary democracy, while an elected one would be superfluous. In 1921, an abolition bill passed the Legislative Assembly, and was later endorsed by the Council thanks to the appointment of a 'suicide squad' of Labour councillors.[44] Like any measure altering the state's constitution, the bill was reserved for the pleasure of the king and sent to London, with a telling remark by Governor Nathan: 'Generally, I am unable to say that there is evidence of any strong or widespread feeling in the country [sic] against this assent being given.'[45] The British government took the view that this was essentially a local matter, and the bill was assented to on 23 March 1922.

Was abolition a good decision? The opinion of the man who was Clerk of the Assembly before and after the Council was abolished, is worth quoting. Abolition, in his opinion:

> has not ... led to any grave or irremediable abuse. Doubtless it has had the effect of accelerating and simplifying legislation, and has enabled the party in power for the time being, to give almost instantaneous effect to its will. If they blunder, or if they are too impulsive, they alone must take the responsibility. No doubt a Legislative Council was a check on unconsidered or insufficiently considered legislation, but it is questionable whether the good it did by occasionally putting on the brake, was not outweighed by the fact that a purely nominee chamber repeatedly checked the manifest will of the people.[46]

On the other hand, the categorical statement by Theodore's biographer that 'there is no evidence to suggest that Queensland has suffered from the absence of a second chamber'[47] is disputed. The sorry state of parliamentary politics under the controversial premiership of Bjelke-Petersen (1968–87) has been attributed in part to the lack of a second chamber,[48] which led a Western Australian academic to conclude that 'the conduct of the unicameral parliament in Queensland speaks powerfully for the costs that may be incurred if legislative councils are removed'.[49]

Part of the explanation for conflicting assessments may well be that some compare Queensland's unicameralism with its own former brand of bicameralism, while others contrast it with the Legislative Councils now existing in other states, which are all directly elected (by PR everywhere except in Victoria) and are more positively evaluated than they used to be 40 years ago.[50]

The vague desire of a subsequent Conservative government for a restoration of the Council[51] alarmed its Labour successor enough to lead to the adoption during the 1930s of legislation, still in force,[52] that requires the holding of a referendum before any kind of second chamber could be restored. This legislation itself cannot be amended without a referendum. Since then, the proverbial reluctance of Australians to endorse constitutional change at referendums seems to have entrenched unicameralism (which, paradoxically, had been rejected by 60.6 per cent of the voters at an earlier referendum!). Despite the poor standing of Queensland's legislative life under Bjelke-Petersen, the restoration of the Council has never been envisaged as a solution by the otherwise reform-minded Labour administrations that followed.

CONCLUSION

What about the future? I would suggest in closing that despite the apparent reversal in recent decades of a secular trend, the prospects for unicameralism are good.

Outside federations, second chambers were often advocated either as a brake against governments pushing radical policies, or as a check against infringements of liberty. Even though many second chambers are likely to be with us for a long time, experience suggests that the same ends can be met with different tools, which for now have not generated as much criticism as second chambers often did or still do.

For example, when it comes to curbing the excesses of the government of the day, especially in parliamentary regimes where the government and the legislative majority go hand in hand, constitutionally entrenched bills of rights combined with judicial review may prove much more effective. In general judges are more credible among the public than politicians. They must ground their decisions on a discourse that is often more convincing than the partisan arguments put forward by senators, provided they behave more shrewdly than the US Supreme Court did during the 1930s.

Providing that their holding does not depend on the wishes of the government, referendums can also to some extent serve as a substitute for a second chamber[53] in order to check illiberal tendencies, as exemplified by the defeat in Australia in 1951 of a proposal to allow the Commonwealth government to ban the Communist Party – a move that interestingly the Senate, albeit dominated by the opposition, had failed to block earlier. The more aggressive tone adopted over recent decades by the media against governments may also be an effective check.

When it comes to a second, less widely accepted, function of second chambers, namely curbing radical legislation adopted by left-wing governments, here again other avenues are now open. Globalisation and the International Monetary Fund (IMF) are today arguably more effective in checking radical moves in developing countries than second chambers would have been, because the check comes from a faceless 'world environment' or 'international markets' rather than from an identifiable group of individuals acting publicly within the country in the legislature. The independence of central banks from the government of the day may insulate monetary policy from the inflationary tendencies sometimes attributed to left-wing governments.

NOTES

Since this article was completed, Senegal has adopted a new Constitution (in early 2001) that abolished the Senate created three years earlier.

1. In a survey of 14 bicameral democratic countries conducted in the early 1980s, bicameralism was found to be 'strong' in four cases, 'weak' in eight cases, and 'insignificant' in two cases. See A. Lijphart, *Democracies. Patterns of Majoritarian and Consensus Government in Twenty-One Countries* (New Haven, CT & London: Yale University Press, 1984), pp.99–101. Since then, the Belgian Senate has arguably gone from weak to insignificant.

2. The Republics of Kabardino-Balkariya, of Kareliya and of Sakha, as well as the *Oblast* (Territory) of Sverdlovsk have bicameral legislatures. See *The Territories of the Russian Federation* (London: Europa, 1999).
3. The Senate of Northern Ireland disappeared in 1972 when Ulster was made subject to direct rule from London, and has not been re-established despite the creation of the Northern Ireland Assembly in 1998.
4. Another confederal legislature, the continental Congress of the United States under the Articles of Confederation, was unicameral, with each state having an equal vote.
5. This standard point has been made in a number of works. See R. Hague and M. Harrop, *Comparative Government and Politics. An Introduction* (Houndmills: Macmillan, 2nd edn. 1987), pp.205–6); M. Ameller, *Parliaments – A Comparative Study on the Structure and Functioning of Representative Institutions in 41 Countries* (London: Cassell and Co., 1962), pp.4–7; J.D. Derbyshire and I. Derbyshire, *Political Systems of the World* (Edinburgh: Chambers, 1989), pp.74–5; D.G. Hitchner and C. Levine, *Comparative Government and Politics* (New York: Dodd Mean & Co., 1975), p.141.
6. Further, on closer examination, the 'Senate' of Micronesia is found to include two categories of members: a few are elected within each state irrespective of population and for a four-year term, while other seats are distributed among states on the basis of population and their members are elected for a shorter term: this looks like two chambers fused into one.
7. D. Shell, *The House of Lords* (New York: Harvester Wheatsheaf, 2nd edn. 1992), p.1.
8. J. Blondel, *An Introduction to Comparative Government* (New York: Praeger, 1969), p.373; Hitchner and Levine, *Comparative Government*, pp.142–3.
9. J.-E. Lane, *Constitutions and Political Theory* (Manchester: Manchester University Press, 1996), p.205, found twice as many bicameral legislatures (23 to 12) among 'firm democracies', while unicameralism was leading 65 to 26 among 'non democratic' countries. Blondel, *Introduction*, p.373, rightly notes, however, that 'not only have these single-chamber countries remained 'liberal', but the larger countries which have second chambers and leave these chambers with effective influence (USA) do not display any differences in 'liberalism' from the countries which do not (France, UK, Germany)'. See also D. Shell, *The House of Lords*, p.1.
10. J. Unruh, 'Unicameralism – The Wave of the Future', in D.C. Herzberg and A. Rosenthal (eds.), *Strengthening the States. Essays on Legislative Reform* (Garden City, NY: Doubleday & Co., 1971), pp.89–97.
11. J.A.R. Marriott, *Second Chambers. An Inductive Study in Political Science* (Freeport, NY: Books for Libraries Press, 1969), pp.1 and 240 (1910).
12. A.J. Peaslee, *Constitutions of Nations* (Concord, NH: The Rumford Press, 1950). According to the same source (vol.1, p.9), countries with bicameral legislatures then included 65% of the world's population.
13. Second chambers existed in Québec, Manitoba, Nova Scotia, New Brunswick and Prince Edward Island, while Newfoundland and part of British Columbia had one before joining Canada. All these bodies were appointed, except the Legislative Council of Prince Edward Island, which was directly elected. Ontario had an appointed upper house until 1840, while Alberta and Saskatchewan never had a second chamber.
14. Seven of the 20 Brazilian state legislatures, covering two-thirds of the total population, were bicameral in the early 1920s. See H.G. James, *The Constitutional System of Brazil* (Washington, The Carnegie Institution of Washington, 1923) pp.179–80. The present Brazilian Constitution provides for unicameral state legislatures.
15. Prior to the 1966 coup, all four regions of the Nigerian federation had bicameral legislatures. See J.P. Mackintosh, *Nigerian Government and Politics* (London: Allen & Unwin, 1966). Unicameral state legislatures are established by the 1999 Constitution.
16. The Kingdoms of Prussia, Bavaria, Wurttemberg, and Saxony; the Grand-Duchies of Baden and Hessen; and the city-states of Hamburg, Bremen and Lubeck. Except for the last three, these were the largest states of the German Empire. See F.K. Kruger, *Government and Politics of the German Empire* (Yonkers-on-Hudson, NY: World Book Company, 1915), pp.311–16.
17. H.W. Koch, *A Constitutional History of Germany in the Nineteenth and Twentieth Centuries* (London: Longman, 1984), p.275.

18. D.P. Conradt, *The German Polity* (New York: Longman, 5th edn. 1993), p.193.
19. They are: Bihar; Jammu and Kashmir; Karnataka; Maharashtra and Uttar Pradesh. Except for Jammu and Kashmir, all are large states. See M.V. Pylee, *Constitutional Government in India* (Bombay: Asia Publishing House, 1960), p.481; B.M. Sharma, *The Republic of India. Constitution and Government* (Bombay: Asia Publishing House, 1966).
20. A.F. Macdonald, *Government of the Argentine Republic* (New York: Thomas Y. Crowell Co., 1942), p.390; Internet site www.parlamericas.qc.ca.
21. W.E. Rappard, *The Government of Switzerland* (Toronto: D. Van Nostrand, 1936), p.21.
22. During the years 1980–99, two second chambers were created but later abolished (in Congo-Brazzaville and the Comoros), while three were abolished but were restored afterwards (in South Africa, Fiji and Liberia).
23. As Donald Shell notes, 'wherever they exist, second chambers have invariably been subject to attack from the political left', in *The House of Lords*, p.5.
24. S.E. Finer, *Comparative Government* (London: Allen Lane, The Penguin Press, 1970), p.72.
25. Three formerly Communist countries (Poland, Romania and the Czech Republic), once free, moved to bicameralism even if they were unitary.
26. See B.C.F. Jarayatne, 'Abolition of the Senate of Ceylon', *The Parliamentarian*, 53/2 (April 1972), pp.104–12.
27. The Congolese Senate disappeared with the breakdown of democracy in 1997.
28. This section is based on K. Jackson, *The New Zealand Legislative Council. A Study of the Establishment, Failure and Abolition of an Upper House* (Dunedin: University of Otago Press, 1972), and K. Jackson, 'The Abolition of the New Zealand Upper House of Parliament', in L.D. Longley and D. Olson (eds.), *Two into One. The Politics and Processes of National Legislative Cameral Change* (Boulder, CO: Westview Press, 1991), pp.43–76.
29. See the section 'A Second Chamber', in L. Cleveland and A.D. Robinson (eds.), *Readings in New Zealand Government* (Wellington: Reed Education, 1972), pp.141–7.
30. G. Palmer, *Unbridled Power? An Interpretation of New Zealand's Constitution & Government* (Wellington: Oxford University Press, 1979), pp.141–6. On Bolger, see Jackson, 'The Abolition', pp.68–72.
31. J. Vowles and P. Aimer (eds.), *Voters' Vengeance. The 1990 Election and the Fate of the Fourth Labour Government* (Auckland: Auckland University Press, 1993), p.220.
32. This section relies on D. Arter, 'One *Ting* Too Many: The Shift to Unicameralism in Denmark', in Longley and Olson (eds.), *Two into One*, pp.77–142.
33. This section is based on B. von Sydow, 'Sweden's Road to a Unicameral Parliament', in Longley and Olson (eds.), *Two into One*, pp.143–201.
34. Von Sydow, 'Sweden's Road', p.194.
35. This summary of the events that led to unicameralism in Nebraska owes much to the chapter by J. Rodgers, R. Sittig and S. Welch, 'The Legislature', in R.D. Miewald (ed.), *Nebraska Government and Politics* (Lincoln & London: University of Nebraska Press, 1984), pp.57–63.
36. C.F. Snyder, *American State and Local Government* (New York: Appleton Century-Crofts, 2nd edn. 1965), p.183.
37. G.S. Blair, *American Legislatures: Structure and Process* (New York: Harper & Row, 1967), p.144.
38. A. Rosenthal, *Legislative Life. People, Process and Performance in the States* (New York: Harper & Row, 1981), p.130–31.
39. M.S. Stedman Jr., *State and Local Governments* (Cambridge, MA: Winthrop, 1976), pp.98–9.
40. Rodgers *et al.*, 'The Legislature', p.85.
41. Rodgers *et al.*, 'The Legislature', pp.61–2.
42. This section is based on the following sources: C.A. Bernays, *Queensland Politics During Sixty Years, 1859–1919* (Brisbane, n.d.), pp.235–82; C.A. Bernays, *Queensland – Our Seventh Political Decade, 1920–1930* (Sydney: Angus & Robertson, 1931), pp.72–8; D.J. Murphy, 'Edward Granville Theodore: Ideal and Reality', in D. J. Murphy, R. Joyce and M. Cribb (eds.), *The Premiers of Queensland* (Brisbane: University of Queensland Press, rev. edn. 1990), pp.320–22; C.A. Hughes, *The Government of Queensland* (Brisbane: University of Queensland Press, 1980) pp.112–13.

43. A.A. Morrison, 'The Government of Queensland', in S.R. Davis (ed.), *The Government of the Australian States* (London: Longman, 1960), p.268.
44. The abolition bill (12 Geo. V No. 32) did not provide for the payment of any compensation to the incumbent councillors. However, section 3 provided that the governor-in-council *may* provide for the continuance of their free rail travel privilege within the state as well as access to the parliamentary library. The outgoing governor had refused to appoint new MLCs in sufficient numbers to secure abolition; pending the arrival of his successor, the government requested the lieutenant-governor, who was also a legislative councillor from their own party, to make the appointments needed for abolition, which he obligingly did, though this meant the elimination of his own job. To the hitherto unpaid position of lieutenant-governor, the government suddenly attached £1,000 salary. See C. Lack, *Three Decades of Queensland Political History 1929–1960* (Brisbane: Government Printer, n.d.), pp.11–13.
45. Murphy, 'Theodore', p. 322.
46. Bernays, 'Queensland – Our Seventh', p.82.
47. Murphy, 'Theodore', p.322.
48. P. Coaldrake, 'Parliament and the Executive', in A. Patience (ed.), *The Bjelke-Petersen Premiership 1968–1983. Issues in Public Policy* (Melbourne: Longman Cheshire, 1985), pp.219–37. For a contrary opinion, see M.B. Cribb and P.J. Boyce (eds.), *Politics in Queensland. 1977 and Beyond* (Brisbane: University of Queensland Press, 1980), pp.10 and 272.
49. C. Sharman, 'Coping with the Future: The Political Apparatus of the States', in M. Birrell (ed.), *The Australian States. Towards a Renaissance* (Melbourne: Longman Cheshire, 1987), pp.39–52.
50. See S. Bennett, *Affairs of State. Politics in the Australian States and Territories* (North Sydney: Allen & Unwin, 1992), pp.95–110.
51. See B. Costar, 'Arthur Edward Moore: Odd Man In', in Murphy *et al.* (eds.), *The Premiers of Queensland*, pp.375–96.
52. *Constitution Act Amendment Act 1934* (24 Geo. V No. 35). On the background of this legislation, see Lack, *Three Decades*, pp.115–16 and 131–2.
53. The widespread use of the referendum in Swiss cantons has been advanced as a justification for the unicameralism of cantonal legislatures. See R.C. Brooks, *Government and Politics of Switzerland* (London: George C. Harrap, 1920), p.315.

APPENDIX 1
COUNTRIES THAT NEVER HAD A SECOND CHAMBER (NUMBER: 79)

Andorra
Angola
Armenia
Azerbaidjan
Bangladesh
Benin
Bhutan
Botswana
Bulgaria
Cameroon
Cape Verde
Central African Republic
Chad
Côte d'Ivoire
Cyprus
Djibouti
Dominica
Equatorial Guinea
Eritrea
Finland
Gambia
Georgia
Ghana
Guatemala
Guinea-Conakry
Guinea-Bissau
Indonesia
Israel
Kiribati
Kuwait
Latvia
Lebanon
Liechtenstein
Lithuania
Luxembourg
Macedonia
Malawi
Maldives
Mali
Marshall Islands
Mauritius
Micronesia
Moldova
Monaco
Mongolia
Mozambique
Nauru
Niger
North Korea
Panama
Papua New Guinea
Rwanda
St.Kitts & Nevis
St.Vincent & Grenadines
Samoa
San Marino
Sao Tome & Principe
Seychelles
Sierra Leone
Singapore
Slovakia
Slovenia
Solomon Islands
Suriname
Syria
Togo
Tonga
Tunisia
Turkmenistan
Tuvalu
Uganda
Ukraine
United Arab Emirates
Tanzania
Uzbekistan
Vanuatu
Vietnam
Yemen
Zambia

APPENDIX 2
UNICAMERAL COUNTRIES
THAT FORMERLY HAD A SECOND CHAMBER (NUMBER: 31)

Albania (until 1928)
Burundi (from 1965 to 1966)
China (until 1925)
Congo-Kinshasa (until 1965)
Costa Rica (until 1847, and from 1859 to 1869)
Cuba (until 1960)
Denmark (until 1953)
Ecuador (until 1979)
Egypt (until 1952)
El Salvador (until 1886)
Estonia (from 1934 to 1940)
Greece (until 1862, and from 1927 to 1935)
Honduras (until 1865)
Hungary (until 1918, and from 1926 to 1945)
Guyana (until 1966)
Iceland (until 1991)
Iran (until 1979)
Iraq (until 1958)
Kenya (from 1963 to 1966)
Laos (until 1975)
Libya (until 1969)
Malta (from 1921 to 1936)
New Zealand (until 1951)
Nicaragua (until 1979)
Peru (until 1992)
Portugal (until 1974)
South Korea (from 1960 to 1961)
Sri Lanka (until 1971)
Sudan (from 1953 to 1958)
Sweden (until 1970)
Turkey (until 1923, and from 1961 to 1980)
Venezuela (until 1999)
Zimbabwe (from 1969 to 1989)

Concluding Observations

NICHOLAS D.J. BALDWIN

Notwithstanding the fact that in the past it was said that 'experience, no less than philosophy, has declared unmistakably in favour of the bicameral system',[1] from the studies contained within this collection it is apparent that although it is far from uncommon to find a second chamber present within a nation's body politic, the majority of countries today do not in fact have a second chamber. Indeed, of the 177 countries around the world currently classified by the Inter-Parliamentary Union as having parliaments, 63 per cent (111) are unicameral (see Massicotte) and only 37 per cent (66) are bicameral.

Among the 66 parliaments which do have second chambers, these second chambers as institutions are far from uniform in either composition (see Borthwick and Rush), focus, approach, function, powers or influence (see Patterson/Mughan, Russell, Scully and Russell). These differences – one second chamber to another, one political culture to another (and not forgetting one time-frame to another) – have been and are accompanied by different analyses and justifications for their form, functions and powers – indeed, for their very existence as institutions. Different purposes have been given different weight at different times in different circumstances and situations in different countries (see Shell, 'The History').

Broadly speaking, however, when considering the topic of second chambers two schools of opinion are, in general, discernable: one regarding a second chamber to be a useless complexity which hinders and upsets the course of good government in a state, the other believing a second chamber to be both useful and necessary. The most obvious proponent from within the first school of thought was the Abbe Sieyes, that indefatigable drafter of constitutions for revolutionary France, who – as Donald Shell pointed out in his chapter on the history of bicameralism – dismissed the second chamber question with the oft-quoted observation that 'if a second chamber dissents from the first it is mischievous; if it agrees, it is superfluous'.[2] The countervailing point of view was perhaps best advanced by John Stuart Mill when he declared that:

Nicholas Baldwin is Dean of Wroxton College of Fairleigh Dickinson University

> a majority in a single assembly, when it has assumed a permanent character – when composed of the same persons habitually acting together, and always assured of victory in their own House – easily becomes despotic and overweening, if released from the necessity of considering whether its acts will be concurred in by another constitutional authority. The same reason which induced the Romans to have two consuls, makes it desirable there should be two chambers: that neither of them be exposed to the corrupting influence of undivided power, even for the space of a single year.[3]

Despite Maine's view that 'almost any sort of second chamber was better than none', the second chamber question – how to strike the right balance – has been a perennial one:

> to devise a good second chamber; to discover for it a basis which shall be at once intelligible and differentiating; to give it powers of revision without powers of control; to make it amenable to permanent public sentiment and yet independent of transient public opinion; to erect a bulwark against revolution without interposing a barrier to reform – this is the task which has tried the ingenuity of constitution makers from time immemorial.[4]

– and it continues so to do.

Different fundamental purposes for second chambers have been given weight at different times, while – as has been shown in the preceding chapters – second chambers, both in theory and practice, can fulfil a variety of roles. First and foremost in this has been the belief of many that the power of government should not be concentrated either in a single individual or in a single institution, or even in a single class of people. It is this belief that gave rise to the desire for a system of checks and balances within a political and governmental system, with a second chamber being seen as one of the checks and balances. Also important was the view that there was a need for wisdom in government, namely that it was desirable to have the counsel of the wise and the experienced. Hence the emergence in Britain of the so-called classical theory of mixed government, the constitutional trinity balancing Crown, Lords and Commons – although an emergence more through chance than by design. With the spread of mass representative democracy in the nineteenth century many feared the elected majority – the power of the masses – and turned to the second chamber to keep the nation 'safe from democracy'. As part of this, second chambers themselves came to be seen as bodies to be given special responsibilities for and safeguards over constitutional issues, institutions and human rights – for instance, safeguarding the rights of minorities (after all, as has been observed, individuals of property and wealth are minorities) and having specific powers to protect the constitution (see Russell). In the case of Britain, the House of Lords came to be seen – certainly by some – as a barrier against a possible 'elective dictatorship' and its consequences, not least of all by being in a position to guarantee regular elections and to safeguard the independence of the judiciary. Lord Crowther-Hunt explained the position as he saw it:

> [The] constitutional functions [of the House of Lords] are so important that they are worth dying at the stake for. Because ... if [the Lords] is abolished there is nothing to stop a House of Commons extending its own life indefinitely and dismissing any judges the Government found inconvenient. Here [the House of Lords has] ... a total veto, and in a country without a written constitution guaranteeing regular elections and the independence of the judiciary, it is crucial for [the House of Lords] to continue to exist to fill what would otherwise be a dangerous gap in our constitutional system. We must have some mechanism which at present is only [the House of Lords], to stop a transient majority in [the House of Commons] from extending its own life indefinitely and from dismissing any judge that sought to defend our liberties against what [the Commons] might want to do to them.[5]

It was at the time of the American Revolution and the birth of the United States Constitution that – as Donald Shell points out in 'The History of Bicameralism' – a whole new justification for a second chamber came to be formulated, namely as a result of the 'great compromise' whereby the interests of both large and small states could be reconciled, with the second chamber – the Senate – providing for an equality of representation for the states, irrespective of their size or populations. The concept of federalism was born, with the second chamber playing an important territorial role. Consequently, territorial representation came to be seen as one of the classic functions of, and justification for, a second chamber (see Russell, 'Territorial Role'). Nonetheless, as has been written, the concept of check and balance was still very much to the forefront:

> Federalism, in its earliest form, was designed as a bulwark against turbulent democracy in a land where equality was something more than a philosopher's phrase. The Supreme Court, the President, the Senate and House of Representatives were set up as four federal

> powers checking one another. The first three were all checks upon the fourth democratic power, while the first, and to a certain extent the third, checked the executive powers of the President. Moreover, all four were to ensure by their federal activity that the state legislatives did not democratically destroy the natural rights of man. Though federal powers were limited, they were limited precisely to such things as foreign trade, foreign policy, currency control and command of the armed forces which were necessary to keep the turbulent democracy of the states within harmless limits.... In the first place ... the Constitution could be modified by the interpretation of expert lawyers, but an amendment of it was made as difficult as possible. In the second place the will of the people was split into a Federal and State will and thereby weakened. In the third place foreign policy was removed from the control of the House of Representatives. In the fourth place the Senate was set up as the most refined expression of the popular will.[6]

Thirdly, a second chamber can provide for the representation of elements within society – for example the landed aristocracy, as was for centuries the role of the British House of Lords, or white, male, property owners, as was the justification of some for an American Senate at the time of the constitutional settlement following the revolution against Britain – which are either unlikely to be a part of the democratically representative chamber or, if a part, only a minority in it.

Fourth, and developing on from this point, legislatures in states involved in the process of liberalisation and democratisation have to strike a difficult balance between simultaneously offering mass representation and maintaining stability through safeguarding elite and minority interests. As James Ketterer shows in the case of Morocco, a bicameral legislature can provide structure for this balance. Consequently, the existence of a second chamber – of bicameralism – can further increment democratisation.

Fifth, the very existence of a second chamber within a political system can provide time for reflection and second thought. Hence the idea of a second chamber as a means whereby what has been termed 'the ill-conceived, sometimes rash, and often muddled legislation of the other chamber'[7] can be checked. Winston Churchill sought to draw an analogy between bicameralism and a motor car, observing that 'if you have a motor car ... you have to have a break. There ought to be a break ... it prevents an accident through going too fast'.[8] In a similar vein, George Washington had illustrated the need, as he saw it, for a second chamber by pouring hot liquid into a saucer, thereby allowing it to cool, remarking that, in the same way 'we pour legislation into the senatorial saucer to cool it'.[9] It was for this very concept that, as Laurence Sterne wrote: 'The ancient Goths of Germany … had … a wise custom of debating everything of importance to their state twice; that is, once drunk and once sober: drunk – that their councils might not want vigour; and sober – that they might not want discretion.'[10]

Sixth, a second chamber can be extremely useful in tidying up and improving legislation from the first chamber and by relieving pressures of congestion in the first chamber. Walter Bagehot in his work *The English Constitution* has a well-known passage in which he offers a justification for the existence of the House of Lords by the deficiencies of the House of Commons:

> With a perfect Lower House it is certain that an Upper House would be scarcely of any value. If we had an ideal House of Commons perfectly representing the nation, always moderate, never passionate, abounding in men of leisure, never omitting the slow and steady forms necessary for good consideration, it is certain that we should not need a higher chamber. The work would be done so well that we should not want any one to look over or revise it … But though beside an ideal House of Commons the Lords would be unnecessary … beside the actual House a revising and leisured legislature is extremely useful.[11]

This argument if used in isolation is not perhaps the best defence for a second chamber as it does rather suggest that if the first chamber could be made more efficient then there would be no need – certainly in this regard – for a second chamber.

The classic statement of the functions of a second chamber within the British polity were given by the Bryce Commission Report of 1918,[12] and one can certainly see the extent to which the report drew upon the theory and practise. Bryce stipulated four functions, namely:

1. The examination and revision of bills brought from the first chamber, a function which he declared had become more needed since, on many occasions the first chamber (in this respect the House of Commons) was often obliged to act under special rules limiting debate.

2. The initiation of bills dealing with subjects of a practically non-controversial character which may have an easier passage through the first chamber if they have been fully discussed and put into a well-considered shape before being submitted to it.

3. The interposition of so much delay (and no more) in the passage of a Bill into law as may be needed to enable the opinion of the nation to be adequately expressed upon it. Bryce argued that this would be especially needed with regard to bills which affected the fundamentals of the constitution or introduced new principles of legislation, or raised issues whereon the opinion of the country may appear to be almost equally divided.

4. Full and free discussion of large and important questions, such as those of foreign policy, at moments when the first chamber may happen to be so much occupied that it cannot find sufficient time for them. Such discussions may often be all the more useful, Bryce concluded, if they were to be conducted in an assembly whose debates and discussions do not involve the fate of the executive government.

Much more recently – and again in the British context – the subject has been addressed by a Royal Commission,[13] the report of which highlighted what it described as four distinct and separate strands of thinking which had long dominated discussions about the possible roles of second chambers. These were described and explained in the following way:

1. 'Counsel from a range of sources', namely to provide a means whereby a range of different experiences and points of view – different from those of the first chamber – could be brought to bear on proposed legislation and on public affairs generally.

2. 'Estates of the realm', namely to be broadly representative of a society as it is now (as opposed to as it was in the past) – ideally, considerably more representative than are the members of the first chamber – and to reflect the diverse experiences and traditions of a society.

3. 'Checks and balances', namely to act as a check on the government with its majority in the popular assembly. The report observed that – in the British case - the House of Commons often finds it difficult both to sustain in power the government of the day and to act as an effective check upon it. A second chamber – so the report argued – could enhance the ability of parliament as a whole to provide an effective check on the executive. Three specific areas were identified in this regard. Firstly by scrutinising the actions of the executive and holding it to account; secondly, by participating in the legislative

process; and thirdly, by playing a role in connection with proposed constitutional change.

4. 'The representation of regions', namely giving a direct voice to the nations, regions, provinces, states or other territorial units of a country, as distinct from simply representing population, although it should be noted that none of these positively require bicameral representation.

Constitutional framers, having decided upon the purposes of a second chamber, then set out to determine not only what powers a second chamber needed to fulfil these purposes (see Patterson/Mughan), but also what method of composition would secure a body fit to exercise its prescribed powers (see Borthwick) and the resources (see Rush) and proceedings (see Wheeler-Booth) required to do so. Often what resulted was a dispute between those who advocated a 'strong' or 'activist' or even 'interventionist' second chamber – namely a second chamber that would be capable of standing up to the first chamber and/or the government of the day – and those who advocated a 'weak' or 'limited' or at most simply a 'useful' second chamber, namely a second chamber with only limited powers in relation to the first chamber and/or the government of the day (see Patterson/Mughan and Scully).

From the studies contained within this collection it is apparent that second chambers are important for legislative policies and outcomes, and that this is so even in those parliamentary democracies where second chambers are endowed with only a few, limited, legislative, political or constitutional powers. Indeed, in some countries their role in the legislative process has increased, is increasing and is likely to increase further. For example, in the member states of the European Union domestic parliaments have had to deal with a growing number of legislative initiatives emanating from Brussels and Strasbourg. Both the German Bundesrat and the British House of Lords are good examples of second chambers that have already turned the flow of European legislation to their advantage. In the case of the House of Lords for example, following the accession of the United Kingdom to the European Community in January 1973, a Select Committee was appointed:

> to consider Community proposals whether in draft or otherwise, to obtain all necessary information about them, and to make reports on those which, in the opinion of the Committee, raise important questions of policy or principle, and on other questions to which the Committee consider that the special attention of the House should be drawn.

Today, the terms of reference of the European Union Committee (as it is now called) are 'to consider the European Union documents and other matters relating to the European Union'. It is comprised of 19 full members and another 51 co-opted members and is organised into six sub-committees covering:

- Economic and Financial Affairs, Trade and External Relations;
- Energy, Industry and Transport;
- Common Foreign and Security Policy;
- Environment, Agriculture, Public Health and Consumer Protection;
- Law and Institutions;
- Social Affairs, Education and Home Affairs.

Since it was established the Committee has scrutinised in great depth and scope and reported on a wide range of issues – some 30 to 40 items of EU business each year – from the protection of personal data to genetically modified food, and from airline competition to economic and monetary union, and is generally regarded as having made an extremely positive contribution to the scrutinising ability of the British parliament as a whole. One recent report noted that 'their reports are widely regarded, throughout Europe, as being of extremely high quality and are capable of having a significant influence on policy development'.[14] Indeed, the Royal Commission on the Reform of the House of Lords concluded that a reformed second chamber should in fact build on the high quality work done by the House of Lords in this regard.

While focusing on second chambers in the context of the European Union it is worth noting that the British Prime Minister, Tony Blair, speaking in Warsaw (Poland) in October 2000, called for the creation of a second chamber for the European Parliament, one to be made up of representatives of national parliaments thereby involving them much more on European matters, whose function it would be to review the EU's work in the light of an agreed 'Statement of Principles', a political as opposed to a legal document, which would outline what is best done at the European level and what should be done at the national level; in short a second chamber providing for political review within the European Union by a body of democratically elected politicians.[15]

Certainly, for some, the future points to second chambers having not only a more apparent place in, but perhaps also a growing importance in, the legislative, parliamentary and political processes within which they exist and operate. Indeed, in this regard it is interesting to note – as Michael Wheeler-Booth has done – that the Report of the Royal

Commission on the Reform of the House of Lords saw new, additional duties, and responsibilities for a second chamber in the British context, namely:

- in protecting the constitution – advocating that an authoritative Constitutional Committee be set up to scrutinise the constitutional implications of all legislation and to keep the operation of the constitution under review (this was in fact something the House of Lords agreed to establish in July 2000);
- in protecting human rights – advocating that a Human Rights Committee be set up to scrutinise all bills and Statutory Instruments for human rights implications; and
- in holding the government to account – advocating that a committee be set up to scrutinise treaties laid before parliament and draw attention to any implications which merit parliamentary consideration before ratification takes place.

Because of the greater visibility and perhaps the growing importance of second chambers the role that they play needs to be better understood in at least two respects. Firstly with regard to their own internal dynamics (see Wheeler-Booth and Cockerell), as entities in their own right and not merely in relation to their interactions with first chambers and governments which has very much tended to be the focus to date. Secondly, with regard to their relationship to and standing with the wider public – public opinion, with the implication that this has not merely for the legitimacy of a second chamber, but for the parliamentary system within which it functions and, indeed, for the wider political system within which it operates. It is hoped that this collection of articles will contribute towards that greater understanding.

NOTES

1. J.A.R. Marriott, *Second Chambers* (Oxford: Clarendon Press, 1910), p.298.
2. Abbe Sieyes, cited by Marriott, *Second Chambers*, p.1.
3. John Stuart Mill, citied by Marriott, *Second Chambers*, p.1.
4. Marriott, *Second Chambers*, p.298.
5. Lord Crowther-Hunt, 415 *H.L. Debs.*, c607 (8 Dec. 1980).
6. R.H.S. Crossman, *Government and the Governed* (London: Chatto and Windus, 1969), pp.97–8.
7. Former Conservative MP – confidential to author.
8. Winston Churchill, 444 *H.C.Debs*, c208 (11 Nov. 1947).
9. George Washington, cited by Lord Crowther-Hunt, 'Altering the House of Lords', *The Listener*, 104/2690, 4 Dec. 1980, p.742.
10. Laurence Sterne, cited by S.D. Bailey (ed.), *The Future of the House of Lords* (Hansard Society, 1953), p.7.

11. W. Bagehot, *The English Constitution* (London: Fontana/Collins, 1975; 1867/1915), pp.133–4.
12. 'Report of the Conference on the Reform of the Second Chamber', Cmnd 9038 (London: HMSO, 1918).
13. 'A House for the Future', the Report of the Royal Commission on the Reform of the House of Lords, *Cm* 4534 (London: 50, 2000).
14. 'A House for the Future', p.83.
15. See Prime Minister's speech to the Polish Stock Exchange, 6 Oct. 2000. www.number-10.gov.uk/speeches.

Abstracts

The History of Bicameralism, *by Donald Shell*

The ideas which underlie bicameralism may be traced back to the theories developed in ancient Greece and Rome, though recognisable bicameral institutions arose first in medieval Europe where they were associated with separate representation of different estates of the realm. The American Founding Fathers eschewed any notion of separate representation for a social aristocracy, but accepted the prevailing disposition towards bicameralism. However, they then invented a new rationale for bicameralism linked with federalism. In subsequent constitution-making, federal states have invariably adopted bicameralism, but the older justification for second chambers as providing opportunities for second thoughts about legislation has survived. A trend towards unicameralism in the twentieth century appears now to have been halted. Growing awareness of the complexity of the notion of representation and the multi-functional nature of modern legislatures may be affording incipient new rationales for second chambers though these do generally remain contested institutions in ways that first chambers are not.

Methods of Composition of Second Chambers, *by R.L. Borthwick*

Interest in the composition of second chambers has been given a boost by the debates in the United Kingdom about reform of the House of Lords. Despite the fact that the Royal Commission that examined the question paid some attention to other second chambers, there is little indication that practice elsewhere will have much impact on what happens. Other second chambers show a considerable diversity but are generally smaller than their country's first chamber. Their members tend to have longer legislative terms (where these are fixed) but rarely longer than 5–6 years. The most common basis of representation in second chambers is territorial but a number of others can be found. A majority of members of second chambers are elected, either directly or indirectly, but appointed second chambers are not uncommon.

Socio-Economic Composition and Pay and Resources in Second Chambers, *by Michael Rush*

Although less information is available on the socio-economic composition of second chambers and the resources available to their members than is the case for first chambers, there is sufficient data to allow useful comparisons to be made. Members of second chambers tend to be older, partly because of widespread minimum age qualifications and partly because of different political career patterns. Women are generally under-represented, but are more numerous where PR systems and some appointment systems facilitate their membership. Socio-economically members of second chambers are overwhelmingly middle class. Most are regarded as full-time and consequently fully salaried, with appropriate pension schemes. They are generally well-resourced. However, the German Bundesrat, the UK House of Lords and the Irish Senate are, to varying degrees, exceptions. Overall, in terms of composition and resources first and second chambers have much in common. The major exception is the House of Lords.

Fundamentals of Institutional Design: The Functions and Powers of Parliamentary Second Chambers, *by Samuel C. Patterson and Anthony Mughan*

Well over one-third of the national parliaments in the world are bicameral. The upper houses of these parliaments, alternatively called second chambers or senates, vary in their geographical location, size, membership selection and constitutional context. Moreover, second chambers vary in their intercameral roles and powers, analysed here as 'symmetrical vs. asymmetrical bicameralism'. Finally, the relative power of upper houses is circumscribed differently in federal versus unitary systems, dependent on the powers accorded to executive authority, shaped by the houses' role in law-making, and marked by the strength of the bodies' internal structure. This analysis offers a preliminary probe into these institutional features.

Responsibilities of Second Chambers: Constitutional and Human Rights Safeguards, *by Meg Russell*

Second chambers – even those which are otherwise weak – are often given particular responsibility for protecting the constitution. This responsibility flows naturally from both of the original models of second chambers – as either conservative or federal houses. This study discusses the constitutional and human rights roles of second chambers in seven Western democracies. The chambers selected are intended to represent a spectrum of different models, and a range from effective to ineffective upper houses. The countries considered are Australia, Canada, France, Germany, Ireland, Italy, and Spain.

Procedure: A Case Study of the House of Lords, ***by Sir Michael Wheeler-Booth***

This article first describes briefly the procedure of the Lords in the reign of James I, as 1621 saw the writing down of the then procedures in the first edition of *Public Business Standing Orders* or '*Remembrances*'. Then jumping briskly forward three and a half centuries to the period 1960–99, current Lords procedures are described in the later twentieth century before the passage of the House of Lords Act 1999 and the exclusion of the majority of hereditary peers. Finally, we examine the procedural problems which the half reformed 'interim House' of Lords faces on several fronts.

Dealing with Big Brother: Relations with the First Chamber, ***by Roger Scully***

An issue central to an understanding of second chambers – their relationship with the first chamber in a bicameral system – is examined. Drawing on a variety of real-world illustrations, consideration is given to how inter-chamber relations may be shaped by variance in three key factors: the relative powers of the two chambers, the balance of party competition between them, and the degree of party unity prevailing. The inter-relationship between these factors may often be complicated; what is more certain is that inter-cameral relations both reflect and influence wider processes in a political system.

The Territorial Role of Second Chambers, ***by Meg Russell***

Territorial representation is one of the classic functions of an upper house. Whilst the lower house is elected on a popular basis to represent the nation's citizens, the upper house may represent regions, provinces or states. Often this representation is of sub-national governments or assemblies, rather than citizens. The origins of the territorial upper house model, and its current day use are examined. Using diverse examples such as the upper houses of

Australia, Canada, South Africa, Spain, Germany and Italy, the extent to which these chambers perform a truly territorial function is questioned. The conclusion considers the spread of the territorial model, and how this can best be harnessed to play a useful territorial function in federal or devolved states.

The Politics of Second Chamber Reform: A Case Study of the House of Lords and the Passage of the House of Lords Act 1999, *by Michael Cockerell*

This case study of the politics of second chamber reform examines the way in which the Labour government set about achieving the removal of hereditary members in the House of Lords Act in 1999. The author had unique access to confidential meetings of Baroness Margaret Jay, Leader of the Lords, and her team during the passage of this legislation. Consequently, the twists and turns of a tale of pure politics are outlined. The result of this extraordinary sequence of behind-the-scenes deals and arguments is an historic compromise whereby some of the hereditary peers still remain as members of the House of Lords. Interviewees include Baroness Jay of Paddington and Lord Richard, former Labour Leader of the Lords, Lord Irvine of Lairg, the Lord Chancellor, and Lords Cranbourne and Strathclyde, the Conservative Leaders at the time.

From One Chamber to Two: The Case of Morocco, *by James P. Ketterer*

In the mid-1990s, Morocco shifted from a unicameral to bicameral parliament, thereby highlighting the role of the parliament in the nation's self-declared democratisation project. While many scholars of Morocco have examined the political process surrounding the constitutional ratification of this new institution, little attention has been paid to the institutional implications of the cameral shift. In legislative studies, there has been a resurgence of interest in bicameralism, but little attention has been paid to bicameralism as it relates to ongoing democratisation processes. Accordingly, this article seeks to fill the void in both Moroccan and legislative studies, focusing on the role that Morocco's bicameral parliament plays in ending a zero-sum game between the opposition and centre-right forces; creating enough political space for an opposition-led government to take power; strengthening the multi-party system; expanding representation; and reassuring ambivalent parties that the democratisation process will not unduly threaten their interests. All of these elements support Morocco's incremental democratisation effort and add to our understanding of bicameralism as a component of such an effort.

Legislative Unicameralism: A Global Survey and a Few Case Studies, *by Louis Massicotte*

This survey of unicameralism in sovereign countries and within federations finds that unicameralism is correlated with the absence of federalism, small populations and size, and not being a stable democracy. Since 1914, unicameralism has been on the rise. The predominance of unicameralism among IPU members today is explained mostly by the accession of scores of former colonies to independence in the 1960s and 1970s, while most countries that were bicameral in 1950 still are. The article discloses, however, that throughout the 1980s and 1990s far more second chambers have been created or restored than abolished, notably because many new democracies have opted for bicameralism. Case studies of democratic countries (New Zealand, Denmark, and Sweden) and subnational jurisdictions (Nebraska, Québec, and Queensland) that abolished their second chambers are provided. In all these cases, it appears that the move towards unicameralism has not been regretted, in contrast with moves towards unicameralism that occurred in non-democratic countries, which have sometimes been followed by a restoration of the second chamber.

Index

For Product Safety Concerns and Information please contact our EU representative GPSR@taylorandfrancis.com
Taylor & Francis Verlag GmbH, Kaufingerstraße 24, 80331 München, Germany

www.ingramcontent.com/pod-product-compliance
Lightning Source LLC
Chambersburg PA
CBHW050712280326
41926CB00088B/2947

* 9 7 8 1 1 3 8 9 8 1 5 2 2 *